Mastering Firebase for Android Development

Build real-time, scalable, and cloud-enabled Android apps
with Firebase

Ashok Kumar S

BIRMINGHAM - MUMBAI

Mastering Firebase for Android Development

Commissioning Editor: Kunal Chaudhari
Acquisition Editor: Reshma Raman
Content Development Editor: Francis Carneiro
Technical Editor: Sachin Sunilkumar
Copy Editor: Safis Editing
Project Coordinator: Hardik Bhinde
Proofreader: Safis Editing
Indexer: Rekha Nair
Graphics: Jason Monteiro
Production Coordinator: Nilesh Mohite

First published: June 2018

Production reference: 1270618

Published by Packt Publishing Ltd.
Livery Place
35 Livery Street
Birmingham
B3 2PB, UK.

ISBN 978-1-78862-471-8

www.packtpub.com

To my father, Mr. Srinivas Achar, and to his memory, a letter I couldn't write or the words I couldn't acknowledge when he was around me and looking after me. He was an ordinary bus driver who thrived through the holy book of Bhagavad Gita. He was a great fan of Kannada literature. I remember every story my father used to tell us. He never clipped my wings; he taught me to be a unique and constructive person. I may not be able to describe in any number of pages how humble and awesome a father I had.

My father was suffering from chronic illness. I could see my mother praying every day for his health. We tried everything from expensive hospitals to strangers' advice of visiting temples. At the beginning of this book, my father was so excited, and he blessed and wished me to accomplish the book successfully. A few days after, we visited the temple far from home, and he unfortunately took his last breath in the temple's premises.

My father always used tell me to be a lifetime learner, because "The best cannot happen through luck, it needs years of hard work and dedication". I will continue to be the best I can and will be a lifetime learner.

Though he may not be with me physically, all his ideologies that feed the hunger—work hard, be the best you can, and more—will continue through me and through all my work.

– Ashok Kumar Srinivas

`mapt.io`

Mapt is an online digital library that gives you full access to over 5,000 books and videos, as well as industry leading tools to help you plan your personal development and advance your career. For more information, please visit our website.

Why subscribe?

- Spend less time learning and more time coding with practical eBooks and Videos from over 4,000 industry professionals

- Improve your learning with Skill Plans built especially for you

- Get a free eBook or video every month

- Mapt is fully searchable

- Copy and paste, print, and bookmark content

PacktPub.com

Did you know that Packt offers eBook versions of every book published, with PDF and ePub files available? You can upgrade to the eBook version at `www.PacktPub.com` and as a print book customer, you are entitled to a discount on the eBook copy. Get in touch with us at `service@packtpub.com` for more details.

At `www.PacktPub.com`, you can also read a collection of free technical articles, sign up for a range of free newsletters, and receive exclusive discounts and offers on Packt books and eBooks.

Contributors

About the author

Ashok Kumar S has been working in the mobile development domain for about eight years. He is a Google-certified engineer, a speaker at global scale conferences, and he also runs a YouTube channel called AndroidABCD for Android developers. He is an early Firebase adopter before Google acquires Firebase.

He is a computer science and engineering graduate who is passionate about innovation in technology. He contributes to open source heavily to improve his e-karma.
He has also written a book on Wear OS programming using a project-based approach, titled *Android Wear Projects*.

I would like to express my deepest appreciation and special gratitude to all those from the Packt Editorial team who helped me complete this book, especially Francis Savio Carneiro, Sachin Sunilkumar, and Roshan Ravi Kumar.

I'd also like to thank T. Subhash Chandra and Mohan B.A. for all the motivation. Finally, my deepest thanks to my mother Lalitha Srinivas, and my friends and family who helped manifest the book.

About the reviewers

Houssem Yahiaoui is full stack JavaScript developer and consultant based in Algeria. He has worked for many local and international agencies, and now has an interest in new technologies and machine learning with JavaScript. He's the author of *Firebase Cookbook* and is also a meetup and community advocate, conference speaker, and bootcamp mentor. In his free time, Houssem is a blockchain advocate, backpacker, and traveler, with a keen eye for local food experiments.

I would like to thank my family, mostly my mother for her infinite support in every possible way. Without you, I would never be where I am now.

Harmeet Singh is a senior associate working for Synechron with varied experience in UI. He hails from the holy city of Amritsar, India. His expertise includes HTML5, CSS, JavaScript, jQuery, Angular, ReactJS, Redux, Firebase, MongoDB, and Node.js. His interests include music, sports, and adventure. Harmeet has given various presentations and conducted many workshops on UI development. On the academic front, Harmeet is a graduate in IT and is a GNIIT diploma holder from NIIT, specializing in software engineering. He can be reached on Skype and LinkedIn at *harmeetsingh090*.

I would like to thank my best friend, Srishti Gajbhiye, for her tremendous support and motivation to make this work possible.

Packt is searching for authors like you

If you're interested in becoming an author for Packt, please visit `authors.packtpub.com` and apply today. We have worked with thousands of developers and tech professionals, just like you, to help them share their insight with the global tech community. You can make a general application, apply for a specific hot topic that we are recruiting an author for, or submit your own idea.

Table of Contents

Preface   1

Chapter 1: Keep It Real – Firebase Realtime Database   7
  Firebase Realtime Database   8
  Setting up a development environment   9
    Prerequisites   9
    Configuring Firebase in Android projects   9
  Reading and writing to Realtime Database   10
    Database reference   10
    Writing into Realtime Database   11
    Reading from Realtime Database   12
    Structuring the data with objects   13
    Reading the objects from Firebase   15
    Reading value changes   16
      Parsing the DataSnapshot object   17
    Updating data   17
    Writing HashMaps to Realtime Database   18
    Realtime Database and lists   19
    Deleting data   21
      Offline capabilities   22
  Realtime Database rules   22
    Default security rules   22
    Database rules and types   25
      Customizing database rules   26
      Data security   27
    Custom variables   28
    Default variables   28
      RuleDataSnapshot and its methods   29
  Creating an Android application using Realtime Database   30
    User interface design   30
    Logic   35
  Summary   42

Chapter 2: Safe and Sound – Firebase Authentication   43
  Firebase Authentication   44
  Setting up Firebase Authentication   45
    FirebaseUI Auth authentication   46
    Firebase SDK Authentication   47
  FirebaseUI Email Authentication   48
    Configuring for Email Authentication   48

Enabling Email/Password Authentication in Console 52
Initializing Firebase Authentication 53
Finalizing the project 54
Firebase SDK Email Authentication 57
Sign up new users 57
Sign in existing users 58
Managing users 59
Provider-specific user profile details 60
Profile updating 60
Sending a verification Email 61
Forgot password 61
Deleting a user 62
Managing users through console 63
Smart Lock 65
FirebaseUI social networking site authentication 65
Google Sign-in 66
SHA-1 fingerprint 66
Code for Google provider 68
Facebook Login 71
Facebook App ID and App secret 71
Project configuration 75
Twitter Sign-in 77
Twitter Api key 78
Project Configuration 80
Phone number sign-in 82
Project configuration 82
Firebase SDK social networking site authentication 84
Google sign-in 84
Facebook login 85
Twitter sign-in 87
Phone number sign-in 89
Anonymous Authentication 90
Link multiple Auth providers 91
Firebase Authentication failures 92
Firebase Authentication exceptions 92
Summary 93
Chapter 3: Safe and Sound – Firebase Crashlytics 95
Firebase Crash Reporting and Crashlytics 96
Firebase Crash Reporting setup 97
Creating crash reports 98
Creating custom logs 100
Deobfuscating ProGuard labels 100
Crash Report support for multiple APK 101
Disabling Crash Reporting 102
Firebase Crashlytics 103

Firebase Crashlytics setup and upgrading from Crash Reporting   103
Migrating from Firebase Crash Reporting to Crashlytics   105
Validating Crashlytics implementation   106
Enabling Crashlytics debug mode   107
Customizing Crashlytics reports   107
Crashlytics and functions   109
Summary   110

Chapter 4: Genie in the Cloud – Firebase Cloud Functions   111
  Firebase Cloud Functions   112
    Set up the development environment   113
      Project structure   116
        Required modules   117
        Deploying Cloud functions project   118
        Custom logs and reviewing functions   119
  Trigger functions   122
    Cloud Firestore Triggers   122
      Specific documents   123
      Creating a document   123
      Updating documents   124
      Deleting a document   124
      Changes in a document   125
    Realtime Database Triggers   126
    Firebase Authentication Triggers   127
    Analytics and Crashlytics Triggers   127
    Cloud Storage Triggers   129
    HTTP Triggers   129
    Cloud Pub/Sub Triggers   131
  Writing Firebase functions   131
    Cloud Functions to fire a push notification   133
  Summary   138

Chapter 5: Arsenal for Your Files – Firebase Cloud Storage   139
  Firebase a Cloud Storage   140
  Creating storage reference   141
    Storage reference properties   142
    Limitations of reference   142
  Uploading and downloading files   143
    Uploading files   144
      Uploading existing files   144
      Uploading files as a stream   145
      Uploading from data in memory   146
      Managing file upload   147
      Monitoring file upload   148
      Beyond monitoring and managing   149
    Downloading files   152
      Creating a reference   153

Downloading into memory	153
Downloading into a local file	154
Downloading data through a URL	155
Downloading images using FirebaseUI	155
Beyond downloading files	156
File metadata	158
Retrieving File Metadata	158
Update the metadata of the file	158
Deleting files	161
Handling common errors	161
Security and rules	162
The general syntax for storage security rules	163
Securing user files	166
Request and Resource Evaluation	168
Storage and functions	169
Firebase Storage in practice	170
Summary	181
Chapter 6: Not Just a Keeper, Firebase Hosting	183
Firebase Hosting	184
Deploying a website	185
Connecting to custom domain	191
Connecting Firebase cloud functions	193
Customizing hosting behavior	197
Custom 404/Not Found page	197
Redirects	198
Rewrites	198
Headers	199
Hosting priorities	199
Reserved URLs	200
Summary	200
Chapter 7: Inspection and Evaluation – Firebase Test Lab	201
Firebase Test Lab	202
Test Lab for Android	203
Choosing the testing method	205
Robo testing	205
Choosing device type and reviewing test results	206
Test Lab with Firebase Console	206
Test Lab with gcloud CLI	212
Google Cloud SDK environment	212
Choosing test configurations	212
Scripting gcloud commands with Test Lab	213
Test Lab with CI systems	214
Creating a Jenkins project	216
Test Lab with Android Studio	217

Firebase Test Lab results 219
  Available devices in Test Lab 220
Firebase Test Lab Game Loop testing 221
  Test Loop Manager 222
  Game loop in Test Lab 223
Prelaunch reports 224
Summary 224
Chapter 8: A Smart Watchdog – Firebase Performance Monitoring 225
Firebase Performance Monitoring 226
  Performance Monitoring for Android 227
    Automatic traces 229
  Custom trace and counters 230
    Performance Monitoring for Android performance 231
    Monitoring for specific network requests 232
  Monitoring custom attributes 232
    Enabling Logcat output 233
    Firebase Console for Performance Monitoring 235
Summary 237
Chapter 9: Application Usage Measuring and Notification, Firebase Analytics, and Cloud Messaging 239
Firebase Analytics 240
  Firebase Analytics for Android 241
    Setting user properties 242
    Analytics in a WebView 242
    Debugging events 244
    Firebase Analytics and functions 245
Cloud Messaging 246
  Firebase Cloud Messaging in Android 248
    Accessing the device registration token 249
  Cloud Messaging explained 251
    Sending the first notification 251
Summary 256
Chapter 10: Changing Your App – Firebase Remote Config and Dynamic Links 257
Firebase Remote Config 258
  Setting up Remote Config on Android 259
    Remote Config's singleton object 259
    In-app parameters 260
    Accessing the Remote Config parameters 261
    Server-side parameters 261
    Fetching the parameters 263
    Activating parameters 265
    Conditions, rules, and values 265
    Remote Config and Google Analytics 267

A/B Testing with Remote Config | 268
Firebase Dynamic Links | 274
Dynamic Links use cases | 275
Converting mobile web users to native app users | 276
Sharing content between users | 277
Rewarding referrals using Firebase | 278
The anatomy of Dynamic Links | 282
Creating Dynamic Links | 283
Receiving Dynamic Links | 284
Summary | 285

Chapter 11: Bringing Everyone on the Same Page, Firebase Invites, and Firebase App Indexing | 287
Firebase Invites | 288
Sending and receiving invites from Android applications | 289
Firebase App Indexing | 293
Enabling public content indexing | 295
Enabling personal content indexing | 298
Logging user actions | 301
Testing your implementation | 302
Search performance and latest APIs | 303
Summary | 306

Chapter 12: Making a Monetary Impact and Firebase AdMob and AdWords | 307
Firebase AdWords | 308
Creating an AdWords account | 309
Linking AdWords to Firebase | 310
Tracking app conversions with Firebase | 312
AdMob | 312
Android Studio and initializing the SDK | 315
Summary | 316

Chapter 13: Flexible NoSQL and Cloud Firestore | 317
Cloud Firestore | 318
Adding and managing data | 321
Choosing a data structure for your Firestore project | 322
Querying data | 328
Securing data | 330
Offline data support | 331
Summary | 332

Chapter 14: Analytics Data, Clairvoyant, Firebase Predictions | 333
Firebase Predictions | 334
Setting up Firebase Predictions | 336
Optimizing monetization | 338
Optimizing promotions | 341

Preventing churn	343
Predefined predictions	344
Predictions and risk tolerance	345
Summary	346
Chapter 15: Training Your Code and ML Kit	347
Firebase ML Kit	348
Vision	350
Recognizing text	350
Setting up ML Kit for recognizing text	351
On-device text recognition	352
Cloud-Based text recognition	353
Face detection	355
Setting up ML Kit for face detection	355
Barcode scanning	358
Setting up ML Kit for barcode scanning	358
Custom models	359
ML Kit and text recognition	361
Summary	367
Other Books You May Enjoy	369
Index	373

Preface

Firebase is a very popular Backend-as-a-Service (**BaaS**) tool launched in April 2012. Because of its state-of-the-art capabilities and technology such as its real-time database, it caught the interest of Google and was acquired by Google in 2014. I started to explore Firebase technologies before Google's acquisition. Now, Firebase has transformed into a powerful tool, containing support for most of the use cases of real-world software development. Firebase divides the toolchain into three distinct categories: build your application, improve the application's quality, and grow your business.

The book introduces all the tools with quick code snippets, and also, in a couple of chapters you get to run programs as quick simple projects. The book will give you complete comprehension of what Firebase has to offer for Android developers by tailoring features and code snippet examples in every chapter.

Since Firebase, it has become easy to build a great mobile application, be it iOS or Android. Firebase has a lot of things to offer, from analytics to user acquisition and A/B testing, and the list goes on. This book will cover the most up-to-date information on Firebase, including the latest tools that were introduced in Google IO 2018.

Who this book is for

The book can be used by any developer who has basic knowledge of building mobile or web applications. Though the book targets Android developers, there are chapters on Firebase functions and hosting that can help web developers too.

What this book covers

Chapter 1, *Keep It Real – Firebase Realtime Databaset*, will introduce configuring the development environment and deep dive into the popular Firebase feature, the real-time database.

Chapter 2, *Safe and Sound – Firebase Authentication*, demonstrates how to use the multi-platform sign-in feature available in Firebase. Developers will be able to explore email authentication, social login, phone number authentication, and more.

Chapter 3, *Safe and Sound – Firebase Crashlytics*, demonstrates the Firebase crash reporting feature in detail, along with how to diagnose and fix bugs, and how to generate detailed error reports

Chapter 4, *Genie in the Cloud – Firebase Cloud Functions*, contains comprehensive examples and an overview of Firebase functions. Firebase functions is still in beta and the active development phase, but it is already a jaw-dropping technology.

Chapter 5, *Arsenal for Your Files – Firebase Cloud Storage*, consists of comprehensive examples and an overview of Firebase cloud storage. Firebase cloud storage helps store and serve content with ease. This chapter will show how to store different mime type files ranging from photographs to videos.

Chapter 6, *Not Just a Keeper, Firebase Hosting*, comprises comprehensive examples and an overview of Firebase Hosting. Firebase Hosting is a very handy feature for hosting websites. Firebase Hosting has low latency and Global CDN with a free SSL certificate.

Chapter 7, *Inspection and Evaluation – Firebase Test Lab*, contains comprehensive examples and an overview of Firebase Test Lab for Android. This cloud-based infrastructure helps developers to test their products on different use cases. Test Lab can test applications remotely on different devices.

Chapter 8, *A Smart Watchdog – Firebase Performance Monitoring*, explains the process of diagnosing an application's performance issues. Using the trace feature, we will be able to monitor specific bugs and avoid performance setbacks.

Chapter 9, *Application Usage Measuring and Notification, Firebase Analytics, and Cloud Messaging*, explains how to measure an application's usage and send and receive push notifications.

Chapter 10, *Changing Your App – Firebase Remote Config and Dynamic Links*, explains that Firebase Remote Config lets you change the behavior and appearance of your application. Dynamic links are very useful in terms of presenting the content to different platforms.

Chapter 11, *Bringing Everyone on the Same Page, Firebase Invites, and Firebase App Indexing, and Firebase App Indexing*, explores sending and receiving invites from your mobile app. Also, App index helps get public and personal content from your app into users' search results.

Chapter 12, *Making a Monetary Impact and Firebase AdMob and AdWords*, helps developers inflate in-app advertisements and improve the user experience. You will access monetization reports using AdWords developer, and will learn how to reach potential customers with online ads.

Chapter 13, *Flexible NoSQL and Cloud Firestore*, helping developers to write next-generation Firebase applications.

Chapter 14, *Analytics Data, Clairvoyant, Firebase Predictions*, demonstrates the power of Firebase Predictions, which runs the advanced machine learning algorithms by predicting the next action before it takes place.

Chapter 15, *Train Your Code and ML-kit*, illustrates the power of ML-kit by explaining its features. You also will write an application to perform text recognition in a photograph captured through your phone's camera.

To get the most out of this book

To master Firebase, you need to have fundamental knowledge of platforms such as iOS, web, and Android. The book mostly targets Android developers, and at the time of writing, the following assumptions were made for the reader:

1. How to install the latest version of Android Studio
2. Has Google official credentials for Firebase
3. An intermediate developer who can understand Java and Kotlin syntax
4. Little experience of CLI tools and Node.js syntax

The book also has a little for web developers if you are a beginner and want to explore how to host your website and you want to understand a little bit about writing Node.js code that can trigger an action.

Download the example code files

You can download the example code files for this book from your account at www.packtpub.com. If you purchased this book elsewhere, you can visit www.packtpub.com/support and register to have the files emailed directly to you.

You can download the code files by following these steps:

1. Log in or register at www.packtpub.com.
2. Select the **SUPPORT** tab.
3. Click on **Code Downloads & Errata**.
4. Enter the name of the book in the **Search** box and follow the onscreen instructions.

Once the file is downloaded, please make sure that you unzip or extract the folder using the latest version of:

- WinRAR/7-Zip for Windows
- Zipeg/iZip/UnRarX for Mac
- 7-Zip/PeaZip for Linux

The code bundle for the book is also hosted on GitHub at https://github.com/PacktPublishing/Mastering-Firebase-for-Android-Development. In case there's an update to the code, it will be updated on the existing GitHub repository.

We also have other code bundles from our rich catalog of books and videos available at https://github.com/PacktPublishing/. Check them out!

Conventions used

There are a number of text conventions used throughout this book.

CodeInText: Indicates code words in text, database table names, folder names, filenames, file extensions, pathnames, dummy URLs, user input, and Twitter handles. Here is an example: "Mount the downloaded WebStorm-10*.dmg disk image file as another disk in your system."

A block of code is set as follows:

```
FirebaseUser user = FirebaseAuth.getInstance().getCurrentUser();
if (user != null) {
    // When User is signed in
} else {
    // When user is not signed in
}
```

When we wish to draw your attention to a particular part of a code block, the relevant lines or items are set in bold:

```
myTrace = FirebasePerformance.getInstance().newTrace("packt_trace")
myTrace?.start()
val bundle = Bundle()
bundle.putString("oncreate", "created")
mFirebaseAnalytics?.logEvent(FirebaseAnalytics.Event.SELECT_CONTENT,
bundle)
myTrace?.stop()
```

Any command-line input or output is written as follows:

```
npm install -g firebase-tools
```

Bold: Indicates a new term, an important word, or words that you see onscreen. For example, words in menus or dialog boxes appear in the text like this. Here is an example: "Select **System info** from the **Administration** panel."

Warnings or important notes appear like this.

Tips and tricks appear like this.

Get in touch

Feedback from our readers is always welcome.

General feedback: Email feedback@packtpub.com and mention the book title in the subject of your message. If you have questions about any aspect of this book, please email us at questions@packtpub.com.

Errata: Although we have taken every care to ensure the accuracy of our content, mistakes do happen. If you have found a mistake in this book, we would be grateful if you would report this to us. Please visit www.packtpub.com/submit-errata, selecting your book, clicking on the Errata Submission Form link, and entering the details.

Piracy: If you come across any illegal copies of our works in any form on the Internet, we would be grateful if you would provide us with the location address or website name. Please contact us at copyright@packtpub.com with a link to the material.

If you are interested in becoming an author: If there is a topic that you have expertise in and you are interested in either writing or contributing to a book, please visit authors.packtpub.com.

Reviews

Please leave a review. Once you have read and used this book, why not leave a review on the site that you purchased it from? Potential readers can then see and use your unbiased opinion to make purchase decisions, we at Packt can understand what you think about our products, and our authors can see your feedback on their book. Thank you!

For more information about Packt, please visit packtpub.com.

1
Keep It Real – Firebase Realtime Database

It has always been a dream to produce a hassle-free backend that will help in providing profound solutions to build better mobile and web applications. In April, 2012, James Tamplin and Andrew Lee launched Firebase. In its early stage, Firebase provided an API that helped to integrate the online chat modules to websites. Now Firebase is one of the dominant **BaaS** (**Backend as a Service**) platforms that is continuously improving the cloud experience by introducing new features and functionalities. Firebase is the only provider with autosyncing database functionality. It lets you grow great applications, develop your consumer base, and acquire more monetary value. Each feature works freely, and they work far superior together. Firebase has created a massive buzz in the developer community. Most of the traditional backend services are quite easy to implement and get into production. Firebase is the best fit when there is a short development time and the application demands data in real time as it is easy to scale. We can also mix and match Firebase products to solve everyday app development challenges.

In this chapter, we will cover the following topics:

- Overview of the Firebase Realtime Database
- Setting up the development environment for the Firebase toolchain
- Creating our first Firebase Android project and structuring the data
- Reading and writing the data and enabling offline capabilities
- Working with different structures of data in the Realtime Database
- Pros and cons of using the Realtime Database

Firebase Realtime Database

The Firebase Realtime Database gives you a chance to fabricate rich, community-oriented applications by enabling secure access to the database specifically from client-side code. Data will continue to be cached locally, and even while disconnected to the internet, real-time events keep on firing, giving the end client a responsive ordeal. At the point when the device recaptures connection, the Realtime Database synchronizes the local data changes with the remote updates that happened while the client was disconnected, consolidating any data contentions consequently.

The Realtime Database gives an adaptable, expression-based rules language, called Firebase Realtime Database Security Rules, to characterize how your data ought to remain organized and when data can be fetched from or written over. At the point when incorporated with Firebase Authentication, engineers can characterize on who approaches what information, and how they can get to it.

The Realtime Database is a very powerful NoSQL database and, in that capacity, it has several advancements and usefulness when compared with a relational database. The Realtime Database API is intended just to permit operations that can continue to be executed rapidly. Firebase allows the developer to assemble an impressive real-time experience that can serve millions of clients without bargaining on responsiveness. Along these lines, it is critical to consider how clients need to get to your information and after that structure it accordingly.

The Firebase Realtime Database supports Android, iOS, web, and more. All data is put away in JSON format and any change in data is reflected promptly by performing a sync operation across every platform. Realtime Database enables us to construct more adaptable real-time applications effortlessly. It helps users to collaborate with one another. At the point when clients are disconnected from the internet, the Realtime Database SDKs employ local cache on the device to store changes. Later when the device comes online, the local data is automatically synchronized to Realtime Database. The Realtime Database incorporates with Firebase Authentication to give basic and instinctive authentication for developers. You can utilize the Firebase security model to permit access-based client identity or with pattern coordinating on your data.

In October, 2017, Google announced Cloud Firestore, the latest real-time, scalable NoSQL database from Firebase and Google Cloud Platform. Since Firestore is still in the beta program, we will learn about Firestore, and the last chapter is dedicated to it.

Setting up a development environment

To get started, we need to integrate the Firebase SDK to the project, and it is a one-time integration. Later, we can choose any of the Firebase tools that we want to work with and add the appropriate gradle dependency.

Prerequisites

To develop Firebase applications, you can surely use your development environment; the essential requirements are as follows:

1. Your favorite operating system (Windows, macOS, or Linux)
2. Determine whether you have the latest JRE installed on your operating system
3. Install the latest version of JDK or Open JDK
4. Install the newest version of Android Studio (at the time of writing, the most recent stable version is 2.3.3 and 3.0 is still in beta, or any newer version should also be excellent)
5. Android SDK with one complete API will be very significant

 Before we continue to create our first Firebase Realtime Database Android application, ensure that you have one complete version of Android API installed, and you have the latest version of Android Studio.

Configuring Firebase in Android projects

There are two ways that you can connect Firebase to your Android project, from the Firebase console creating the new project and adding the dependencies and Google config file. The other way is just to add Firebase support to an Android project directly from Android Studio:

1. The usual way of connecting Firebase is to visit the Firebase console at `https://console.firebase.google.com/`
2. Create a new project using the **Add Project** button, and if you already have an existing project, you are free to choose it
3. In the overview section of the console, you can choose to add an Android application by clicking on the relevant button and add the necessary information to the fields

4. Download the `google-services.json` file, add it to your project's `app` folder root, and the classpath gradle dependencies in the project's `gradle` file

5. To reduce the effort, we can make Android Studio do all this for us by choosing the **Tools | Firebase** menu option and clicking on the Firebase tools that you want to integrate from the list

6. After you chose the Firebase tool, tap on **Save** and retrieve data

7. In the next window panel, you will see options such as **Launch in the browser**, **Connect your app to Firebase**, and so on, click on the **Connect your app to Firebase** button and select your project or you can create the new project in the **Connect to Firebase** window

8. Go back to the Firebase panel and click on the **Add the Realtime Database to your application** button

Since we have connected to Firebase, it is as simple as it sounds, all we have to do is select the **Add the Realtime Database to your application** button in the **Firebase assistance** window, you will see a dialog for requesting your authorization to change the gradle file with a few dependencies. Tap on **Accept Changes**, now we are all set to explore Realtime Database abilities.

Reading and writing to Realtime Database

Since the nuts and bolts of the Firebase Realtime Database are set up, the next stage is to explore how data can be composed or written to a database tree from an Android application. This section will give points of interest on the most proficient method to write, how to erase database tree nodes, and furthermore, outline a few strategies for taking care of database write errors.

Database reference

Essentially, a reference to the database is required. Every Firebase project has its own particular devoted Realtime Database items of which can be examined by opening the project inside the Firebase console and picking the **Database** option. Inside the console, panels can be selected to show data trees set away in the database, the rules outlined for fetching the access, database use estimations, and so on.

Firebase databases are usually **Representational State Transfer** (**REST**) endpoint references, which we will use to add the data. We will understand how to fetch the reference with the following code snippet:

```
// fetch reference database
FirebaseDatabase mDatabase = FirebaseDatabase.getInstance();
DatabaseReference mDbRef = mDatabase.getReference("Donor/Name");
```

The preceding code will fetch the reference, on the off chance that the particular path does not exist now, it is composed automatically inside the tree when data is written at that location.

Writing into Realtime Database

Fetch an instance of your database employing `getInstance()` and reference the location you need to write. You can write most of the primitive data types as they also include Java objects:

```
// Write a message to the database
FirebaseDatabase mDatabase = FirebaseDatabase.getInstance();
DatabaseReference mDbRef = mDatabase.getReference("Donor/Name");
mDbRef.setValue("Parinitha Krishna");
```

The following screenshot explains the dashboard changes after running the preceding code:

If you notice that there aren't any changes in the dashboard from the write operation, we shall attach an `onFailure` callback like the following for identifying what's stopping it:

```
// Write a message to the database
FirebaseDatabase mDatabase = FirebaseDatabase.getInstance();
DatabaseReference mDbRef = mDatabase.getReference("Donor/Name");
mDbRef.setValue("Parinitha Krishna").addOnFailureListener(new
OnFailureListener() {
    @Override
    public void onFailure(@NonNull Exception e) {
        Log.d(TAG, e.getLocalizedMessage());
    }
});
```

Before we compile the preceding code snippet, we need to change the rules to be `true` since we are no longer using any authentication service. Go to the **Rules** tab and change the read and write service to be `true`. When we do this, remember that the endpoint is publicly accessible by anybody who has the URL:

```
{
"rules": {
".read": true,
".write": true
}
}
```

Reading from Realtime Database

After writing the data into Firebase now it's time to read what we have written. Firebase Realtime Database syncs all the data in real time across platforms and devices. So we have an `onDatachanged()` callback to read the data:

```
// Read from the database
mDbRef.addValueEventListener(new ValueEventListener() {
    @Override
    public void onDataChange(DataSnapshot dataSnapshot) {
        // This method is called once with the initial value and again
        // whenever data at this location is updated.
        String value = dataSnapshot.getValue(String.class);
        Log.d(TAG, "Value is: " + value);
    }

    @Override
```

```
    public void onCancelled(DatabaseError error) {
        // Failed to read value
        Log.w(TAG, "Failed to read value.", error.toException());
    }
});
```

Structuring the data with objects

Create a model class with constructors and declare a string to fetch the database reference for a unique key to add the list of objects. The model class is as follows:

```
public class Users {

    private String Name;
    private String Email;
    private String Phone;

    public Users() {
    }

    public String getName() {
        return Name;
    }

    public void setName(String name) {
        Name = name;
    }

    public String getEmail() {
        return Email;
    }

    public void setEmail(String email) {
        Email = email;
    }

    public String getPhone() {
        return Phone;
    }

    public void setPhone(String phone) {
        Phone = phone;
    }

    public Users(String name, String email, String phone) {
        Name = name;
```

```
            Email = email;
            Phone = phone;
        }

    }
```

Now in the activity class using the `DatabaseReference` class we can set the object value to Firebase, as follows:

```
public class MainActivity extends AppCompatActivity {

    private static final String TAG = "MainActivity";
    private FirebaseDatabase mDatabase;
    private DatabaseReference mDbRef;
    private String userId;

    @Override
    protected void onCreate(Bundle savedInstanceState) {
        super.onCreate(savedInstanceState);
        setContentView(R.layout.activity_main);

        // Write a message to the database
        mDatabase = FirebaseDatabase.getInstance();
        mDbRef = mDatabase.getReference("Donor/Name");

        //Setting firebase unique key for Hashmap list
        String userId = mDbRef.push().getKey();
        // creating user object
        Users user = new Users("Hillary", "hillary@xyz.com", "90097863873",
"Tokyo");

        mDbRef.child(userId).setValue(user);

    }
}
```

The preceding code will add the object into Firebase as follows:

Reading the objects from Firebase

To read the object data from Firebase Realtime `ValueEventListner()` whenever there is an update in the database in `onDatachanged` callback we can read the data changes:

```
mDbRef.child(userId).addValueEventListener(new ValueEventListener() {
    @Override
    public void onDataChange(DataSnapshot dataSnapshot) {

        Users user = dataSnapshot.getValue(Users.class);

        Log.d(TAG, "User name: " + user.getName() + ", email " +
user.getEmail());
    }

    @Override
    public void onCancelled(DatabaseError error) {
        // Failed to read value
        Log.w(TAG, "Failed to read value.", error.toException());
    }
});
```

When the code is executed, it will result in fetching the data tree to your project. It is up to us how we make use of the data.

Since we are using unique key mechanism the data will be added under the **Name** reference with a unique identifier:

Reading value changes

In Firebase Realtime Database to listen to the data changes, we have `addValueEventListener` for listening to the multiple nodes. In case you want to check the single value by adding `addListenerForSingleValueEvent()`, we can do that as well:

```
mDbRef = mDatabase.getReference("/Donor/name");


ValueEventListener changeListener = new ValueEventListener() {
    @Override
    public void onDataChange(DataSnapshot dataSnapshot) {
    }

    @Override
    public void onCancelled(DatabaseError databaseError) {
    }
};

mDbRef.addValueEventListener(changeListener);
```

When a listener is not required, it should be detached from the database reference object as follows:

```
mDbRef.removeEventListener(changeListener);
```

Parsing the DataSnapshot object

In a simple way, DataSnapshot can be accessed through the getValue method. We can use the child() method to reach to a specific path of a snapshot. Consider the following example code snippet that fetches the title:

```
String title =
mDataSnapshot.child("message1").child("title").getValue(String.class);
```

And all the children can be accessed using the getChildren() method. Consider the following code that is reading all the child details inside a for each loop:

```
for (DataSnapshot child : mDataSnapshot.getChildren()) {
    Log.i(TAG, child.getKey());
    Log.i(TAG, child.getValue(String.class));
}
```

Updating data

To update data, we can use the setValue() method by passing updated values. You can likewise utilize updateChildren() by passing the way to update data without exasperating other child nodes:

```
String newEmail = "ashokslsk@gmail.com";
mDbRef.child(userId).child("email").setValue(newEmail);
```

The following screenshot illustrates the updated value for the **email** field:

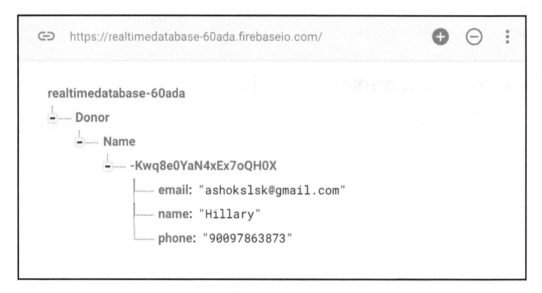

Writing HashMaps to Realtime Database

By using the updateChildren() method of the database reference class, we can write the HashMap data structure into Firebase Realtime Database. Let's create a HashMap and add different key-value pairs, each should be reflected in the Realtime Database:

```
// Write a message to the database
mDatabase = FirebaseDatabase.getInstance();
mDbRef = mDatabase.getReference("Donor/Name");

//Writing Hashmap
Map<String, Object> mHashmap = new HashMap<>();

mHashmap.put("Name 1/title", "Ashok");
mHashmap.put("Name 1/content", "Parinitha");
mHashmap.put("Name 2/title", "Krishna");
mHashmap.put("Name 2/content", "Sumuthra");

mDbRef.updateChildren(mHashmap);
```

The following screenshot illustrates the HashMap writing in the Firebase console:

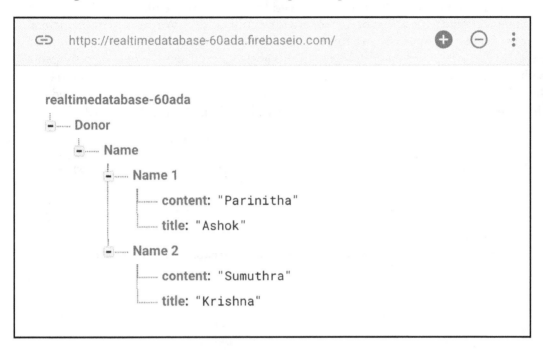

Realtime Database and lists

Lists are compelling data structures and they help in numerous use cases. Firebase has excellent support for HashMap and lists. Users can append the data according to the unique key from Firebase, or you can create your logic to create a unique identifier. Using the `push()` method a user can insert the data, and there are many ways to filter and match the data pushed. Let's see how the `push()` method helps in creating a list. As usual first grab the reference to the database and then using the `push()` method get the unique key. Using the `push()` method we can add a new child:

```
// Write a message to the database
mDatabase = FirebaseDatabase.getInstance();
mDbRef = mDatabase.getReference("Donor/Name");

//Setting firebase unique key for Hashmap list
String key = mDbRef.push().getKey();

mDbRef.child(key).setValue("First item");
```

Apart from allowing a database to create a list, it is also necessary to receive a data-changed notification from the list. This can be achieved through adding child event listeners. These listeners will notify the app when there is a new child added. We need to implement a couple of callbacks when we use this listener. Most commonly there is the onChildAdded() method when a child is added, and it sends a new data snapshot with data added. Note that onChildChanged() is called when there is an update to the existing node, and onChildRemoved() is called when a child node is removed. However onChildMoved() is called when any alterations change the list order:

```
ChildEventListener childListener = new ChildEventListener() {
    @Override
    public void onChildAdded(DataSnapshot dataSnapshot, String s) {
    }
    @Override
    public void onChildChanged(DataSnapshot dataSnapshot, String s) {
    }
    @Override
    public void onChildMoved(DataSnapshot dataSnapshot, String s) {
    }
    @Override
    public void onChildRemoved(DataSnapshot dataSnapshot) {
    }
    @Override
    public void onCancelled(DatabaseError databaseError) {
    }
};

mDbRef.addChildEventListener(childListener);
```

There are many ways to perform the query on the list. Firebase has a class named Query to access the database inside the application on specified criteria:

```
Query mQuery = mDbRef.orderByKey();

ValueEventListener mQueryValueListener = new ValueEventListener() {
    @Override
    public void onDataChange(DataSnapshot dataSnapshot) {
        Iterable<DataSnapshot> snapshotIterator =
dataSnapshot.getChildren();
        Iterator<DataSnapshot> iterator = snapshotIterator.iterator();
        while (iterator.hasNext()) {
            DataSnapshot next = (DataSnapshot) iterator.next();
            Log.i(TAG, "Value = " + next.child("name").getValue());
        }
    }
    @Override
```

```
        public void onCancelled(DatabaseError databaseError) {
        }
};

mQuery.addListenerForSingleValueEvent(mQueryValueListener);
```

Deleting data

To delete data, you can call the `removeValue()` method onto database reference. You can likewise pass null to the `setValue()` method, which does the same delete operation:

```
//Removes the entire child
mDbRef.child(userId).removeValue();
//Passing null to remove the calue
mDbRef.chile(userId).child("name").setValue(null);

// Similarly Hashmap can also be removed
Map<String, Object> mHashmap = new HashMap<>();

mHashmap.put("Name 1/title", null);
mHashmap.put("Name 1/content", null);
mHashmap.put("Name 2/title", null);
mHashmap.put("Name 2/content", null);
```

The following screenshot shows the Firebase console reaction for the delete operation:

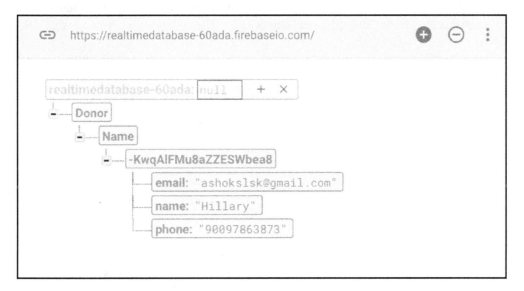

Offline capabilities

At the point when clients are disconnected from the internet, the Realtime Database SDKs employ local cache on the device to store changes. Later when the device comes online, the local data is automatically synchronized to Realtime Database. We can enable disk persistence to save the data offline from the following lines of code:

```
//Offline support
FirebaseDatabase.getInstance().setPersistenceEnabled(true);
```

Realtime Database rules

Firebase database rules control the process in which the data is put away in a Firebase Realtime Database, data is secured, approved, and indexed. These rules are characterized, utilizing a rules articulation language, such as JSON that might be arranged on each project basis, utilizing either the Firebase console or Firebase command-line interface.

In this section, we will explore Firebase rules in detail through the Firebase console.

Default security rules

By default, Firebase sets the rules for users to authenticate before writing or reading operations. We can go to our project in Firebase console and choose the **Database** option in the left-hand options panel and go to the **Rules** tab in the **Main** panel. The default rules are as follows:

```
{
 "rules": {
 ".read": "auth != null",
 ".write": "auth != null"
 }
}
```

The following screenshot shows the default security configurations for any Realtime Database project:

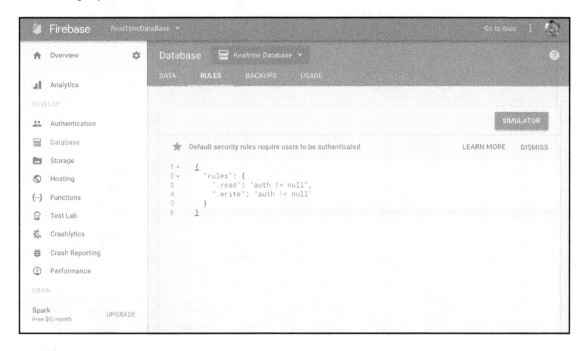

Firebase offers a unique way to examine rules in the simulator. In the right-hand corner of the Firebase console's **Main** window, you will notice a blue button labelled as **SIMULATOR**, click on it to have a perceptible familiarity. Now we can see that there are two checkboxes and one input field to enter the URL and a toggle button indicating **Authenticated**. If you toggle it towards the right side, you will see a drop-down allowing you to choose the security provider, and it will also show UID and auth token payload. When we click on the **RUN** button, it will show the possible responses.

The following screenshot shows the **Simulator** in a default state:

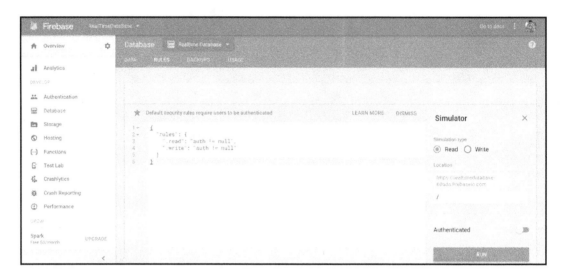

If we press the **RUN** button, the simulator assumes that the user continues not-authenticated, and it will return a **Simulated read denied** error.

The following screenshot illustrates the not-authenticated user's state:

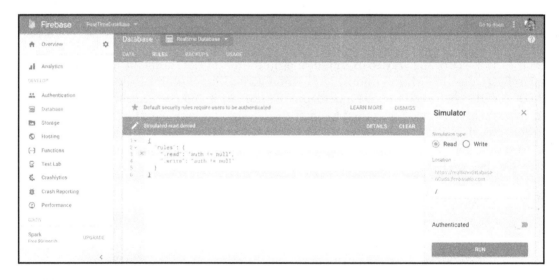

If you want to allow the user to access the database without authentication then you need to set the rules to `true`.

Since now we know what a simulator is, let's check what happens when we push the toggle button and choose a provider:

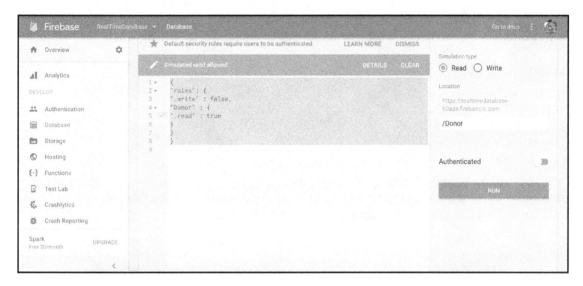

It will grant the access to the database. Likewise, we can run the test on the write operation and understand what happens behind the screen.

Database rules and types

Typically, there are four types of database rules. These rules dictate different responsibilities:

- Read and write rules: As already seen, the .read and .write rule types are utilized to pronounce the conditions under which the data in a Realtime Database might be perused and written by clients.
- Data validation rules: The .validate rule type enables standards to be used that approve data values before they are written to the database. This gives an adaptable approach to guarantee that data sent to the database meets the precise form. This includes ensuring that the data sent to a specific database node is string and does not surpass a particular length, child node limits, and so on.
- Indexing rules: The .indexOn rule type gives a system by which you, as the application engineer, have database nodes to be indexed, so intern helps you in arranging your child nodes as indexes, and it will help in ordering and querying.

Customizing database rules

Database rules are versatile and powerful and if we want to customize certain operations we can achieve it through rules. For instance, if we require giving access to read all the data and no write access to users, we can achieve this by using the following rules:

```
{
"rules": {
".read": true,
".write": false
}
}
```

The preceding rules will allow the user to have a read access to the database. Since there isn't any path specified, the complete database is readable, but not writable. If we want to customize on node basis we can take the node name into the rules and we can give the rules as follows. Test the rules in the simulator before publishing them:

```
{
"rules": {
".write" : false,
"Donor" : {
".read" : true
}
}
}
```

The following screenshot illustrates custom rules for read-write access to a particular node:

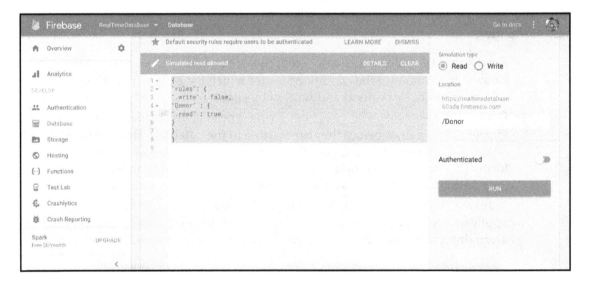

We can customize the rules to a level where we can specify which node needs to be read, which node can be written, which cannot be written, and a lot more.

Data security

Another outstanding feature of Firebase is security. Ensuring that no data is being given access to the unapproved or not-authenticated users. For this problem there is a variable named `auth`. It is a predefined variable within the database rules. It contains the auth provider, used auth ID, and token and user's UID. Using this we can restrict the database access and grant the application on a use case basis. Consider the following diagram for apprehending the security. There are blood donors and the details are helpful for having authentic donor information:

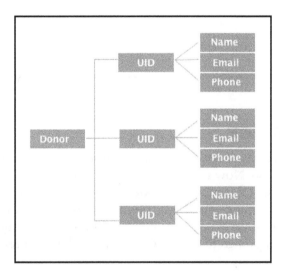

Consider the following rules that allow only authenticated users to read the data:

```
{
"rules": {
".write" : false,
"Donor" : {
"$uid": {
".read": "auth != null && auth.uid == $uid"
}
}
}
}
```

The following screenshot shows the simulated authenticated user:

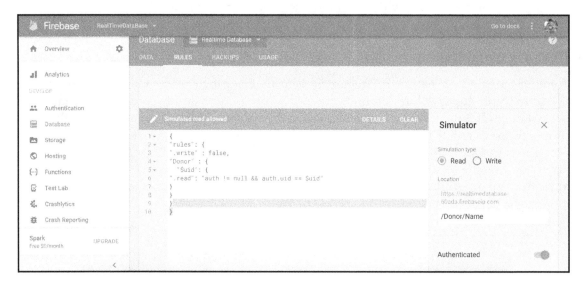

Custom variables

In previous examples, we have seen how to set the rules, how to use the predefined variables of rules, and so on. Now let's understand what custom variables are. Anything that has $ and the name that describes the node will be a variable that we can use in rule expressions. Say for instance, the value allocated to the UID will, obviously, rely upon which node is being read, since every user ID node will have a unique value doled out to it. The $ variable gives an approach to store the value to the key and reference rule expressions.

Default variables

With the ability to create custom variables, Firebase has predefined variables that can be used in database rules in many use cases. The following is a list of predefined variables:

- `auth`: This variable contains all the authentication related data, including UID and provider information. A null value in auth variable indicates that a user is not-authenticated.

- `now`: This variable has the current timestamp in milliseconds elapsed from a few decades (January 1, 1970).
- `data`: This is the reference of current data associated with a read or write request. Data supplies a `RuleDataSnapshot` instance for different methods to find the data content.

- `newData`: When a write request is approved it creates a `RuleDataSnapshot` instance to write.
- `root`: This denotes `RuleDataSnapshot` of the tree from the current database tree.

RuleDataSnapshot and its methods

`RuleDataSnapshot` is accessible from data and `newData` predefined variables. `RuleDataSnapshot` offers a variety of methods to perform operations on. They are enlisted as follows:

Method name	What it does
`Child()`	`Child()` returns a `RuleDataSnapshot` at the specified path.
`parent()`	It will return a parent node from the current node.
`hasChild(childpath)`	This method will return true or false on a specified child existence.
`hasChildren([children])`	This method will return true or false on a specified array of children existence.
`exists()`	This method will return true or false on `RuleDataSnapShot` whether it contains any data.
`getPriority()`	It will return the priority data from the snapshot.
`isNumber()`	It will return true or false if the snapshot has numeric value.
`isString()`	It will return true or false if the snapshot has a String value.
`isBoolean()`	It will return true or false if the snapshot has a boolean value.
`val()`	Used with the `child()` method to extract the associated value from the child node.

Consider the following code snippet that checks whether email fields exist or not, this will be very handy when you have huge datasets:

```
".write" :
"data.child('Donor').child('Name').child('userid').child('email').exists()"
```

Creating an Android application using Realtime Database

We have explored all the possibilities of Realtime Database. Now let's build a small application using what we have learned. Ideating on the health and medical field is something that helps in the long term. In this project, we will build an Android mobile application that is crowdsourced to fetch email addresses of blood donors.

User interface design

In this application, we will keep the user interface simple and informative. All we have is one `RecyclerView` and two buttons for adding and loading the data. The following xml layout code dictates the UI design:

```xml
<?xml version="1.0" encoding="utf-8"?>
<LinearLayout xmlns:android="http://schemas.android.com/apk/res/android"
    xmlns:tools="http://schemas.android.com/tools"
    android:id="@+id/activity_main"
    android:layout_width="match_parent"
    android:layout_height="match_parent"
    android:orientation="vertical">

    <TextView
        android:textColor="@color/colorPrimaryDark"
        android:textStyle="bold"
        android:textSize="25dp"
        android:gravity="center"
        android:text="Packt Blood Bank"
        android:layout_width="match_parent"
        android:layout_height="wrap_content" />
    <View
        android:layout_marginLeft="50dp"
        android:layout_marginRight="50dp"
        android:layout_width="match_parent"
        android:layout_height="5dp"
        android:background="@color/colorAccent" />
```

The following code adds the vertical `LinearLayout` to support the `DynamicData`:

```
<LinearLayout
    android:layout_marginTop="10dp"
    android:layout_width="match_parent"
    android:layout_height="match_parent"
    android:orientation="vertical">
    <LinearLayout
        android:layout_width="match_parent"
        android:layout_height="match_parent"
        android:layout_weight="1"
        android:orientation="vertical">

        <android.support.v7.widget.RecyclerView
            android:id="@+id/peopleList"
            android:layout_width="match_parent"
            android:layout_height="match_parent" />
</LinearLayout>
```

The above code sets the dynamic lists that load the data from `RecyclerView`. lets continue updating the same layout to make the UI complete.

```
<View
    android:layout_width="match_parent"
    android:layout_height="5dp"
    android:background="@color/colorPrimary" />
<LinearLayout
    android:layout_width="match_parent"
    android:layout_height="match_parent"
    android:layout_weight="1"
    android:orientation="vertical">
```

The following layout adds a scrollable layout for the input controls.

```
<ScrollView
    android:scrollIndicators="right"
    android:scrollbarStyle="insideOverlay"
    android:layout_width="match_parent"
    android:layout_height="match_parent"
    android:scrollbars="vertical">
    <LinearLayout
        android:layout_width="match_parent"
        android:layout_height="150px"
        android:layout_marginTop="40px"
        android:gravity="center"
        android:orientation="vertical">
        <LinearLayout
            android:layout_width="match_parent"
```

```xml
                android:layout_height="150px"
                android:layout_marginTop="40px"
                android:gravity="center"
                android:orientation="horizontal">
                <EditText
                    android:id="@+id/donorNameInput"
                    android:layout_width="match_parent"
                    android:layout_height="wrap_content"
                    android:layout_weight="1"
                    android:hint="Full name"
                    android:textColor="#000000"
                    android:textSize="16dp" />
                <EditText
                    android:id="@+id/donorCityInput"
                    android:layout_width="match_parent"
                    android:layout_height="wrap_content"
                    android:layout_weight="1"
                    android:hint="City"
                    android:textColor="#000000" />
            </LinearLayout>
```

The following code adds the donor blood group type and email address:

```xml
            <LinearLayout
                android:layout_width="match_parent"
                android:layout_height="150px"
                android:layout_marginTop="40px"
                android:gravity="center"
                android:orientation="horizontal">
                <EditText
                    android:id="@+id/donorBloodGroupInput"
                    android:layout_width="match_parent"
                    android:layout_height="wrap_content"
                    android:layout_weight="1"
                    android:hint="Blood Group"
                    android:textColor="#000000"
                    android:textSize="16dp" />
            </LinearLayout>

            <LinearLayout
                android:layout_width="match_parent"
                android:layout_height="150px"
                android:layout_marginTop="40px"
                android:gravity="center"
                android:orientation="horizontal">

                <EditText
                    android:id="@+id/donorEmailInput"
```

```
                    android:layout_width="match_parent"
                    android:layout_height="wrap_content"
                    android:layout_weight="1"
                    android:hint="Email address"
                    android:textColor="#000000"
                    android:textSize="16dp" />

            </LinearLayout>
```

The following code adds the buttons to act on the data received from the input fields:

```
            <RelativeLayout
                android:layout_width="match_parent"
                android:layout_height="wrap_content"
                android:background="#36FFFFFF">
                <Button
                    android:id="@+id/loadBtn"
                    android:layout_width="500px"
                    android:layout_height="150px"
                    android:text="Load Donors info"
                    android:textColor="#000000"
                    android:textStyle="bold" />
                <Button
                    android:id="@+id/addBtn"
                    android:layout_width="500px"
                    android:layout_height="150px"
                    android:layout_marginLeft="30px"
                    android:layout_toRightOf="@id/loadBtn"
                    android:text="Add Donor info"
                    android:textColor="#000000"
                    android:textStyle="bold" />
            </RelativeLayout>
          </LinearLayout>
        </ScrollView>
      </LinearLayout>
    </LinearLayout>
</LinearLayout>
```

We also need each item layout for the `RecyclerView`, which is defined as follows. In this layout, all we have is four `TextView`:

```
<?xml version="1.0" encoding="utf-8"?>
<LinearLayout xmlns:android="http://schemas.android.com/apk/res/android"
    android:layout_width="match_parent"
    android:layout_height="wrap_content"
    android:orientation="vertical">

    <TextView
```

```
        android:id="@+id/donorName"
        android:layout_width="match_parent"
        android:layout_height="match_parent"
        android:gravity="center_vertical"
        android:padding="10px"
        android:textColor="@color/colorPrimary"
        android:textSize="25dp"
        android:textStyle="bold" />

    <TextView
        android:id="@+id/donorCity"
        android:layout_width="match_parent"
        android:layout_height="match_parent"
        android:gravity="center_vertical"
        android:padding="10px"
        android:text="+216 54 821 200"
        android:textSize="14dp"
        android:textStyle="italic" />

    <TextView
        android:id="@+id/donorBloodGroup"
        android:layout_width="match_parent"
        android:layout_height="match_parent"
        android:gravity="center_vertical"
        android:padding="10px"
        android:text="+216 54 821 200"
        android:textSize="14dp"
        android:textStyle="italic" />

    <TextView
        android:id="@+id/donorEmail"
        android:layout_width="match_parent"
        android:layout_height="match_parent"
        android:gravity="center_vertical"
        android:padding="10px"
        android:text="+216 54 821 200"
        android:textSize="14dp"
        android:textStyle="italic" />

</LinearLayout>
```

Now that we have our user interface in place, let's dive deep into the Java part. Let's create a class called `Donor`. This class is a **Plain Old Java Object (POJO)** class that we will use throughout the application, and the POJO class dictates the structure of the data.

Logic

The following POJO class expresses the idea and the data format that we will save in Firebase. Using the POJO class we will pass the data to the adapter:

```
package com.ashok.packt.realtime.database.model;

/**
 * Created by ashok.kumar on 20/10/17.
 */
public class Donor {

    private String FullName;
    private String Email;
    private String City;
    private String BloodGroup;
    public Donor(){

    }
```

Now within the same class lets create a constructor for passing the data to the POJO:

```
    public Donor(String fullName, String email, String city, String
bloodGroup) {
        FullName = fullName;
        Email = email;
        City = city;
        BloodGroup = bloodGroup;
    }

    public String getFullName() {
        return FullName;
    }

    public void setFullName(String fullName) {
        FullName = fullName;
    }

    public String getEmail() {
        return Email;
    }
```

```
    public void setEmail(String email) {
        Email = email;
    }

    public String getCity() {
        return City;
    }

    public void setCity(String city) {
        City = city;
    }

    public String getBloodGroup() {
        return BloodGroup;
    }

    public void setBloodGroup(String bloodGroup) {
        BloodGroup = bloodGroup;
    }
}
```

Now let's write our `Adapter` class. The `Adapter` class requires POJO, view holder, and row layout. Consider spending some time on understanding the `RecyclerView` adapter:

```
package com.ashok.packt.realtime.database.adapter;

import android.content.Context;
import android.support.v7.widget.RecyclerView;
import android.view.LayoutInflater;
import android.view.View;
import android.view.ViewGroup;
import android.widget.TextView;
import com.ashok.packt.realtime.database.R;
import com.ashok.packt.realtime.database.model.Donor;

import java.util.List;

/**
 * Created by ashok.kumar on 20/05/18.
 */

public class RecyclerViewAdapter extends
RecyclerView.Adapter<RecyclerViewAdapter.View_Holder>{

    private Context mContext;
    private List<Donor> ItemList;
```

```
public RecyclerViewAdapter(Context mContext, List<Donor> itemList) {
    this.mContext = mContext;
    ItemList = itemList;
}
```

The constructors require context and the list of donor object for setting the data in `RecyclerView` callbacks.

```
@Override
public View_Holder onCreateViewHolder(ViewGroup parent, int viewType) {
    View itemView = LayoutInflater.from(parent.getContext())
            .inflate(R.layout.donor_list_row, parent, false);
    return new View_Holder(itemView);
}
```

The above `Override` method will be responsible for inflating the donor list item row.

```
@Override
public void onBindViewHolder(View_Holder holder, int position) {

    Donor Item = ItemList.get(position);
    holder.Name.setText(Item.getFullName());
    holder.City.setText(Item.getCity());
    holder.BloodGroup.setText(Item.getBloodGroup());
    holder.Email.setText(Item.getEmail());

}

@Override
public int getItemCount() {
    return ItemList.size();
}

public class View_Holder extends RecyclerView.ViewHolder {

    TextView Name;
    TextView City;
    TextView BloodGroup;
    TextView Phone;
    TextView Email;

    View_Holder(View itemView) {
        super(itemView);

        Name = (TextView) itemView.findViewById(R.id.donorName);
        City = (TextView) itemView.findViewById(R.id.donorCity);
        BloodGroup = (TextView)
    itemView.findViewById(R.id.donorBloodGroup);
```

```
            Email = (TextView) itemView.findViewById(R.id.donorEmail);
        }
    }

}
```

Now, `MainActivity` holds the complete logic for the application by adding the data to Firebase, fetching the data from Firebase, and loading that in `RecyclerView`. I have also written methods to update, find, and delete for your future reference:

```
package com.ashok.packt.realtime.database;

import android.os.Bundle;
import android.support.v7.app.AppCompatActivity;
import android.support.v7.widget.LinearLayoutManager;
import android.support.v7.widget.RecyclerView;
import android.util.Log;
import android.view.View;
import android.widget.EditText;

import com.ashok.packt.realtime.database.adapter.RecyclerViewAdapter;
import com.ashok.packt.realtime.database.model.Donor;
import com.google.firebase.database.ChildEventListener;
import com.google.firebase.database.DataSnapshot;
import com.google.firebase.database.DatabaseError;
import com.google.firebase.database.DatabaseReference;
import com.google.firebase.database.FirebaseDatabase;
import com.google.firebase.database.Query;
import com.google.firebase.database.ValueEventListener;

import java.util.ArrayList;
import java.util.Iterator;
import java.util.List;

public class MainActivity extends AppCompatActivity {

    private DatabaseReference myDatabaseReference;
    private String personId;
    private List<Donor> ItemList;
    private RecyclerView mRecyclerview;
    private RecyclerViewAdapter mAdapter;
```

Lets initialise all the above code in the `onCreate` method as shown below:

```
@Override
protected void onCreate(Bundle savedInstanceState) {
    super.onCreate(savedInstanceState);
    setContentView(R.layout.activity_main);

    mRecyclerview = (RecyclerView) findViewById(R.id.peopleList);
    RecyclerView.LayoutManager mLayoutManager = new
LinearLayoutManager(this);
    mRecyclerview.setLayoutManager(mLayoutManager);

    // for data persistence
    FirebaseDatabase.getInstance().setPersistenceEnabled(true);
myDatabaseReference=FirebaseDatabase.getInstance().getReference("Donor");
    personId= myDatabaseReference.push().getKey();


    (findViewById(R.id.addBtn)).setOnClickListener(new
View.OnClickListener() {
        @Override
        public void onClick(View view) {

            String FullName =
((EditText)findViewById(R.id.donorNameInput)).getText().toString();
            String Email =
((EditText)findViewById(R.id.donorEmailInput)).getText().toString();
            String City =
((EditText)findViewById(R.id.donorCityInput)).getText().toString();
            String BloodGroup =
((EditText)findViewById(R.id.donorBloodGroupInput)).getText().toString();


            addPerson(FullName,Email, City, BloodGroup);
        }
    });


    (findViewById(R.id.loadBtn)).setOnClickListener(new
View.OnClickListener() {
        @Override
        public void onClick(View view) {
            readData();
        }
    });
}
```

After adding the views its now time to work on the adding and retrieving the data as shown below:

```
private void addPerson(String name, String Email, String city, String
Bloodgroup){
    personId= myDatabaseReference.push().getKey();
    Donor person = new Donor(name, Email, city, Bloodgroup);
    myDatabaseReference.child(personId).setValue(person);
}

 private void updatePerson(String name,int phoneNumber){
 myDatabaseReference.child(personId).child("fullName").setValue(name);
myDatabaseReference.child(personId).child("phoneNumber").setValue(phoneNumb
er);
 }

 private void removePerson(String name){
 myDatabaseReference.child(personId).removeValue();
 }
 private void readData(){
 ItemList = new ArrayList<>();
 myDatabaseReference.addValueEventListener(new ValueEventListener() {
 @Override
 public void onDataChange(DataSnapshot dataSnapshot) {
 Iterable<DataSnapshot> snapshotIterator = dataSnapshot.getChildren();
 Iterator<DataSnapshot> iterator = snapshotIterator.iterator();
 while((iterator.hasNext())){
 Donor donor = iterator.next().getValue(Donor.class);
 ItemList.add(donor);
 mAdapter.notifyDataSetChanged();
 }
 }

 @Override
 public void onCancelled(DatabaseError databaseError) {

 }
 });

 mAdapter = new RecyclerViewAdapter(this, ItemList);
 mRecyclerview.setAdapter(mAdapter);

 }
```

We also can do the specific person search as shown below:

```
private void findPerson(String name){
Query deleteQuery =
myDatabaseReference.orderByChild("fullName").equalTo(name);
deleteQuery.addChildEventListener(new ChildEventListener() {
@Override
public void onChildAdded(DataSnapshot dataSnapshot, String s) {
Iterable<DataSnapshot> snapshotIterator = dataSnapshot.getChildren();
Iterator<DataSnapshot> iterator = snapshotIterator.iterator();
while((iterator.hasNext())){
Log.d("Item found: ",iterator.next().getValue().toString()+"---");
}
}

@Override
public void onChildChanged(DataSnapshot dataSnapshot, String s) {

}

@Override
public void onChildRemoved(DataSnapshot dataSnapshot) {

}

@Override
public void onChildMoved(DataSnapshot dataSnapshot, String s) {

}

@Override
public void onCancelled(DatabaseError databaseError) {
Log.d("Item not found: ","this item is not in the list");
}
});
}
}
```

When you compile and run the program in your Android device the output will have the following look and feel:

Summary

This chapter is an outstanding exercise intended to show the power of the Firebase Realtime Database, to store and manage data in the list format including saving, erasing, and furthermore, looking for list items. This has included the use of the push() method for the DatabaseReference class with the Query class and both value and child event listeners. We have also understood database rules, and we have built an application using all this knowledge that helps blood seekers by connecting to blood donors.

Safe and Sound – Firebase Authentication

2

"A ship is always safe at the shore - but that is not what it is built for."

- Albert Einstein

The previous chapter was extensive practice in a different way that you can save data in the cloud. However, securing data is an essential process. In this chapter, we will explore Firebase Authentication, which is designed to build a secure authentication framework while enhancing the sign-in and onboarding experience for end users. It gives an end-to-end authentication solution, supporting email and passwords; telephone authentication; and Google, Twitter, Facebook, and GitHub login. FirebaseUI gives us an adaptable, open source, drop-in auth feature that handles the UI flows for signing in. The FirebaseUI Auth fulfills best practices for validation on mobile and web applications, which can improve sign-in and sign-up rates for your application. As it is developed by the same group of developers that created Google Sign-in, Smart Lock, and Chrome Password Manager, Firebase security applies Google's internal skills in overseeing one of the most significant account databases in the tech world. It can take a long time to set up your own particular auth framework, and it requires an engineering team to keep that framework running into the foreseeable future. With this, you can set up the whole Authentication system of your application in less than ten lines of code, notwithstanding complex cases such as account combination.

Firebase Authentication gives backend services simple-to-utilize SDKs and instant UI libraries to authorize users to your application.

In this chapter, let's explore the following topics:

- Overview of Firebase Authentication
- Setting up the development environment for Firebase Authentication
- Firebase Authentication and functionalities
- Firebase AuthUI for authentication
- Managing onboard users
- Firebase for Auth providers
- Anonymous Authentication

The following section is an extensive look at Firebase Authentication, covering the Firebase UI and Firebase SDK to integrate Authentication into your applications. It's time to explore Firebase authentication.

Firebase Authentication

Firebase helps you develop superb applications, grow your user base, and earn more money. As I mentioned in Chapter 1, *Keep it Real - Firebase Realtime Database,* each feature works autonomously, and they work far better together.

Assorted applications and web services need to have some type of authentication framework while keeping in mind the end goal of recognizing users. Use cases include controlling access to premium data and to preserve user information. Without some approach to distinguishing one user from another, it would be impossible for the application to know which information and settings have a place with which user.

Despite the inspiration for adding user authentication to an application, developers usually find that implementing authentication is substantially more intricate than it appears. Not exclusively should verification be performed safely and dependable; it should likewise be taken into consideration for users to change their account settings, offer help for forgotten passwords, and incorporate with a of third-party authentication APIs. Databases must be implemented and put away safely, and a general console provided for managing CRUD operations.

In Chapter 1, *Keep it Real – Firebase Realtime Database,* we integrated the Firebase SDK; now, all we need to do to set up Firebase Authentication is just add the Gradle dependency, if you are continuing from the last chapter. Every feature works autonomously, and we can create a new project and get started with exploring Firebase Authentication.

Setting up Firebase Authentication

As we learned in Chapter 1, *Keep it real – Firebase Realtime Database*, we can make use of Android Studio to integrate Firebase, or we can follow the traditional way of integrating Firebase features through the console by adding configuration files and dependencies manually.

In this chapter, we will explore the complete features and potential of Firebase Authentication. We will later create a new Android project and add the Firebase SDK and authentication Gradle dependency.

Add the following dependency to an already configured project. At the time of writing, Firebase authentication had a version 16.0.1. It may vary in your builds, but the components class names will remain same:

```
implementation 'com.google.firebase:firebase-auth:16.0.1'
```

Firebase Authentication can follow two methods of implementation, one using Firebase Auth UI and the other using the Firebase SDK. The authentication process will make use of the FirebaseAuth shared instance. Reference to this object will allow developers to handle various tasks, such as creating the user account, signing users in and signing users out, and fetching information relating to the signed in user. Another essential role of a FirebaseAuth instance is as an authentication state listener; the AuthStateListener interface application will be able to receive notification of the user's authentication status.

An AuthUI instance helps when the application makes use of the FirebaseUI Auth library for the user interface. It will have all the classes that are necessary for creating the user account to sign in users and so on.

The FirebaseUser class is used to bind the user profile information for signed in users. The getCurrentUser() method from FirebaseAuth will return the FirebaseUser object, and data will be different depending on the auth provider.

The `AuthCredential` class will take care of data marshaling (the process of making the data compatible with Firebase) from all the Auth providers, and also it will bind the user account credentials to Firebase. Using this class, we can exchange tokens from third-party authentication providers for the credentials of the Firebase account. When the user signs in using a third-party authentication provider such as Facebook, Twitter, or GitHub, the application provides a user token for that provider. Using this token, Firebase creates an account for the user. The third-party provider token needs to be converted to the `AuthCredential` object by calling the `getCredential()` method. For popular authentication providers, there are `AuthCredential` subclasses listed here:

- `EmailAuthCredential`
- `PhoneAuthCredential`
- `FacebookAuthCredential`
- `GithubAuthCredential`
- `GoogleAuthCredential`
- `TwitterAuthCredential`

Every authentication provider class has its own provider class helping to manage most of the authentication tasks. Firebase includes these provider classes:

- `EmailAuthProvider`
- `PhoneAuthProvider`
- `FacebookAuthProvider`
- `GithubAuthProvider`
- `GoogleAuthProvider`
- `TwitterAuthProvider`

We will see all these classes in use in a later section of the chapter. Firebase authentication is one of the key components of the Firebase toolchain. It needs a practical approach to excel.

FirebaseUI Auth authentication

There are two approaches we can choose to integrate Firebase Authentication into your project. The prominent one is with the Firebase SDK and the recommended one is to use the FirebaseUI Auth. By covering most of the use cases in FirebaseUI, the developer community voted to use the FirebaseUI library for many reasons:

- The FirebaseUI Auth follows best practices for authentication on mobile devices and websites

- Customizing the UI is very easy
- It also knows how to handle cases such as account recovery and account linking, which can be delicate in terms of security and difficult to handle correctly.

Firebase UI offers all the necessary setup to integrate user authentication, which includes screens such as account creation and sign-in screens. It is also very easy to integrate the FirebaseUI auth, considering the following sequence of steps while using FirebaseUI Auth:

1. Identify the auth provider you will be using in your project (Google, Facebook, Twitter, GitHub and so on).
2. Enable the appropriate provider in the Firebase console.
3. Register the application in the provider's console and obtain a token.
4. `FirebaseAuth` reference or add the dependency in your project.
5. Use the `AuthUI` class to configure and build the FirebaseUI Authentication intent.

Firebase SDK Authentication

Although incorporating authentication utilizing the Firebase SDK is time consuming, it has the upside of adaptability. Unlike FirebaseUI Auth, the Firebase SDK gives full control over the look, feel, and conduct of the verification process (except for any confirmation screens introduced by outsider verification providers). Consider the following sequence of steps while using Firebase SDK authentication:

1. Identify the auth provider that you will be using in your project (Google, Facebook, Twitter, GitHub and so on).
2. Enable the appropriate provider in the Firebase console.
3. Register the application in the provider's console and obtain a token.
4. `FirebaseAuth` reference or add the dependency in your project.
5. Using the AuthUI class, we need to set up and build the FirebaseUI Authentication intent.
6. Attach AuthStateListener to the FirebaseAuth instance for callback methods, using which we can reference them to the click event.
7. We have to design the complete UI for login, registering, and so on.

Authentication is a vital component in any application for protecting user data. Now that we have a fair understanding of Authentication, this is the time to drive it in the practical sense.

FirebaseUI Email Authentication

Email ID is a unique user identity that helps in sending and routing emails and notifications to users. So far, we have learned what authentication is. In this section, we will explore it with the help of working code. We will use the FirebaseUI Auth API, in which we will extend the concepts to apprehend in social login, phone number verification, and so on.

Configuring for Email Authentication

The following steps illustrate what necessary actions are to be taken to integrate the Firebase Authentication:

1. Create a new project with **Empty Activity** as the preferred template. In this project, we will explore social site integration and other authentication services. It is recommended you use the latest version of Android Studio and dependencies:

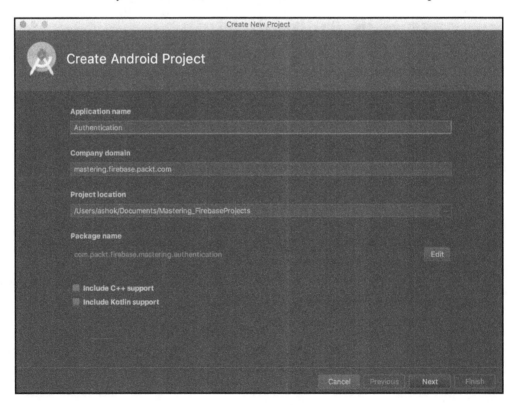

2. After successful project creation, go to **Tools** | **Firebase** within Android Studio and select **Authentication** on the right-hand-side of the assistant panel window.

3. In the **Assistant** window, click on Connect to Firebase. If you have already created a project in the Firebase console, you can choose it. For the scope of exploring the Authentication, it is good if you can create a new project and allow Android Studio to register the clients. After successful creation, Android Studio will notify with the status of the application:

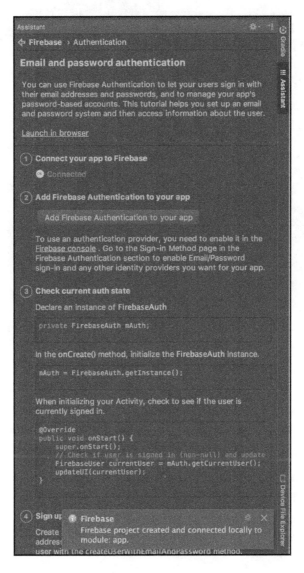

4. After that, click on **Add Firebase Authentication to your app** and accept the changes. After successful project sync, we shall see additional dependencies in your `build.gradle` file and also a `google-services.json` file in the project scope:

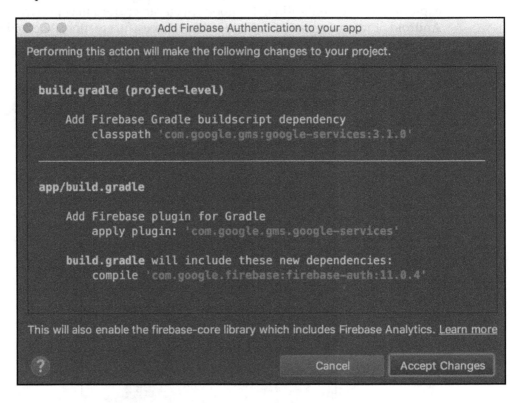

```
//Add this dependency to gradle.build file
implementation 'com.google.firebase:firebase-auth:11.8.0'
```

5. The final step is to add the **FirebaseUI** dependencies. The following table explains the FirebaseUI and Firebase SDK version mapping.

As of the date of writing, the newest dependency version number is 3.1.0. It might be different when you read this book. Please add the latest dependency because most of the syntax remains the same.

FirebaseUI Version	Firebase/Play Services Version
3.1.3	11.8.0
3.1.2	11.6.2
3.1.0	11.4.2
3.0.0	11.4.2
2.4.0	11.4.0
2.3.0	11.0.4
2.2.0	11.0.4
2.1.1	11.0.2
2.0.1	11.0.1
1.2.0	10.2.0
1.1.1	10.0.0 or 10.0.1
1.0.1	10.0.0 or 10.0.1
1.0.0	9.8.0

6. Add the following Gradle dependency to your `build.gradle` file in the module scope:

```
// FirebaseUI for Firebase Auth
   compile 'com.firebaseui:firebase-ui-auth:3.1.3'
```

 Note: Add this Maven URL because the fabric components need to be downloaded from this repository:

```
repositories {
  maven {
      url 'https://maven.fabric.io/public'
      }
}
```

Enabling Email/Password Authentication in Console

Now that we have the Android Project ready for Authentication, we need to enable an option in the Firebase console. Visit `https://console.firebase.google.com` and choose the project you created using Android Studio. After that, choose development, in which you need to select the Authentication option in the console. After that, go to the **Sign-in Method** tab and enable the desired service:

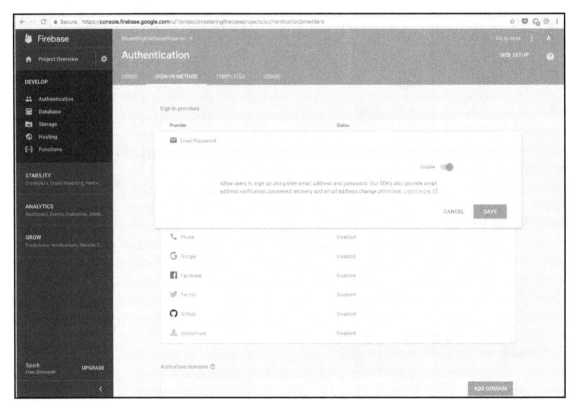

Firebase Console to enable the Authentication provider

Initializing Firebase Authentication

Let's get our hands dirty by instantiating the required classes and methods. In the onCreate(..) method of the Activity, initialize the FirebaseAuth class. Check whether the getCurrentUser method is returning null values. If it returns, ask the user to log in again or else take the user to the next activity:

```
package com.packt.firebase.mastering.authentication;

import android.content.Intent;
import android.support.v7.app.AppCompatActivity;
import android.os.Bundle;

import com.google.firebase.auth.FirebaseAuth;

public class MainActivity extends AppCompatActivity {

    private FirebaseAuth mAuth;

    @Override
    protected void onCreate(Bundle savedInstanceState) {
        super.onCreate(savedInstanceState);
        setContentView(R.layout.activity_main);
        mAuth = FirebaseAuth.getInstance();
        if (mAuth.getCurrentUser() != null) {
            startActivity(new Intent(this, DashBoardActivity.class));
            finish();
        } else {
            Authenticate();
        }
    }
}
```

We have written the preceding code so that if an unauthorized user tries to log in, the application will prompt the user to enter their credentials. If the user is authorized, we will take them to the DashboardActivity.

Finalizing the project

Now, let's write the code for Sign in or Sign up using an Email provider. Already signed up users can enter the email ID and password to start using the application. In the case of new account creation, users should be able to enter the necessary information in the form to create an account. When we use the FirebaseUI library, the bare minimum UI is taken care of. The following code dictates the steps for creating email onboarding:

```
// Add this in global scope
private static final int REQUEST_CODE = 101;

private void Authenticate() {
    startActivityForResult(
            AuthUI.getInstance().createSignInIntentBuilder()
                    .setAvailableProviders(getAuthProviderList())
                    .setIsSmartLockEnabled(false)
                    .build(),
            REQUEST_CODE);
}

private List<AuthUI.IdpConfig> getAuthProviderList() {
    List<AuthUI.IdpConfig> providers = new ArrayList<>();
    providers.add(
            new AuthUI.IdpConfig.Builder(AuthUI.EMAIL_PROVIDER).build());
    return providers;
}
```

The getauthproviderlist method returns the email provider among all the other providers. So, we have set up the required line of codes to onboard, but we have a few more things to ensure, The Authenticate method starting an activity for the result this needs to be handled like shown in the following:

```
@Override
protected void onActivityResult(int requestCode, int resultCode, Intent
data) {
    super.onActivityResult(requestCode, resultCode, data);
    IdpResponse response = IdpResponse.fromResultIntent(data);
    if (requestCode == REQUEST_CODE) {
        if (resultCode == ResultCodes.OK) {
            startActivity(new Intent(this, DashBoardActivity.class));
            return;
        }
    } else {
        if (response == null) {
            // if user cancelled Sign-in
            return;
```

```
        }
        if (response.getErrorCode() == ErrorCodes.NO_NETWORK) {
            // When device has no network connection
            return;
        }
        if (response.getErrorCode() == ErrorCodes.UNKNOWN_ERROR) {
            // When unknown error occurred
            return;
        }
    }
}
```

In `DashBoardActivity`, we need to show who logged in. We can use a simple Toast message to show this information:

```
@Override
protected void onCreate(Bundle savedInstanceState) {
    super.onCreate(savedInstanceState);
    .....

  FirebaseUser currentUser =
  FirebaseAuth.getInstance().getCurrentUser();
  if (currentUser == null) {
  startActivity(new Intent(this, MainActivity.class));
  finish();
  return;
  }
  Toast.makeText(this, " "+currentUser.getEmail()+
currentUser.getDisplayName(),
  Toast.LENGTH_SHORT).show();
}
```

To sign out manually, we can use the following method, which makes use of `AuthUI`. Here, the `AuthUI` class will reach out to the Firebase servers to check the instance. We will subscribe to the `signOut` method, and then we will attach `addOnCompleteListener` to return the task of log in success or failure:

```
public void signOut(View view) {
    AuthUI.getInstance()
            .signOut(this)
            .addOnCompleteListener(new OnCompleteListener<Void>() {
                @Override
                public void onComplete(@NonNull Task<Void> task) {
                    if (task.isSuccessful()) {
                        startActivity(new Intent(
                                DashBoardActivity.this,
                                MainActivity.class));
```

```
                    finish();
            } else {
                    // Report error to user
            }
        }
    });
}
```

If your project needs account removal, `AuthUI` provides all the required details. We will then have to subscribe to the `delete` method and attach the `addOnCompleteListener` callback to check the task for successful account removal:

```
public void removeAccount(View view) {
    AuthUI.getInstance()
            .delete(this)
            .addOnCompleteListener(new OnCompleteListener<Void>() {
                @Override
                public void onComplete(@NonNull Task<Void> task) {
                    if (task.isSuccessful()) {
                        startActivity(new Intent(DashBoardActivity.this,
                                MainActivity.class));
                        finish();
                    } else {
                        // Notify user of error
                    }
                }
            });

}
```

We have now completed exploring Firebase authentication for email providers using Firebase auth UI. In the following section, let's see how to achieve without using any of the libraries; in other words, when we need the ability to customize the UI for the authentication system.

Firebase SDK Email Authentication

Firebase Authentication for email credentials is one of the most simple and powerful onboarding features. To be able to make use of this facility, we need to enable the Email provider in the Firebase console. Using the Android Studio Firebase window, we can set up Firebase Authentication. Alternatively, we can add the configuration `google-play-services.json` file and dependencies manually. In your application level Gradle file, add the following dependency:

```
compile 'com.google.firebase:firebase-auth:11.8.0'
```

We need to declare an instance of the `FirebaseAuth` class, using which we can later get an access to the Firebase `AuthResult` object:

```
private FirebaseAuth mAuth;
```

We need to initialize the `FirebaseAuth` reference in the `onCreate` method, as shown here:

```
mAuth = FirebaseAuth.getInstance();
```

Sign up new users

Now it is time to explore the sign-up process. When the user opts to create an account, we need two pieces of primary information, which is email and password. It might sound a little humorous, but the method we need to use for creating the account is `createUserWithEmailAndPassword`. The method is named because of the functionality and here we need to attach an `addOnCompleteListner` interface with its callbacks:

```
mAuth.createUserWithEmailAndPassword(email, password)
        .addOnCompleteListener(this, new OnCompleteListener<AuthResult>() {
            @Override
            public void onComplete(@NonNull Task<AuthResult> task) {
                if (task.isSuccessful()) {
                    // Successfully account created
                    Log.d(TAG, "Accounted creation:success");
                    FirebaseUser user = mAuth.getCurrentUser();
                    // Your UI logic can be executed now
                    updateUI(user);
                } else {
                    // In case of acount creation failed.
                    Log.w(TAG, "Account creation:failure",
```

```
                task.getException());
                        Toast.makeText(MainActivity.this, "Authentication
failed.",
                                Toast.LENGTH_SHORT).show();
                    updateUI(null);
                }

            // ...
        }
    });
```

This code is self-explanatory and if the task is successful, then we will have
a `FirebaseUser` object as a result; if it is not, then it will show an error message on a
simple toast. Remember, you can pass the email received from `EditText` or Email and
password string.

Sign in existing users

Sign in also looks for two string parameters, which are valid email address and password.
However, here, we will make use of another method
called `signInWithEmailAndPassword`. We need to attach `addOnCompleteListener` and
with its callbacks, as shown:

```
mAuth.signInWithEmailAndPassword(email, password)
        .addOnCompleteListener(this, new OnCompleteListener<AuthResult>() {
            @Override
            public void onComplete(@NonNull Task<AuthResult> task) {
                if (task.isSuccessful()) {
                    // Successful signin
                    Log.d(TAG, "signInWithEmail:success");
                    FirebaseUser user = mAuth.getCurrentUser();
                    updateUI(user);
                } else {
                    // failed for some reason
                    Log.w(TAG, "signInWithEmail:failure",
task.getException());
                        Toast.makeText(MainActivity.this, "Authentication
failed.",
                                Toast.LENGTH_SHORT).show();
                    updateUI(null);
                }

            // ...
        }
    });
```

This code explains that when the task object is successful, we can retrieve the user information through the `FirebaseUser` object; for instance, consider the following code, which retrieves the information from the authorized user:

```
FirebaseUser user = FirebaseAuth.getInstance().getCurrentUser();
if (user != null) {
        // These are the information we will be able to retrieve
        // Name, email address, and profile photo Url

        String name = user.getDisplayName();
        String email = user.getEmail();
        Uri photoUrl = user.getPhotoUrl();

        // Check if user's email is verified
        boolean emailVerified = user.isEmailVerified();

        // The user's ID, unique to the Firebase project.
        // UID shall not be used to server purpose
        // FirebaseUser.getToken() instead.
        String uid = user.getUid();
    }
```

Managing users

After onboarding users, there are many use cases to handle, for example, provider-specific user profile information such as updating the profile, sending a verification email, updating the password, deleting users, and so on. Let's understand them. In standard programming practice, we will check for the currently logged in user's details and if that returns null, then we ask the user to sign in:

```
FirebaseUser user = FirebaseAuth.getInstance().getCurrentUser();
if (user != null) {
    // When User is signed in
} else {
    // When user is not signed in
}
```

Sometimes there could be a not null user object, in which case we need to check for the invalid token.

Provider-specific user profile details

The `FirebaseUser` object returns the provider-specific data in the `getProviderData` method, using which we can access the information of a user:

```
FirebaseUser user = FirebaseAuth.getInstance().getCurrentUser();
if (user != null) {
        for (UserInfo profile : user.getProviderData()) {
                // unique id of the provider (ex: facebook.com)
                String providerId = profile.getProviderId();

                // UID of the provider
                String uid = profile.getUid();

                // Name, email address, and profile photo Url
                String name = profile.getDisplayName();
                String email = profile.getEmail();
                Uri photoUrl = profile.getPhotoUrl();
        };
    }
```

This code snippet explains the details of provider-based information for the logged in user. Using the `UserInfo` class, we will be able to access all the details of a user.

Profile updating

In any of the onboarding services, it is very important to allow the user to update profile-related details such as updating profile pictures, displaying names, and so on. To accomplish this in a FirebaseUser instance, we have a method called `updateProfile` which accepts a `UserProfileChangeRequest` object with updated information:

```
FirebaseUser user = FirebaseAuth.getInstance().getCurrentUser();

UserProfileChangeRequest profileUpdates = new
UserProfileChangeRequest.Builder()
        .setDisplayName("Vinisha Krishna")
.setPhotoUri(Uri.parse("https://example.com/vinisha-k-bengaluru/profile.jpg
"))
        .build();

user.updateProfile(profileUpdates)
        .addOnCompleteListener(new OnCompleteListener<Void>() {
            @Override
            public void onComplete(@NonNull Task<Void> task) {
                if (task.isSuccessful()) {
```

```
                    Log.d(TAG, "User profile updated.");
                }
            }
        });
```

This code is self-explanatory. In the first block, we will get the reference of the currently logged in users. Then we will make use of the `UserProfileChangeRequest` builder class to set the changes, and then we will pass the changed object to the `FirebaseUser` class.

Sending a verification Email

The purpose of verifying the email address is to avoid spam and invalid email addresses. The following code shows how we can send a verification email address using the `sendEmailVerification` method:

```
FirebaseAuth auth = FirebaseAuth.getInstance();
FirebaseUser user = auth.getCurrentUser();

user.sendEmailVerification()
        .addOnCompleteListener(new OnCompleteListener<Void>() {
            @Override
            public void onComplete(@NonNull Task<Void> task) {
                if (task.isSuccessful()) {
                    Log.d(TAG, "Email sent.");
                }
            }
        });
```

We can customize the email templates as well; to customize the email templates you can visit Firebase help center. Also, we can change the language of the mail.

Forgot password

When the user has forgotten their password, he can receive a password reset email using the `sendPasswordResetEmail` method with a string email address as a parameter:

```
FirebaseAuth auth = FirebaseAuth.getInstance();
String emailAddress = "vinisha@krishna.com";

auth.sendPasswordResetEmail(emailAddress)
        .addOnCompleteListener(new OnCompleteListener<Void>() {
            @Override
            public void onComplete(@NonNull Task<Void> task) {
                if (task.isSuccessful()) {
```

```
                    Log.d(TAG, "Email sent.");
                }
            }
        });
```

We can customize the email template and language in the reset mail as well. Once the user receives a mail, he will be able to set the password again. We will explore how to customize the email template in a later section of the chapter.

Deleting a user

Most applications allow freedom to delete an account from the application, and we can achieve that by using the `delete` method of the `FirebaseUser` object:

```
FirebaseUser user = FirebaseAuth.getInstance().getCurrentUser();

user.delete()
        .addOnCompleteListener(new OnCompleteListener<Void>() {
            @Override
            public void onComplete(@NonNull Task<Void> task) {
                if (task.isSuccessful()) {
                    Log.d(TAG, "User account deleted.");
                }
            }
        });
```

Users will not be able to delete their account if they have not signed in recently; a user can also reauthenticate the credentials to delete the account using the `reauthenticate` method:

```
AuthCredential credential = EmailAuthProvider
        .getCredential("Vinisha@Ashok.com", "Secret");

user.reauthenticate(credential)
        .addOnCompleteListener(new OnCompleteListener<Void>() {
            @Override
            public void onComplete(@NonNull Task<Void> task) {
                Log.d(TAG, "User re-authenticated.");
            }
        });
```

Managing users through console

The Firebase Authentication system allows developers to test and customize the application through the Firebase console, so let's make the best use of it. Adding the user is one of the essential operations that can be achieved through the console by entering the information in two fields. In the **Authentication** option, we notice the **Users** tab. Select it. Inside, you will notice a button named **Add User**, which allows entering the email address and password:

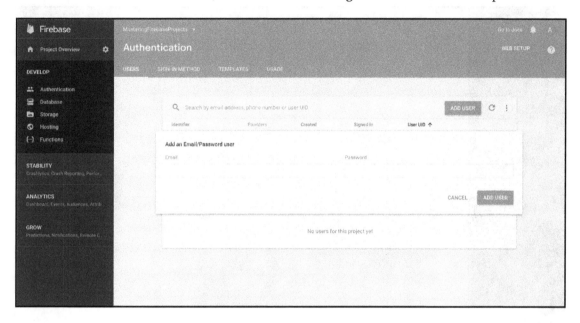

Adding users through Firebase console

After adding users, we can check for invalid email address. And, we also have controls such as disable the account, deleting it, and so on.

We can customize the templates of mail and OTP messages and so on. Choose the **Templates** tab in the authentication window. Here, we can change the format of the mail, we can change email subject, and we can also play with OTP messages.

Customize the email and messages through Firebase console. We can modify all the following parameters with the corresponding values:

- %DISPLAY_NAME%: Usually user's first name
- %APP_NAME%: Application name

- `%LINK%`: The password change URL
- `%EMAIL%`: The user's email address
- `%NEW_EMAIL%`: Used only when the user changes their email address

Using the **Project settings** menu, we can change the public name of the project and we can get access to the web API keys if we want to delete the entire Firebase project:

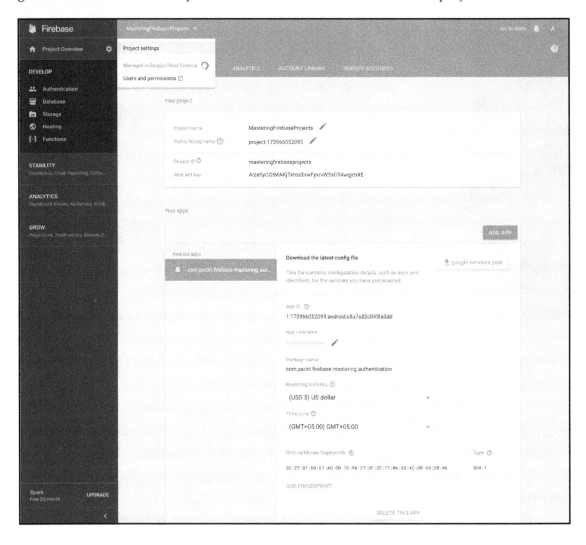

Smart Lock

Up until now, the illustration application has not made use of Smart Lock for Passwords. Smart Lock is the technology behind the Google Chrome browser feature that saves login and password data for the sites used by a client. This feature, when enabled, is also accessible to Android applications utilizing Firebase verification. Smart Lock for Passwords provides the verification framework to exhibit a rundown of the list of credentials saved on the device beforehand by the client utilizing Smart Lock. The client just chooses a formerly saved identity to sign in to or accept access to the application. Smart Lock is enabled when calling the `createSignInIntentBuilder()` method on the `AuthUI` instance as shown here:

```
private void authenticateUser() {
    startActivityForResult(
            AuthUI.getInstance().createSignInIntentBuilder()
                    .setAvailableProviders(getProviderList())
                    .setIsSmartLockEnabled(true)
                    .build(),
            REQUEST_CODE);
}
```

This code helps `AuthUI` to remember the identities used for signing in to the application.

FirebaseUI social networking site authentication

Popular social networking sites include Google+, Facebook, and Twitter, whereas GitHub is more for engineers and software developers. Firebase can work with popular Authentication providers and it also supports non-popular authentication providers. We will explore the popular authentication providers using FirebaseUI. All of these providers use email and password credentials to log in to their services to retrieve user-related information. This means we don't have to enter the sign-up form to account creation all the required information is retrieved from providers. FirebaseUI makes the whole process sweet and simple. Since we have the projects ready to work on Authentication, we will follow the necessary steps to complete them.

Google Sign-in

Google Sign-in expects two valid strings, namely an Email address and a valid password. Once the user enters the valid Google credentials, the application is ready to fetch the information required to create an account or sign in the user. In the event of adding Google Sign-in to our projects, we need to ensure that we have obtained the SHA-1 fingerprint from the developer's computer and enabling Google Sign-in as the Sign-in method in the Firebase console.

Once we have these two things in place, the rest of the process is pretty straightforward since we have already worked with email authentication using FirebaseUI.

SHA-1 fingerprint

Every mobile or Android developer should have an understanding of debug and release certificates for deployment. A debug certificate is for debugging purposes at the time of development, whereas a release certificate is to publish the Android application to the Play Store. These two certificates are dependent on the SHA-1 fingerprint release certificate we can create and store in known paths on the hard drive. The Android debug certificate will be stored in the `.android` directory and `debug.keystore` file. To obtain an SHA-1 fingerprint, we can make use of CLI commands or Android Studio in Windows, we shall use the following commands to get the SHA-1 fingerprint:

- **Windows**: `keytool -exportcert -list -v -alias androiddebugkey - keystore %USERPROFILE%\.android\debug.keystore`
- **macOS and Linux:** `keytool -exportcert -list -v -alias androiddebugkey -keystore ~/.android/debug.keystore`

Another way is to simply use Gradle to do the hard work for us. Go to **Android Studio** and on the right-hand side, you will come across a **Gradle** option. Click on that and go to the project and select **Tasks**; next, choose **Android** and double-click on **signingReport** to access SHA-1 in your Gradle console.
Actions: Android Studio | Gradle | Project | Tasks | Android | singingReport

```
Variant: debugAndroidTest
Config: debug
Store: /Users/ashok/.android/debug.keystore
Alias: AndroidDebugKey
MD5: 92:AA:0A:8B:24:C8:AF:7E:B4:94:15:D2:9D:3A:1A:52
SHA1: 3C:27:01:6B:61:AD:DB:76:98:27:3F:2E:77:06:58:4C:80:60:2B:46
Valid until: Monday, 11 November, 2047
```

Once we obtain the SHA-1 fingerprint, we can go to the Firebase console to paste the fingerprint. Go to the project settings in Firebase console. In the section that says your apps, it will also have an option to add the SHA-1 fingerprint. Add your SHA-1 fingerprint there in the rightful place.

The window that allows adding SHA-1 fingerprint is shown as follows:

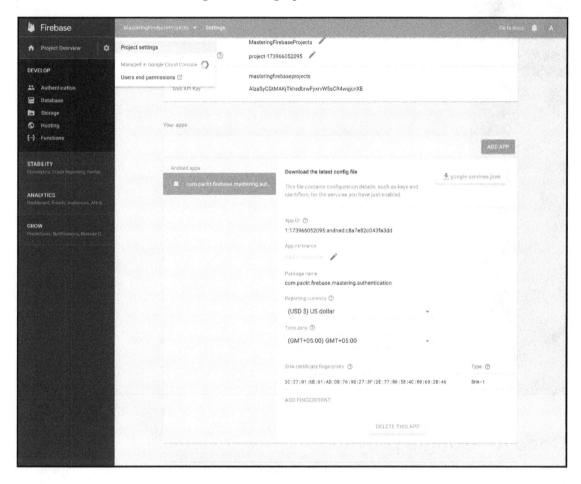

Make sure you have enabled Google Sign-in inside the **SIGN-IN METHOD** tab. If you haven't enabled Google Sign-in, then you will run into exceptions that will be discussed in later sections.

The following screenshot shows enabling Google Sign-in, in the '**SIGN-IN METHOD**' tab:

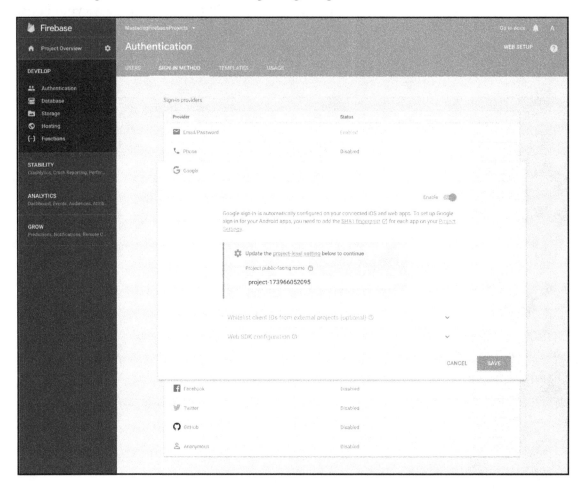

Code for Google provider

Now that we have all the necessary settings in place, the following piece of code helps in initializing Google Sign-in for your project:

```
private List<AuthUI.IdpConfig> getAuthProviderList() {
    List<AuthUI.IdpConfig> providers = new ArrayList<>();
    providers.add(new
            AuthUI.IdpConfig.Builder(AuthUI.EMAIL_PROVIDER).build());
    providers.add(new
            AuthUI.IdpConfig.Builder(AuthUI.GOOGLE_PROVIDER).build());
```

```
        return providers;
    }

    private void authenticate() {
        startActivityForResult(
                AuthUI.getInstance().createSignInIntentBuilder()
                        .setAvailableProviders(getAuthProviderList())
                        .setIsSmartLockEnabled(false)
                        .build(),
                REQUEST_CODE);
    }
```

This code is self-explanatory, as we have just one line of code to enable Google Sign-in. We also have a lot of control over how the application looks by adding a logo and custom theme inside an `AuthUI` builder:

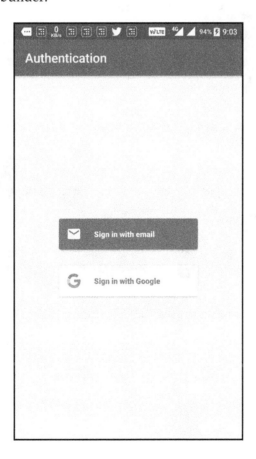

When the user clicks on the **Sign in with Google** method, it will allow the user to log in through their existing accounts on the device or it will ask the user to log in from Google:

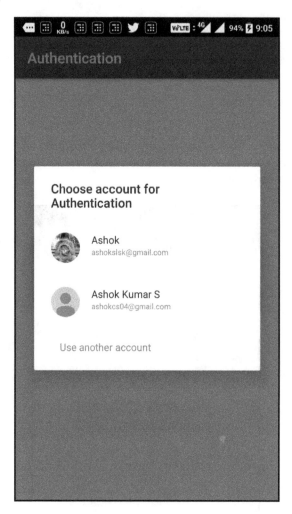

This screenshot shows the email addresses that the user can use to authorize. If there is another account he wishes to choose, he can do that by clicking **Use another account**. On successful signup, you can see user account creation inside the Firebase console.

User added from Google Sign-in will be seen as follows:

Using the `FirebaseUser` object, a developer can access the profile photograph, name, email address, and a lot more profile details.

Facebook Login

Facebook is one of the most popular social networking sites ever created. Most applications feature Facebook login as a service. Similar to the Google login, we will have a Facebook email address and password to sign in. The application can retrieve user-related information. Since we are using FirebaseUI, the code is similar to the Google login, but we need to do extra configuration on the Facebook developer console. The following sequence of steps helps to integrate Facebook with Firebase authentication.

Facebook App ID and App secret

The Facebook login service needs the application ID and application secret to have a secure connection between your application and Facebook. The app ID and secret key are unique and are assigned by Facebook. To create the App ID and secret key, visit the following URL: `https://developers.facebook.com/`. We can add the new application from the **My Apps** option:

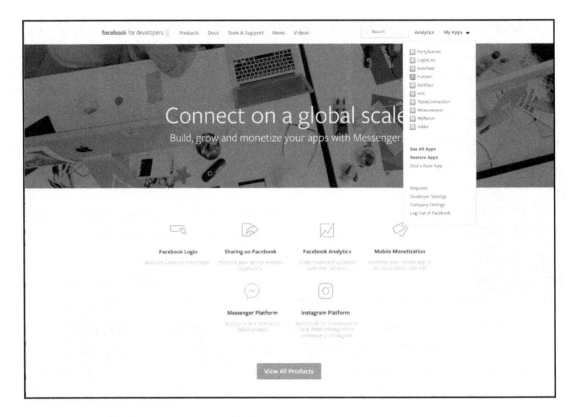

We can visit the following URL to add the new project: `https://developers.facebook.com/apps/`. Here, we will see a button labeled **Add a New App** which enables us to add a new application:

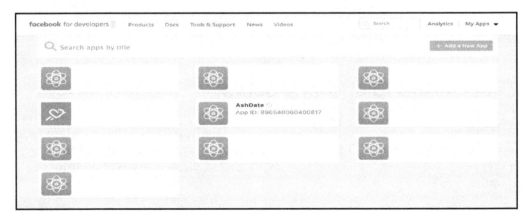

Fill out the form with your application details such as app name, developer email address, and so on. After successful project creation, you will see all the Facebook products; choose **Facebook Login**:

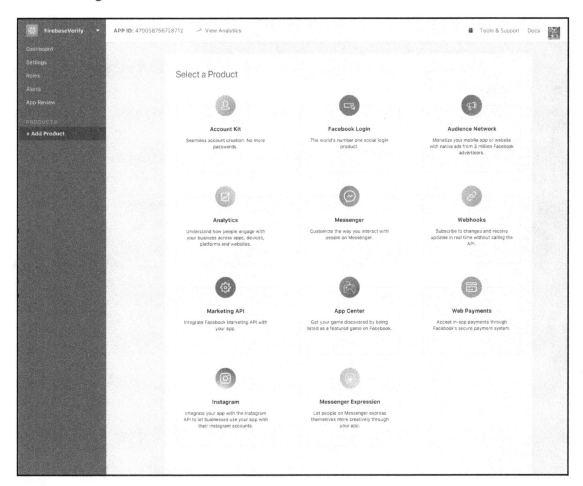

Here, we can copy the latest SDK Gradle dependency in the quick start guide:

```
implementation 'com.facebook.android:facebook-android-sdk:[4,5)'
```

Now, enter the package name and default class, as shown in the screenshot:

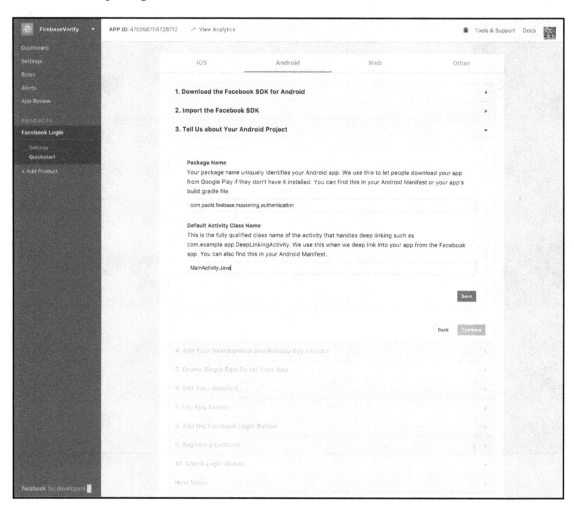

To add the hash key, Mac users should use the following command:

```
keytool -exportcert -alias androiddebugkey -keystore
~/.android/debug.keystore | openssl sha1 -binary | openssl base64
```

We will see the hash key in the terminal:

```
//debug Hash key
ga0RGNYHvNM5d0SLGQfpQWAPGJ8=
```

Windows users can execute the following command:

```
keytool -exportcert -alias androiddebugkey -keystore
"C:\Users\USERNAME\.android\debug.keystore" |
"PATH_TO_OPENSSL_LIBRARY\bin\openssl" sha1 -binary |
"PATH_TO_OPENSSL_LIBRARY\bin\openssl" base64
```

To generate a release key at the time of publishing, the application will use the following command to generate a new hash:

```
keytool -exportcert -alias YOUR_RELEASE_KEY_ALIAS -keystore
YOUR_RELEASE_KEY_PATH | openssl sha1 -binary | openssl base64
```

Single sign-in is enabled when you want to launch the application from Android notifications.

Project configuration

Now, in the manifest of our project, we can add the following code changes.

Open the `string.xml` file and add the Facebook app ID and Facebook protocol scheme ID:

```
Goto /app/res/values/strings.xml

//Add the following strings
<string name="facebook_application_id">470058756728712</string>
<string name="fb_login_protocol_scheme">fb470058756728712</string>
```

Since we already have added internet permissions, we need not worry about it but if you haven't added internet permissions, please do so now:

```
<uses-permission android:name="android.permission.INTERNET"/>
```

We need to add the metadata elements inside the manifest and within the application tag scope:

```
<meta-data android:name="com.facebook.sdk.ApplicationId"
    android:value="@string/facebook_application_id"/>

<activity android:name="com.facebook.FacebookActivity"
    android:configChanges=
        "keyboard|keyboardHidden|screenLayout|screenSize|orientation"
    android:label="@string/app_name" />
<activity
    android:name="com.facebook.CustomTabActivity"
    android:exported="true">
    <intent-filter>
        <action android:name="android.intent.action.VIEW" />
        <category android:name="android.intent.category.DEFAULT" />
        <category android:name="android.intent.category.BROWSABLE" />
        <data android:scheme="@string/fb_login_protocol_scheme" />
    </intent-filter>
</activity>
```

Now, add the following code inside the `getAuthProviderList` method:

```
private List<AuthUI.IdpConfig> getAuthProviderList() {
    List<AuthUI.IdpConfig> providers = new ArrayList<>();
    providers.add(
            new AuthUI.IdpConfig.Builder(AuthUI.EMAIL_PROVIDER).build());
    providers.add(new
            AuthUI.IdpConfig.Builder(AuthUI.GOOGLE_PROVIDER).build());
    providers.add(new
            AuthUI.IdpConfig.Builder(AuthUI.FACEBOOK_PROVIDER).build());

    return providers;
}
```

If there is no Facebook application installed in the device, it will prompt a webview with a Facebook login. The `FirebaseUser` object allows developers to access the profile photograph, name, email address, and other profile details.

Twitter Sign-in

We have explored how to integrate Facebook and Google with an Android application. Now, let's explore another popular social media site: Twitter. Twitter configuration is similar to Facebook, but with a few changes. Since we are using FirebaseUI, the code is similar to Google login or Facebook login, but we need to do extra configuration on the Twitter app creation console. The following sequence of steps helps to integrate Twitter with Firebase authentication.

Twitter Api key

On successful project creation at the following URL `https://apps.twitter.com/`, we will be taken to a window that shows most of our application details:

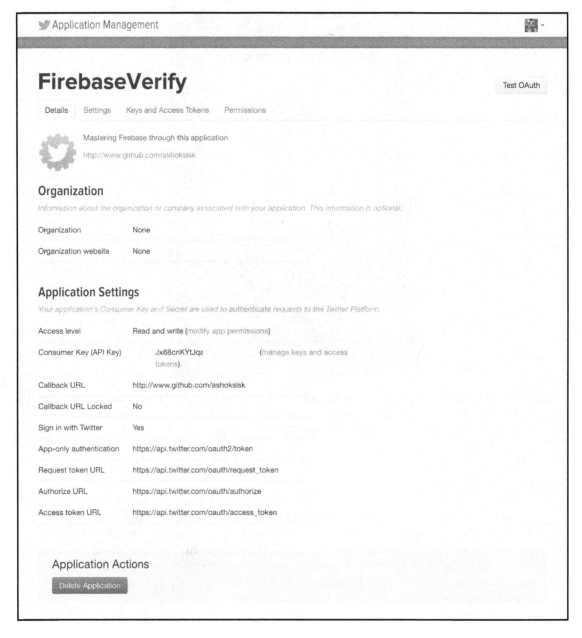

We need to mark **Consumer Key** as an important key. Now, we need to switch to the **Keys and Access Tokens** tab. Here, we have important operations to do. One is to copy all the keys to `string.xml` and create an access token:

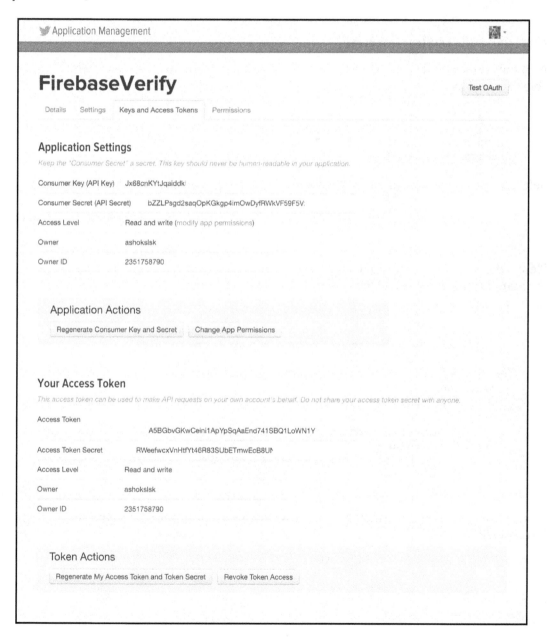

Copy the **Consumer Key** and go to Firebase console to enable the sign-in method for Twitter, inside which you will see API key field to paste the consumer key and consumer secret key into API secret field, enabling Twitter and saving the keys.

Project Configuration

Add the API key and secret key inside a string.xml file. Without these keys, we will not be able to access the Twitter api services. The keys will look like this:

```
<string name="twitter_consumer_key"
translatable="false"><Your_api_key></string>
<string name="twitter_consumer_secret"
translatable="false"><Your_secret_key></string>
```

Before we continue with any further settings, we need to add the Twitter dependency:

```
compile('com.twitter.sdk.android:twitter:3.2.0@aar') {
    transitive = true
}
```

Here, after there is no much of change and we don't have any meta element tags to add to the manifest file, all we need to do is add the provider to the getAuthProviderList method, as follows:

```
private List<AuthUI.IdpConfig> getAuthProviderList() {
    List<AuthUI.IdpConfig> providers = new ArrayList<>();
    providers.add(
            new AuthUI.IdpConfig.Builder(AuthUI.EMAIL_PROVIDER).build());
    providers.add(new
            AuthUI.IdpConfig.Builder(AuthUI.GOOGLE_PROVIDER).build());
    providers.add(new
            AuthUI.IdpConfig.Builder(AuthUI.FACEBOOK_PROVIDER).build());
    providers.add(new
            AuthUI.IdpConfig.Builder(AuthUI.TWITTER_PROVIDER).build());
    return providers;
}
```

Now, we have successfully integrated Twitter with the application, with the support of FirebaseUI:

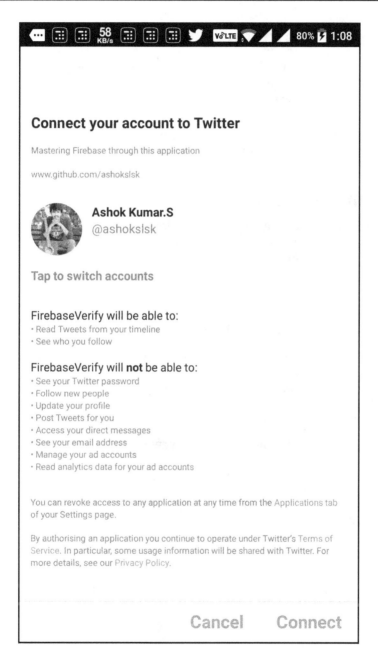

This screenshot explains Twitter integration using FirebaseUI. Let's now move on by exploring phone number sign-in using Firebase UI.

Phone number sign-in

The next popular sign-in method is using a mobile phone number. A user enters their phone number to receive a one-time verification code, also known as OTP, one-time password. There are many use cases in which the application requires two layers of authentication. Even after email login, the business logic of the application expects a phone number verification. To enable phone number sign-in through Firebase UI, all we need to do is enable the phone number sign-in method in Firebase console.

Project configuration

Go to Firebase console and inside the authentication window, go to sign-in method and enable phone number sign- in. Now, we need to add the phone number provider inside the `getAuthProviderList` method:

```
private List<AuthUI.IdpConfig> getAuthProviderList() {
    List<AuthUI.IdpConfig> providers = new ArrayList<>();
    providers.add(
            new AuthUI.IdpConfig.Builder(AuthUI.EMAIL_PROVIDER).build());
    providers.add(new
            AuthUI.IdpConfig.Builder(AuthUI.GOOGLE_PROVIDER).build());
    providers.add(new
            AuthUI.IdpConfig.Builder(AuthUI.FACEBOOK_PROVIDER).build());
    providers.add(new
            AuthUI.IdpConfig.Builder(AuthUI.TWITTER_PROVIDER).build());
    providers.add(new
AuthUI.IdpConfig.Builder(AuthUI.PHONE_VERIFICATION_PROVIDER).build());
    return providers;
}
```

Now that we have successfully integrated phone number verification into the application, let's compile the output:

This screenshot shows the successful integration of the FirebaseUI for phone number sign-in.

Firebase SDK social networking site authentication

As we have understood that popular social networking sites are Google Plus, Facebook, and Twitter, whereas GitHub is more of engineers' and software developers' place. Firebase can work with popular Authentication providers, and it can also support the non-popular authentication providers. We will explore popular authentication providers using the Firebase SDK.

Google sign-in

Google authentication will use the instance of the GoogleSigninOptions class and also it needs a googleApiClient object. Using a builder pattern, we will construct the following code snippet that will be passed to googleApiClient later:

```
GoogleSignInOptions signInOptions = new
        GoogleSignInOptions.Builder(GoogleSignInOptions.DEFAULT_SIGN_IN)
        .requestIdToken(getString(R.string.default_web_client_id))
        .requestEmail()
        .requestProfile()
        .build();
```

This fabricates a GoogleSignInOptions instance by utilizing the default arrangement for a Google Sign-in operation. The instance is arranged to ask for the client's Google account ID token, email address, and profile data. The ID token will be utilized later in return for Firebase authentication credentials.

Now, using the GoogleSignInOption that has been created, we can create the GoogleApiClient class like this:

```
GoogleApiClient googleApiClient = new GoogleApiClient.Builder(this)
        .enableAutoManage(this, this)
        .addApi(Auth.GOOGLE_SIGN_IN_API, signInOptions)
        .build();
```

We need to use the getSignInIntent method for the sign-in, and on successful sign-in, it returns a GoogleSignInResult object:

```
Auth.GoogleSignInApi.getSignInIntent(googleApiClient);
```

Using the following method, we can register Google data with Firebase:

```
private void GoogleFirebase(GoogleSignInAccount googleSignin) {
    AuthCredential credential = GoogleAuthProvider.getCredential(
            googleSignin.getIdToken(), null);
    firebaseAuth.signInWithCredential(credential)
            .addOnCompleteListener(this,
                    new OnCompleteListener<AuthResult>() {
                        @Override
                        public void onComplete(@NonNull Task<AuthResult>
task) {
                            if (!task.isSuccessful()) {
                                Toast.makeText(MainActivity.this, "Firebase
authentication failed.", Toast.LENGTH_SHORT).show();
                            }
                        }
                    });
}
```

To sign out, we can use the `signOut` method of the `GoogleSignInApi` object:

```
public void signOut(View view) {
    FirebaseAuth.signOut();
    Auth.GoogleSignInApi.signOut(googleApiClient).setResultCallback(
            new ResultCallback<Status>() {
                @Override
                public void onResult(@NonNull Status status) {
                }
            });
}
```

Most of the configuration that we did using FirebaseUI will remain the same; for example, adding an SHA-1 fingerprint is a similar process.

Facebook login

The Facebook configuration that we carried out in the FirebaseUI method is very similar, but here we will have to do all the customization according the application. We need the app id and and app protocol scheme ID. Before all of this, we need to add a valid hash key to the Facebook developer console. Once we have done all this configuration, we have to add the meta tag to the manifest:

```
<meta-data android:name="com.facebook.sdk.ApplicationId"
android:value="@string/facebook_application_id"/>
```

Add the Firebase dependency to your app's Gradle file.

```
implementation 'com.facebook.android:facebook-android-sdk:[4,5)'
```

After the library is synced with the project, we will have access to the following button class, which has the button designed for `facebook` login:

```
<com.facebook.login.widget.LoginButton
android:text="Button"
android:layout_width="wrap_content"
android:layout_height="wrap_content"
android:id="@+id/loginButton"
app:layout_constraintRight_toRightOf="parent"
app:layout_constraintLeft_toLeftOf="parent"
app:layout_constraintBottom_toBottomOf="parent"
app:layout_constraintTop_toBottomOf="@+id/statusText" />
```

Now, after this, register a `callbackManager` in the `oncreate` method:

```
callbackManager = CallbackManager.Factory.create();
```

And set the required parameter permissions:

```
loginButton.setReadPermissions("email", "public_profile");
```

Now, we can add these callbacks to the `loginButton`:

```
loginButton.registerCallback(callbackManager,
        new FacebookCallback<LoginResult>() {
    @Override
    public void onSuccess(LoginResult loginResult) {
        Log.d(TAG, "onSuccess: " + loginResult);
    }
    @Override
    public void onCancel() {
        Log.d(TAG, "onCancel: User cancelled sign-in");
    }
    @Override
    public void onError(FacebookException error) {
        Log.d(TAG, "onError: " + error);
    }
});
```

Now, we need to override the onActivityResult method:

```
@Override
protected void onActivityResult(int requestCode, int resultCode, Intent
data) {
    super.onActivityResult(requestCode, resultCode, data);
    callbackManager.onActivityResult(requestCode, resultCode, data);
}
```

We have successfully integrated Facebook with the application; now, we need to register and exchange tokens, and that can be achieved as shown here:

```
private void registerToFirebase(AccessToken token) {
    AuthCredential credential =
            FacebookAuthProvider.getCredential(token.getToken());
    FirebaseAuth.signInWithCredential(credential)
            .addOnCompleteListener(this, new
OnCompleteListener<AuthResult>() {
                @Override
                public void onComplete(@NonNull Task<AuthResult> task) {
                    if (!task.isSuccessful()) {
                        Toast.makeText(FacebookAuthActivity.this,
                                "Authentication failed.",
                                Toast.LENGTH_SHORT).show();
                    }
                }
            });
}
```

This explains how to integrate Facebook and Firebase together without using any UI frameworks.

Twitter sign-in

Firebase user authentication can also be performed using the Twitter SDK. Similar to Google and Facebook integration, the user is told to sign in to a Twitter account, the points of interest of which are then used to create an account in the Firebase authentication user database.

We need to enable the Twitter sign in method in Firebase console. Add the appropriate new Gradle dependency to the project. Since we are using the Firebase SDK, we will have control over creating the user interface. But, we are focusing on the main aspects here.

The Twitter SDK also provides the button designed for Android:

```
<com.twitter.sdk.android.core.identity.TwitterLoginButton
android:id="@+id/loginButton"
android:layout_width="wrap_content"
android:layout_height="wrap_content"
android:text="Button"
app:layout_constraintRight_toRightOf="parent"
app:layout_constraintLeft_toLeftOf="parent"
app:layout_constraintBottom_toTopOf="@+id/button3"
app:layout_constraintTop_toBottomOf="@+id/statusText" />
```

Before loading the layout inside the `oncreate` method, initialize Twitter:

```
TwitterConfig config = new TwitterConfig.Builder(this)
        .logger(new DefaultLogger(Log.DEBUG))
        .twitterAuthConfig(new TwitterAuthConfig(TWITTER_KEY,
            TWITTER_SECRET))
        .debug(true)
        .build();
Twitter.initialize(config);
```

Using Twitter button callbacks, we can have a reference to the success or failure of user data retrieval:

```
loginButton.setCallback(new Callback<TwitterSession>() {
    @Override
    public void success(Result<TwitterSession> result) {
        Log.d(TAG, "loginButton Callback: Success");
    }
    @Override
    public void failure(TwitterException exception) {
        Log.d(TAG, "loginButton Callback: Failure " +
                exception.getLocalizedMessage());
    }
});
```

Now, we can use Firebase to create the account using the Twitter profile details:

```
private void TwitterFirebase(TwitterSession session) {
    AuthCredential credential = TwitterAuthProvider.getCredential(
            session.getAuthToken().token,
            session.getAuthToken().secret);
    FirebaseAuth.signInWithCredential(credential)
            .addOnCompleteListener(this, new
OnCompleteListener<AuthResult>() {
                @Override
                public void onComplete(@NonNull Task<AuthResult> task) {
```

```
                    if (!task.isSuccessful()) {
                        Log.w(TAG, "signInWithCredential",
                                task.getException());
                        Toast.makeText(TwitterAuthActivity.this,
                                "Authentication failed.",
                                Toast.LENGTH_SHORT).show();
                    }
                }
            });
```

Phone number sign-in

We have already seen phone number sign-in earlier. This method allows developers to customize the user interface and functionality. The following code makes use of most of the callbacks:

```
private void setPhoneVerificaton() {
        verificationCallbacks =
                new PhoneAuthProvider.OnVerificationStateChangedCallbacks()
{
                @Override
                public void onVerificationCompleted(
                        PhoneAuthCredential credential) {
                    signInWithPhoneAuthCredential(credential);
                }
                @Override
                public void onVerificationFailed(FirebaseException e) {
                    if (e instanceof
FirebaseAuthInvalidCredentialsException) {
                        // Invalid request
                        Log.d(TAG, "Invalid credential: "
                                + e.getLocalizedMessage());
                    } else if (e instanceof
FirebaseTooManyRequestsException) {
                        // SMS quota exceeded
                        Log.d(TAG, "SMS Quota exceeded.");
                    }
                }
                @Override
                public void onCodeSent(String verificationId,
PhoneAuthProvider.ForceResendingToken token) {
                    phoneVerificationId = verificationId;
                    resendToken = token;
                }
            };
    }
```

The important callback methods of phone number sign-in are:

- `onVerificationCompleted()`: This can be triggered when the verification happens automatically without manual input
- `onVerificationFailed()`: This callback represents a wrongly entered OTP and other errors
- `onCodeSent()`: After code is sent to the number, using this method we can update the UI and other functionalities

Anonymous Authentication

The name clearly states that the application allows users to access the application's features by providing a temporary anonymous identity. We need to enable anonymous login in the Firebase console. Next, the `anonymousSignIn` method calls the `signInAnonymously()` method of the `FirebaseAuth` instance:

```
public void anonymousSignIn() {
    FirebaseAuth.signInAnonymously()
            .addOnCompleteListener(this,
                    new OnCompleteListener<AuthResult>() {
                        @Override
                        public void onComplete(@NonNull Task<AuthResult>
task) {
                            if (!task.isSuccessful()) {
                                Toast.makeText(AnonAuthActivity.this,
                                        "Authentication failed. "
                                                + task.getException(),
                                        Toast.LENGTH_SHORT).show();
                            } else {
                                softButton.setText("Create an Account");
                                buttonMode = CREATE_MODE;
                            }
                        }
                    });
    }
```

Link multiple Auth providers

You can enable clients to sign in to your application utilizing different authentication providers by connecting auth provider credentials to a current user account. Clients are identifiable by a similar Firebase client ID, which pays little respect to the Authentication provider they used to sign in. For instance, a client who signed in with a secret key can connect to a Google record and sign in with either strategy later on. Or on the other hand, an anonymous client can interface a Facebook record and afterward sign in with Facebook to keep utilizing the application.

To achieve this, the user needs to log in from multiple Auth services such as Google, Facebook, and Twitter, as well as anonymously. Now, using the `linkWithCredential` method, we can link all the tokens and can avoid one user creating multiple accounts using different auth providers:

```
mAuth.getCurrentUser().linkWithCredential(credential)
        .addOnCompleteListener(this, new OnCompleteListener<AuthResult>() {
            @Override
            public void onComplete(@NonNull Task<AuthResult> task) {
                if (task.isSuccessful()) {
                    Log.d(TAG, "linkWithCredential:success");
                    FirebaseUser user = task.getResult().getUser();
                    updateUI(user);
                } else {
                    Log.w(TAG, "linkWithCredential:failure",
task.getException());
                    Toast.makeText(AnonymousAuthActivity.this,
"Authentication failed.",
                            Toast.LENGTH_SHORT).show();
                    updateUI(null);
                }

                // ...
            }
        });
```

To unlink the provider, we have a similar mechanism, but the user needs to pass `providerID`. The following code explains the unlinking of a provider:

```
FirebaseAuth.getInstance().getCurrentUser().unlink(providerId)
        .addOnCompleteListener(this, new OnCompleteListener<AuthResult>() {
            @Override
            public void onComplete(@NonNull Task<AuthResult> task) {
                if (!task.isSuccessful()) {
                    // Auth provider unlinked from account
                }
```

```
            }
    });
```

Firebase Authentication failures

Platforms as powerful as Firebase tend to fail at times, for many reasons such as no network, poor memory, and so on. To provide a seamless user experience, we need to know the fail cases firmly. All interface callbacks have a method for failure scenarios and we need to handle it for a better user experience. If a failure occurs and the failure handler is not doing its expected job, then we can manually attach an `addOnFailureListener` to extend the controls:

```
firebaseAuth.signInWithEmailAndPassword(email, password)
        .addOnCompleteListener(this, new OnCompleteListener<AuthResult>() {
@Override
public void onComplete(@NonNull Task<AuthResult> task) {
        if (!task.isSuccessful()) {
                // Notify user of failure
                }
            }
        }).addOnFailureListener(new OnFailureListener() {
                @Override
                public void onFailure(@NonNull Exception e) {
                    }
                });
```

Firebase Authentication exceptions

The Firebase SDK throws exceptions at the time of Authentication failure, which allows developers to identify the cause of failure quickly and find the solution. The following exceptions are thrown at any given specific failure event as enlisted below:

- `FirebaseAuthInvalidUserException`: This indicates that the account is not available in the database

- `FirebaseAuthInvalidCredentialsException`: This indicates invalid credentials

- `FirebaseAuthUserCollisionException`: This indicates a problem with email and account creation

- `FirebaseAuthWeakPasswordException`: When a user enters a weak password, such as a one-digit number
- `FirebaseAuthRecentLoginRequiredException`: Time interval before the user needs to re-authenticate

Firebase also provides certain error codes such as **ERROR_USER_DISABLED** and **ERROR_USER_NOT_FOUND** to indicate major errors.

Summary

As we continue to explore the Firebase toolchain, Authentication turned out to be the biggest chapter. It is a practical chapter; we have seen how to work with different auth providers and we have experience in using the FirebaseUI library. We have explored how to create an account using an email address, phone number, Google, Facebook, and Twitter. We have learned to fetch the API key for different providers, and we also learned how to retrieve the SHA-1 fingerprint inside Android Studio. All the code snippets that we have seen in this chapter are Android community recommended code. We have extensively used the Firebase SDK and FirebaseUI to build most of the authentication use cases. Customizing the email address, we have also understood the Firebase console, managing users, and so on. Overall social networking and phone number login, anonymous login and linking the providers. In the next chapter, let's explore Firebase crash reporting.

Safe and Sound – Firebase Crashlytics

3

"There is no such thing as an accident, only a failure to recognize the hand of fate"

– Napoleon

Monitoring crashes in your application will help you to identify runtime issues and failures of the application in different environments. Like every developer, you have written the code, and you have tested the app and published it in Play Store for everyone to use. As a developer, of course, you are aware that there are many use cases or errors that are merely exposed to you after you publish the application in the Play Store. Although you want your users to have seamless user experience without any performance failures and crashes or any **Application Not Responding (ANR)** errors, if there is bug that causes a problem for the application user you need to know that as soon as possible so you can fix it. To help with this, we can integrate Firebase Crash Reporting or Firebase Crashlytics. Firebase Crash Reporting is robust and it creates detailed reports of the errors by grouping errors based on the issues. It also has the feature of automatic reporting and developers can log custom events that are leading up to a crash. Google also has Google Stackdriver Error Reporting for the web, which supports modern languages such as Node, Python, Go, Java, and so on. Firebase Crashlytics is a light-weight, realtime crash reporter. Crashlytics can give the actionable insights of the application issues. Google and Firebase recommend Crashlytics for an excellent Crash Reporting solution. Crashlytics helps developers to track, prioritize and fix the issues to improve your application quality. It saves time by grouping the crashes and highlighting the circumstances that caused the crash.

In this chapter, we will cover the following topics:

- Firebase Crash Reporting and Crashlytics overview
- Firebase Crash Reporting setup

- Reporting crashes using Firebase Crash Reporting
- Firebase Crashlytics overview
- Firebase Crashlytics setup and upgrading from Crash Reporting
- Customizing crash reports
- Testing your Crashlytics implementation

Firebase Crash Reporting and Crashlytics

Within the Firebase toolchain, Crash Reporting was a robust tool for collecting the nitty gritty report of errors and crashes. Despite the fact that it was powerful, it had its pros and cons. Crash analysis is a crucial ingredient of daily errands, and it aims at solving issues that users experienced with our app by looking by the side of the stack trace and, composed with its context, fixing problematic bugs and troublesome conditions. Firebase Crash Reporting will add 900 kilobytes of size to the APK (Android binary executable), whereas Crashlytics is close to 100 kilobytes. Keeping all of this in mind there are numerous technical factors that are accountable to make Crashlytics as the primary tool. Firebase officially declared that Crashlytics would be the primary solution for Crash Reporting soon. Overtime, Crashlytics has improved and eventually superseded Firebase Crash Reporting. There are a couple of user experience glitches in Firebase crash reporting, such as when we choose 50 issues per page, after a page refreshes we are back to 20 issues per page, whereas in Crashlytics it is an infinite scroll and this issue doesn't exist.

Crashlytics offers a feature for marks an issue as resolved, this feature doesn't exist in Firebase Crash Reporting. Crashlytics integrates plenty of crashes into a flexible list of issues, providing contextual data, and highlighting the fact and ubiquity of crashes so you can pinpoint the origin problem faster. Crashlytics detailed reporting mechanisms can filter the reports by platform, version, and hardware configurations. It will be an excellent opportunity for identifying whether the application is failing on some particular manufacturer's device.

In the following section, we will explore integrating Firebase Crash Reports and Crashlytics.

 Remember that we cannot plug both the tools into your application. Instead, learn to migrate your Firebase Crash Reports to Crashlytics.

Firebase Crash Reporting setup

Firebase Crash Reporting will be obsolete soon, so why are we exploring it? Well, Firebase Crash Reporting still has some features that are worth trying, and Crashlytics will surely take some time to be the primary tool. There are hundreds and thousands of application in the market still relying on the Firebase Crash Reporting. You might also get a request to integrate Firebase Crash Report over Crashlytics. Until Google shuts down the tool we have to understand how to work with principles of Firebase Crash Reporting. Though integrating Firebase Crash Report is straightforward and easy there are a few places where we end up making mistakes, so here are the complete steps for a successful Firebase Crash Reports integration.

Android Studio is the most straightforward option for integrating any of the Firebase toolchains. We can also go to the Firebase console and create the project and follow the configuration from there or let Android Studio do the necessary work for us.

The following steps illustrate how to integrate the Firebase Crash Reporting into an Android project:

1. Set up Firebase in your project from Android Studio. Go to **Tools** and choose **Firebase** and inside select the tool that you want to use (Chapter 1, *Keep It Real, Firebase Realtime Database* explains Firebase integration in detail).
2. In the Firebase window panel when we select an option to **Connect Firebase**, the dialog window prompts for creating a new project or using an existing project.
3. After a successful application creation in the Firebase console, add the **Crash Reporting** dependency and you are free to create the custom log. Also, Firebase automatically starts capturing the events of the application.

At the time of writing, the Firebase Crash Reporting had the following version and dependency:

```
//Android Studio 2.0 or later
compile 'com.google.firebase:firebase-crash:11.8.0'

Or

//Android Studio 3.0 or later
implementation 'com.google.firebase:firebase-crash:11.8.0'
```

Even if you see an updated version number most of the processes that we follow here are going to be identical.

Creating crash reports

We have already understood that Firebase automatically monitors and generates reports in case of any fatal errors or uncaught exceptions. Also, Firebase allows developers to create custom log events to fire when a crash or an error of any means occurs.

Let's create a custom error when the app starts, which will fire an error that we can define and we can see that in the Firebase console with the maximum delay of minutes. In the following code, when the app reaches the onCreate method, it fires a custom error that we have passed:

```
package com.packt.crashreport;

import android.support.v7.app.AppCompatActivity;
import android.os.Bundle;
import com.google.firebase.crash.FirebaseCrash;

public class MainActivity extends AppCompatActivity {

    @Override
    protected void onCreate(Bundle savedInstanceState) {
        super.onCreate(savedInstanceState);
        setContentView(R.layout.activity_main);
        FirebaseCrash.report(new Exception("Firebase crash report is really handy"));
    }
}
```

After running the preceding code in an emulator or actual device, let's now go to the Firebase console that is synced with the project:

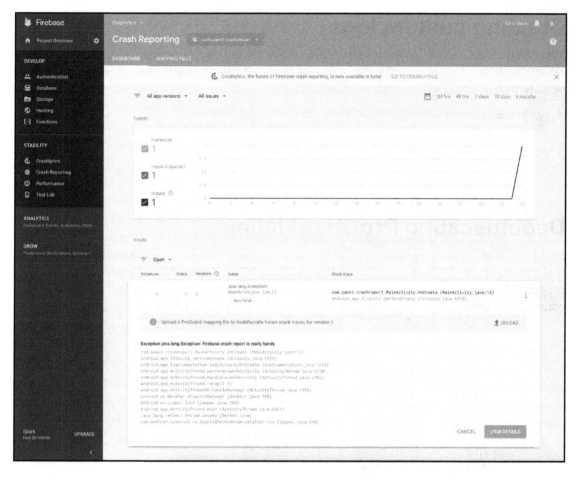

Crash Reporting console displaying the triggered error and stack trace

In the preceding screenshot, we can clearly see the stack trace showing the error that we passed. Here in the console, we can filter the issues and errors and we can also see the charts of error occurrence. We also can filter the issues to **24 hrs**, **48 hrs**, **7 days**, **30 days**, and **6 months** of detailed reports.

Creating custom logs

You can utilize Crash Reporting to log custom events in your error reports and alternatively the logcat. If you wish to log an event and don't need logcat output, you just need to pass a string as the argument, as follows:

```
//Firebase log
FirebaseCrash.log("Firebase crash report is really handy");

//Firebase logcat
FirebaseCrash.logcat(1,"MainActivity", "Errors are not boring");
```

Deobfuscating ProGuard labels

ProGuard produces a `mapping.txt` document that maps ProGuard-obfuscated symbols to their unique names. On the off chance that you have ProGuard enabled, uploading your mapping documents allows you to see deobfuscated stack traces in the Crash Reporting console. For testing, configure ProGuard for debug build types and use the `./gradlew assembleDebug` command:

```
buildTypes {
    release {
        minifyEnabled false
        proguardFiles getDefaultProguardFile('proguard-android.txt'),
'proguard-rules.pro'
    }

    debug {
        minifyEnabled true
        proguardFiles getDefaultProguardFile('proguard-android.txt'),
                'proguard-rules.pro'
    }
}
```

To upload ProGuard mapping files:

1. In the project gradle file, add the following Crash Reporting plugin:

   ```
   // For Android Studio 2.x, use firebase-plugins version 1.1.1
       classpath 'com.google.firebase:firebase-plugins:1.1.1'

   Or

   // For Android Studio 3.0, use firebase-plugins version 1.1.5
       classpath 'com.google.firebase:firebase-plugins:1.1.5'
   ```

2. In the `build.gradle` file, apply the plugin:

```
apply plugin: 'com.google.firebase.firebase-crash'
```

3. Generate a **Service** account and private key. In Crash Reporting, go to the **Mapping files** tab and select **Generate new private key**.

4. In your project `gradle.properties` add `FirebaseServiceAccountFilePath` with a downloaded JSON file as follows:

```
./gradlew -
PFirebaseServiceAccountFilePath=/usr/Ashok/ServiceAccount/Crashlyti
cs-a378fsk34.json :app:firebaseUploadReleaseProguardMapping
```

5. Now we can use the following command to build the APK and upload the mapping file to Firebase:

```
./gradlew :app:firebaseUploadReleaseProguardMapping
```

You can also do a lot of customization by specifying the changes in `gradle.properties`. In case you are not using a `google-service.json` file, you will have to use `FirebaseCrashApiKey` and `FirebaseCrashAppId` in gradle properties.

Crash Report support for multiple APK

The Firebase plugin that we saw in the previous section will work with multiple APK renders with different flavors and variants. The gradle task will upload the mapping files to Firebase for all the APK variants.

For instance, suppose we have two different versions of the APK, namely paid and free, we can customize the processor architecture that the application is going to run and we can include or exclude a specific architecture:

```
productFlavors {
        paid {
            applicationId "com.google.firebase.packt.crashlytics"
            versionName "1.0-Paid"
        }
        free{
          applicationId "com.google.firebase.packt.crashlytics"
            versionName "1.0-Free"
        }
    }

    splits {
```

```
abi {
    enable true
    reset()
    include 'armeabi', 'armeabi-v7a'
    universalApk true
}
}
```

When we run the `./gradlew` command, we can see the following output:

```
Successfully uploaded proguard mapping file for app fullArmeabiRelease with
versionCode: 1!
```

Disabling Crash Reporting

Developers can programmatically disable Crash Reporting or do so in a manifest file. It is great practice for a user to be part of the Crash Reporting process since the user will be paying for the network.

In manifest, if we add the following metadata, Crash Reporting will be disabled:

```
<meta-data android:name="firebase_crash_collection_enabled"
android:value="false" />
```

Programatically we can do this to the future of Firebase Crash Reporting, which is the go-to solution for clear and actionable insight into application issues. When using the `FirebaseCrash` class, when it is set to `false` it is disabled and when it is set to `true` it is enabled:

```
FirebaseCrash.setCrashCollectionEnabled(false);
```

So far we have seen how to integrate the Crash Report and we have explored a decent amount of features of Firebase Crash Report. Now it's time to get ready to understand and explore Crashlytics.

Firebase Crashlytics

For the future of Firebase Crash Reporting, go to solution for clear and actionable insight into application issues. Firebase Crashlytics will save troubleshooting time with smart crash grouping and the causes that lead to the crash. Developer can efficiently identify the crashes, how many users are affected by the crash, and so on. There are numerous capabilities of Crashlytics. Perhaps the most widely accepted capabilities are covered here. Curated crash reports, known as Crashlytics, process the manageable list of issues and also give the context for the issue. It also addresses the impact and shows the cause faster. Crashlytics also provides the tips and resolves the issue more quickly. Crashlytics allows filtering the report based on the platform, version, and hardware configuration. Crashlytics will enable developers to identify particular manufacturer devices that are resulting in the crash. Getting real-time alerts on new issues is faster and manageable. As a feature, Crashlytics automatically starts obtaining the crash related details as soon as we add the SDK to our project. It also allows customizing the report.

Firebase Crashlytics setup and upgrading from Crash Reporting

Firebase Crashlytics cannot be integrated through Android Studio at the time of writing, but we can surely expect an update with Crashlytics, Firestore, Predictions and all the latest arrivals of the toolchain very soon. Nevertheless, let's learn how to integrate Crashlytics newly and migrating from an existing Crash report:

1. Add the Crashlytics plugin dependency in the project level `build.gradle` file:

```
//Add the maven repository url
repositories {
    google()
    jcenter()
    maven {
        url 'https://maven.fabric.io/public'
    }
}

// Add the following classpath under the dependency section
        classpath 'io.fabric.tools:gradle:1.24.4'
```

2. Crashlytics requires Google plugin 3.1.2 or higher to work smoothly:

```
classpath 'com.google.gms:google-services:3.1.2'
```

3. Now add the following dependency to the application-level `build.gradle` file:

```
apply plugin: 'com.android.application'
apply plugin: 'io.fabric'
...
dependencies {
// Crashlytics
compile('com.crashlytics.sdk.android:crashlytics:2.7.1@aar') {
transitive = true
}
compile 'com.google.firebase:firebase-core:11.8.0'
}
```

Once we have added all the preceding dependencies, Crashlytics starts monitoring the application. In case you are using the old setup of fabric Crashlytics, you need to remove all the API keys since Firebase is configured in the project, and we need not worry about the API keys.

Hurray! Crashlytics has been successfully integrated and has started monitoring the app in real time.

The following screenshot illustrates the successful Crashlytics integration with a crash recorded in the console:

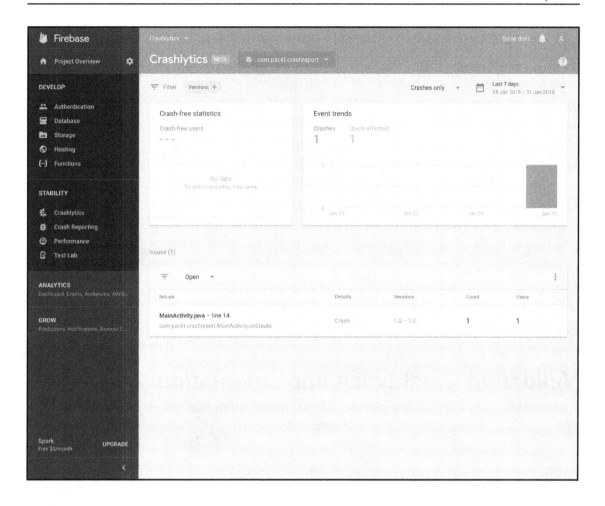

Migrating from Firebase Crash Reporting to Crashlytics

Crashlytics migration is straightforward and has a similar process to Firebase Crash Reporting. It has more useful features than Firebase Crash Reporting. The following steps illustrate how to migrate from Crash Reporting to Crashlytics:

1. Upgrade your project dependencies with Crashlytics dependencies.
2. Remove the Firebase Crash Reporting dependency.

3. Migrate the log calls in your project as follows:

Firebase Crash Reporting	Firebase Crashlytics
FirebaseCrash.log	Crashlytics.log()
FirebaseCrash.logcat()	Crashlytics.log()
FirebaseCrash.report()	Crashlytics.logException()

4. We can initialize Crashlytics in two ways, adding a manifest entry and programmatically. Before adding the following metatag remove any metatag related to Firebase Crash Reporting:

```
<meta-data android:name="firebase_crashlytics_collection_enabled"
android:value="false" />
```

5. Replace the initialization with the following code:

```
Fabric.with(this, new Crashlytics());
```

The application will monitor crashes and send it to Crashlytics until a user closes the application.

Validating Crashlytics implementation

Instead of waiting to validate a successful Crashlytics integration, we can make use of the `Crashlytics` class to crash the application, as follows:

```
package com.packt.crashreport;

import android.os.Bundle;
import android.support.v7.app.AppCompatActivity;
import android.view.View;
import android.widget.Button;
import com.crashlytics.android.Crashlytics;
import io.fabric.sdk.android.Fabric;

public class MainActivity extends AppCompatActivity {
    private Button mCrashbtn;

    @Override
    protected void onCreate(Bundle savedInstanceState) {
        super.onCreate(savedInstanceState);
        setContentView(R.layout.activity_main);
        Fabric.with(this, new Crashlytics());
        mCrashbtn = findViewById(R.id.crashbtn);
        mCrashbtn.setOnClickListener(new View.OnClickListener() {
```

```
        @Override
        public void onClick(View view) {
            Crashlytics.getInstance().crash(); // Force a crash
        }
    });
    }
}
```

After you run the code, open the application to send the crash reports to Crashlytics. All the crashes are grouped and flagged for user basis on the Firebase Console dashboard. Although the UI looks similar to Firebase Crash Report, there exists a lot of functionality differences.

Enabling Crashlytics debug mode

To enable debug mode we need to disable the automatic Crashlytics initialization by adding the following meta tag to the manifest:

```
<meta-data android:name="firebase_crashlytics_collection_enabled"
android:value="false" />
```

Now we are free to enable Crashlytics with `debugger`:

```
final Fabric fabric = new Fabric.Builder(this)
        .kits(new Crashlytics())
        .debuggable(true)          // Enables Crashlytics debugger
        .build();
Fabric.with(fabric);
```

This feature is very handy and will be very helpful to your app testers to work with debug builds.

Customizing Crashlytics reports

Having fine grained crash reports is very important at times. Crashlytics starts sending the crash report to the Firebase console as soon as we integrate it. You can allow the user to make the choice of opting in to the reporting or not, which helps us to identify the bugs and issues in a more personalized fashion.

To opt into reporting we need to disable the automatica collection by adding the meta tag:

```
<meta-data android:name="firebase_crashlytics_collection_enabled"
android:value="false" />
```

We can enable the crash report only from a particular activity or fragment by adding the following code:

```
Fabric.with(this, new Crashlytics());
```

Custom logs play a major role in Crash Reporting and Crashlytics offers a powerful set of functionalities and log methods:

- Crash Report and `log.println()`:

```
Crashlytics.log(int priority, String tag, String msg);
```

- Crash Report only:

```
Crashlytics.log(msg);
```

We can set up a custom key to identify a crash based on the application's state and hardware configuration:

```
Crashlytics.setString(key, value);

Crashlytics.setBool(String key, boolean value);

Crashlytics.setDouble(String key, double value);

Crashlytics.setFloat(String key, float value);

Crashlytics.setInt(String key, int value);
```

Crashlytics supports up to 64 key/value pairs at the moment and each key value can be 1 kilobytes.

If we take a look at many problems, it is very helpful when we can identify the crash based on the user ID. In Crashlytics, we can use the following method to pass the user ID:

```
void Crashlytics.setUserIdentifier(String identifier);
```

Any non fatal exceptions or generic exceptions can be logged with the help of the `Crashlytics` class. Check out the following example:

```
try {
    methodThatThrows();
} catch (Exception e) {
    Crashlytics.logException(e);
    // handle your exception here
}
```

The preceding exceptions are logged as non fatal errors in the Firebase Crashlytics console. With all the details such as network condition, memory leak information, and so on.

 Crashlytics only saves the recent eight exceptions in the app session. Older exceptions are ignored and it only stores the latest eight exceptions for any app session.

Crashlytics and functions

Firebase functions is one of the promising tools in the Firebase toolchain. Crashlytics and functions will be a great combination to work with. Developers can get a notification when there is a new issue and different sets of alerts can be triggered. There are many use cases that we can achieve from Firebase functions and we can send notification to users if and when there are interesting updates. We have a complete chapter dedicated to Firebase functions.

We need to generate an `IssueBuilder` using the `functions.crashlytics.issue()` method, then we can use the following methods in Firebase functions:

- `onNewDetected()`: When there is a new issue this callback triggers:

```
exports.sendOnNew = functions.crashlytics.issue()
                                      .onNewDetected(event => {
// ...
});
```

- `onRegressed()`: When issues reoccur even after fixing the issue and closing it in Crashlytics:

```
exports.sendOnRegressed = functions.crashlytics.issue()
                                      .onRegressed(event
=> {
// ...
});
```

- `onVelocityAlert()`: This event triggers when there are lots of crashes in the app session it notifies:

```
exports.sendOnVelocityAlert = functions.crashlytics.issue()
.onVelocityAlert(event => {
// ...
});
```

Every event triggered from `IssueBuilder` returns an issue, with the issue properties such as name, ID, application information, and so on. The following code sends a slack message with issue ID:

```
exports.postOnIssueCreate =
functions.crashlytics.issue().onNewDetected(event => {
  const { data } = event;
  issueId = data.issueId;
  issueTitle = data.issueTitle;
  const slackMessage = ` There's a new issue (${issueId}) ` +
      `in your app – ${issueTitle}`;
  return notifySlack(slackMessage).then(() => {
    console.log(`Posted new issue ${issueId} successfully to Slack`);
  });
});
```

Overall, Crashlytics and functions are the best in class Crash Reporting and utility tools for collaboration, communication, and a lot more use cases.

Summary

Understanding application failure is very important. Firebase Crash Reporting is a great tool and we have learned how to integrate it, working with Crash Reporting, sending custom log events, and so on. Crashlytics is the future of Firebase Crash Reporting and we have explored it from integrating Crashlytics, creating custom reports, migrating from Firebase Crash Reporting, and so on. Crashlytics and functions are the great combo tools to work and collaborate with.

4
Genie in the Cloud – Firebase Cloud Functions

"Oh what a tangled web we weave when we first practice to deceive"

— *Sir Walter Scott*

The mighty genie who fits inside a lamp, and does jaw-dropping magic when he pops out. Firebase Cloud Functions is the powerful wizard in the Firebase tools spectrum. Functions are essentially JavaScript code running on the Google Cloud Platform, but not inside a bottle. It handles an action when an event trigger occurs. Triggers occur within Firebase and Google platform by supported toolchain, for instance, when there is data written to a Realtime Database or Firestore, at the time of user creation inside Firebase Authentication, and so on.

Firebase Cloud Functions are nothing but server-side programs that respond to an event triggered by one or many of the Firebase services. Functions can be used to send an email when the user clicks on the forgot password link. Functions could fire a welcome email immediately after account creation. They can fire an FCM notification when the Realtime/Firestore database has a new value. Functions can fire notifications if and when, in your analytics cohort, you reach the positive expected results, and so on.

Cloud Functions are written using JavaScript inside a Node environment. They use the Functions SDK, which helps developers to host the code in Google Cloud with the help of CLI tools.

In this chapter, we will cover the following topics:

- An overview of Cloud Functions and setting up a Node environment
- Various Triggers supported by Functions
- Writing and testing Functions

Firebase Cloud Functions

Firebase Cloud Functions is a serverless computing solution to building event-driven applications. The intricate process of hosting code in the cloud virtual machine or inside your server is usually time-consuming and requires expertise in configurations and so forth. Firebase Cloud Functions helps developers to develop solutions quickly and efficiently, without the trouble of managing the server. Although the product is in beta stage, it has so many things to offer developers. Google and Firebase teams have built numerous features in Firebase Cloud Functions, and the tool is continuously evolving. Within the Google Cloud platform, there exists another Cloud Function tool called Google Cloud Functions targeting Google Cloud platform services. These two products are mutual efforts between the Google Cloud Platform team and the Firebase team.

Firebase Cloud Functions, at the time of writing this book, supports almost all significant tools within the Firebase tools. The following tools listed are those currently recommended for using Cloud Functions:

- Cloud Firestore Triggers
- Realtime Database Triggers
- Firebase Authentication Triggers
- Google Analytics for Firebase Triggers
- Crashlytics Triggers
- Cloud Storage Triggers
- Cloud Pub/Sub Triggers
- HTTP Triggers

Server-side programming using Firebase requires an Admin SDK, which allows developers to have admin access over the toolchain, for instance when the Realtime Database adds a new child firing notification using your server, sending payment gateway transaction-related, messages, and so on. When we use the Admin SDK and Cloud Functions, we can write the webhooks for third-party services. Firebase Cloud Functions helps us to improve code quality by reducing boilerplate code.

Functions also help in hosting JavaScript and TypeScript codes in Firebase servers through the command line. Firebase keeps an eye on the user's usage pattern and scales computing resources to match their needs. Also, developers need not worry about anything related to server configuration, creating new server provisions, or decommissioning old servers.

Firebase functions are secure, and the business logic code can remain private and secure, allowing zero chance of reverse engineering. Also, Functions are adequately protected from client-side code.

Set up the development environment

The Firebase Cloud Function CLI is written and developed in Node.js. The CLI requires the Node.js environment. To install Node.js, visit `https://nodejs.org/`. The Node.js binary file will also include Node Package Manager. Google recommends working with Node v.6.11.5 (LTS: Long Term Support) since cloud functions run the same version. You can download this version from `https://nodejs.org/en/blog/release/v6.11.5/`. After a successful Node.js installation through Node Package Manager, we can continue the rest of the process.

1. Install Firebase tools followed by the following command. Enter it inside Terminal or Command Prompt:

    `npm install -g firebase-tools`

    This installs the Firebase tools and commands on your computer. If it fails to install the package, we have to change the permission and retry with the same commands:

    `sudo npm install -g firebase-tools`

    Linux and macOS X users have to give the superuser privilege before installing the Firebase tools:

```
Last login: Thu Feb  8 14:01:19 on ttys000
Ashoks-iMac:~ ashok$ npm --version
5.6.0
Ashoks-iMac:~ ashok$ npm update
Ashoks-iMac:~ ashok$ node --version
v6.11.5
Ashoks-iMac:~ ashok$ sudo so
Password:
sudo: so: command not found
Ashoks-iMac:~ ashok$ sudo su
sh-3.2# clear
sh-3.2# npm install -g firebase-tools
npm WARN deprecated node-uuid@1.4.8: Use uuid module instead
/usr/local/bin/firebase -> /usr/local/lib/node_modules/firebase-tools/bin/firebase
/usr/local/lib
└── firebase-tools@3.17.4

sh-3.2#
```

2. Following successful Firebase tool installation, we need to authenticate the CLI with Firebase console credentials via the browser. Use the following command to authenticate: `firebase login`. And if you want to switch to another account you can use `firebase logout`:

```
                                    1. bash
Ashoks-iMac:Chapter Functions ashok$ firebase login
? Allow Firebase to collect anonymous CLI usage and error reporting information? Yes

Visit this URL on any device to log in:
https://accounts.google.com/o/oauth2/auth?client_id=563584335869-fgrhgmd47bqnekij5i8b5p
r03ho849e6.apps.googleusercontent.com&scope=email%20openid%20https%3A%2F%2Fwww.googleap
is.com%2Fauth%2Fcloudplatformprojects.readonly%20https%3A%2F%2Fwww.googleapis.com%2Faut
h%2Ffirebase%20https%3A%2F%2Fwww.googleapis.com%2Fauth%2Fcloud-platform&response_type=c
ode&state=511309139&redirect_uri=http%3A%2F%2Flocalhost%3A9005

Waiting for authentication...

✓  Success! Logged in as ashokcs04@gmail.com
Ashoks-iMac:Chapter Functions ashok$ 
```

3. Now, create a working directory, navigate to the directory, and use the following command: `firebase init functions`. When you enter the command, if you have an expertise in managing npm dependencies you could switch the directories, it is completely safe:

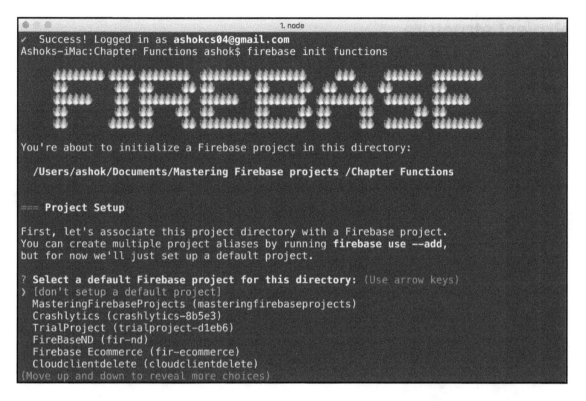

```
1. node
✓  Success! Logged in as ashokcs04@gmail.com
Ashoks-iMac:Chapter Functions ashok$ firebase init functions

[FIREBASE logo]

You're about to initialize a Firebase project in this directory:

  /Users/ashok/Documents/Mastering Firebase projects /Chapter Functions

=== Project Setup

First, let's associate this project directory with a Firebase project.
You can create multiple project aliases by running firebase use --add,
but for now we'll just set up a default project.

? Select a default Firebase project for this directory: (Use arrow keys)
> [don't setup a default project]
  MasteringFirebaseProjects (masteringfirebaseprojects)
  Crashlytics (crashlytics-8b5e3)
  TrialProject (trialproject-d1eb6)
  FireBaseND (fir-nd)
  Firebase Ecommerce (fir-ecommerce)
  Cloudclientdelete (cloudclientdelete)
(Move up and down to reveal more choices)
```

4. After the commands have set up the project, we could use TypeScript or
   JavaScript to write our program and business logic. Also, we are free to use any
   editor that we are comfortable with.

5. In the latter part of the chapter, we will explore how to deploy the functions
   project in Firebase Cloud.

Project structure

Firebase CLI creates the project. The project folders and files will contain the following important configurations:

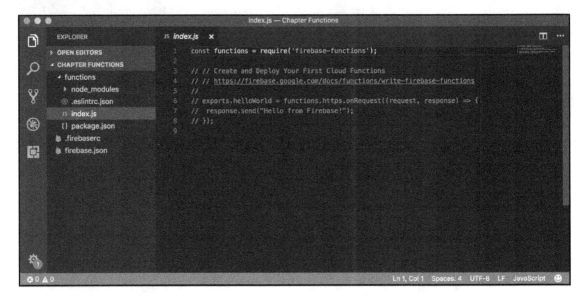

- `.firebaserc`: Reference the current project, allows Firebase to distinguish the project from staging and production, and can also be used to switch between projects.
- `firebase.json`: This file is the property configuration file
- `functions/package.json`: Dependency information and the project configuration details
- `functions/index.js`: Source code file for writing code related to functions
- `functions/node_modules`: Modules configured and installed with the help of `package.json`

Once we complete our code inside `index.js`, we can host the project in cloud functions.

Required modules

Firebase cloud functions require certain important modules, which are the admin SDK module and the functions module itself:

```
// Cloud functions modules for trigger
const functions = require('firebase-functions');

// Admin SDK to access the toolchains like Realtime DB, Firestore and so on
const admin = require('firebase-admin');
admin.initializeApp(functions.config().firebase);
```

The functions module will initialize the functions-related components, and the Admin SDK initializes the FCM, Authentication, Realtime Database, and other Firebase toolchains. The Firebase CLI automatically configures and installs all the Node modules in the project using `funtions/package.json`. We can install third-party node libraries. For example, inside the `package.json` file, there exists a block of code labeled Dependencies that looks like this:

```
{
  "name": "functions",
  "description": "Cloud Functions for Firebase",
  "scripts": {
    "lint": "./node_modules/.bin/eslint .",
    "serve": "firebase serve --only functions",
    "shell": "firebase experimental:functions:shell",
    "start": "npm run shell",
    "deploy": "firebase deploy --only functions",
    "logs": "firebase functions:log"
  },
  "dependencies": {
    "firebase-admin": "~5.8.1",
    "firebase-functions": "^0.8.1"
  },
  "devDependencies": {
    "eslint": "^4.12.0",
    "eslint-plugin-promise": "^3.6.0"
  },
  "private": true
}
```

Inside the dependencies block, we can add our new dependency and run the `npm install` command to install the new library modules:

```
{
  "dependencies": {
    "uuid": "^3.0.1"
  }
}
```

We could also directly run `npm install` commands with module details. The node community has a website for central node module distribution, `https://www.npmjs.com/`, for all the popular and useful libraries.

Using the npm commands `npm install --save uuid.`, we can perform the same operation. `--save` dictates the `package.json` file changes.

Deploying Cloud functions project

Once we write the functions, we could host them in a few simple commands. In simple terms, we will host a `Hello World` program. Your `index.js` file by default will have a hello world program. Uncomment the code and pass the string you want as the function's output:

```
const functions = require('firebase-functions');

// // Create and Deploy Your First Cloud Functions
// // https://firebase.google.com/docs/functions/write-firebase-functions

exports.helloWorld = functions.https.onRequest((request, response) => {
response.send("Packt mastering firebase!");
});
```

Now, we can deploy the the complete project with the following command:

```
$ firebase deploy --only functions
```

If you wanted to deploy one particular method, you can do that by executing this method:

```
$ firebase deploy --only functions:helloWorld
```

These commands and code should work flawlessly. In the case of a deployment error in any platform, check the path of the functions; if any directory has a white space, you might have to change the path and redo the commands with another folder without any white spaces in it.

Here's a successful hello world Deployment in Firebase function:

```
1. bash

=== Deploying to 'realtimedatabase-60ada'...

i  deploying functions
Running command: npm --prefix $RESOURCE_DIR run lint

> functions@ lint /Users/ashok/Documents/codes/chap/functions
> eslint .

✓  functions: Finished running predeploy script.
i  functions: ensuring necessary APIs are enabled...
✓  functions: all necessary APIs are enabled
i  functions: preparing functions directory for uploading...
i  functions: packaged functions (38.34 KB) for uploading
✓  functions: functions folder uploaded successfully
i  functions: creating function helloWorld...
✓  functions[helloWorld]: Successful create operation.
Function URL (helloWorld): https://us-central1-realtimedatabase-60ada.cloudfunct
ions.net/helloWorld

✓  Deploy complete!

Project Console: https://console.firebase.google.com/project/realtimedatabase-60
ada/overview
Ashoks-iMac:chap ashok$
```

The function URL in the output will have the result for `Hello World`. Copy the URL and open it in a browser. It should print the string inside.

Custom logs and reviewing functions

When the function URL is refreshed, we can see the auto-generated logs in the Firebase console. The logs can be accessed from Firebase CLI and Firebase console. In Firebase CLI, use the following command to see the log:

```
$ firebase functions:log
```

This is the output:

```
                                    1. bash
i  functions: creating function helloWorld...
✓  functions[helloWorld]: Successful create operation.
Function URL (helloWorld): https://us-central1-realtimedatabase-60ada.cloudfunct
ions.net/helloWorld

✓  Deploy complete!

Project Console: https://console.firebase.google.com/project/realtimedatabase-60
ada/overview
Ashoks-iMac:chap ashok$ firebase functions:log
2018-02-08T18:26:27.153Z N helloWorld: undefined
2018-02-08T18:28:02.261Z N helloWorld: undefined
2018-02-08T18:35:32.225699631Z D helloWorld: Function execution started
2018-02-08T18:35:32.225768939Z D helloWorld: Billing account not configured. Ext
ernal network is not accessible and quotas are severely limited. Configure billi
ng account to remove these restrictions
2018-02-08T18:35:32.396511389Z D helloWorld: Function execution took 171 ms, fin
ished with status code: 200
2018-02-08T18:44:44.917816731Z D helloWorld: Function execution started
2018-02-08T18:44:44.917858354Z D helloWorld: Billing account not configured. Ext
ernal network is not accessible and quotas are severely limited. Configure billi
ng account to remove these restrictions
2018-02-08T18:44:44.997753395Z D helloWorld: Function execution took 81 ms, fini
shed with status code: 304
2018-02-08T18:44:59.498676002Z D helloWorld: Function execution started
```

Custom logs can be triggered by using JavaScript's very own `console.log()` method. Let's write code that accepts a string as a URL parameter, which is reflected in the log:

```javascript
const functions = require('firebase-functions');

// // Create and Deploy Your First Cloud Functions
// // https://firebase.google.com/docs/functions/write-firebase-functions
//
        exports.helloWorld = functions.https.onRequest((request, response)
=> {
        const UserName = request.query.UserName;
        console.log("Name = " + UserName);
        response.send("Hello from Firebase, " + UserName);
        });
```

Redeploy this code with the changes. Copy the function URL and append the string as shown here:

```
https://us-central1-realtimedatabase-60ada.cloudfunctions.net/helloWorld?Us
erName=Sundar Pichai
```

A simple mouse hover over Firebase console shows a tooltip of the project name. We can filter the result to info, error, debug, and so on.

Logs within Firebase console are as follows:

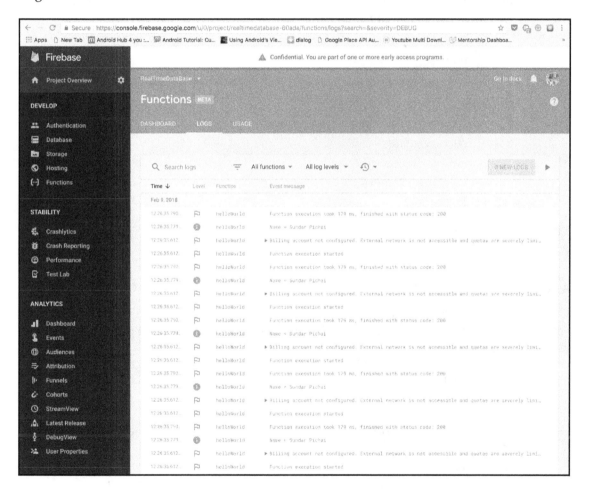

We have seen how to set up our node development environment, and we have also explored the Firebase CLI tool for creating a functions project and deploying it in Firebase cloud. Now, it's time to get our hands dirty by exploring Trigger functions.

Trigger functions

Triggers are the mechanisms that allow a Firebase function to detect a change in the state in Firebase tools. For instance, when the Realtime Database adds a new entry, it triggers a function. Essentially, Triggers are event suppliers. In this section, we will explore the following triggers:

- Cloud Firestore Triggers
- Realtime Database Triggers
- Firebase Authentication Triggers
- Google Analytics for Firebase Triggers
- Crashlytics Triggers
- Cloud Storage Triggers
- Cloud Pub/Sub Triggers
- HTTP Triggers

Let's understand each tool in detail.

Cloud Firestore Triggers

Cloud Firestore is a recent release of the Firebase toolchain. Google labels it as the flexible, scalable NoSQL. To work with Function triggers for Firestore, you don't need to write extra code on the client side. Changes to Firestore can be achieved via `DeltaDocumentSnapshot`, which is an interface representing Cloud Firestore documents. The Cloud Firestore Function typically does the following actions:

- It anticipates changes to Firestore documents
- It triggers the function when an event fired and performs the task of the specific function
- Functions receive the data object with two snapshots of the data stored in Firestore, one with the old data and another with the new data

To trigger a Cloud Firestore function, Firebase SDK offers the `functions.firestore` object for handling specific events. Functions for Firestore support four distinct events: `onCreate`, `onUpdate`, `onDelete` and `onWrite`.

Event	Trigger
onCreate	When a Firestore document is created for the first time
onDelete	When document data is deleted
onUpdate	When a document value is changed
onWrite	When all the events are triggered

Specific documents

Firebase developers can trigger a function for particular document changes. In many cases, monitoring all documents is a waste of computing and also time consuming. If we know which document to monitor, it's best to use trigger for that document:

```
// Anticipates the changes `Teachers` in collection `College`
exports.myFunctionName = functions.firestore
        .document('College/teachers').onWrite((event) => {
        // ... When new teacher joins the institution
        });
```

This code dictates that when a new teacher created in the college collection, it triggers a function that performs a specific action.

Creating a document

Functions for Firestore allows developers to use a wildcard to trigger when a new document is created. Whenever a new user created Firestore, the `createuser` method is called:

```
exports.createUser = functions.Firestore
        .document('users/{userId}')
        .onCreate(event => {
        // Object referencing to the document
        // e.g. {'name': 'Patinitha', 'age': 4}
        var newValue = event.data.data();

        // fetching a particular field.
        var name = newValue.name;

        // perform any actions ...
        });
```

When you have a complex collection structure and you don't know what the identifier is, then we will make use of {wildcard} in place of the document ID. Firebase understands the data through wildcards and fetches the data for us.

Updating documents

Functions for Firestore allow developers to use the onUpdate function with a wildcard to trigger a function when a document is updated or has some change values. The following example illustrates the onUpdate function and its event callbacks:

```
exports.updateUser = functions.firestore
        .document('users/{userId}')
        .onUpdate(event => {
        // e.g. {'name': 'Srinivasa', 'age': 61}
        //indicates the new value
        var newValue = event.data.data();

        // indicates the old value
        var previousValue = event.data.previous.data();

        var name = newValue.name;

        // perform desired operations ...
        });
```

This code is very straightforward; we can perform the desired task based on this data.

Deleting a document

Functions for Firestore offer another function, called onDelete(). This takes a wildcard as a parameter and deletes the appropriate document:

```
exports.deleteUser = functions.firestore
        .document('users/{userID}')
        .onDelete(event => {
        // e.g. {'name': 'Srinivas', 'age': 61}
        var deletedValue = event.data.previous.data();

        // perform desired operations ...
        });
```

This code fetches the value deleted from the Firestore and we could perform an action based on this data.

Changes in a document

If you want to listen to all kinds of events occurring in Firestore and trigger a function, we can make use of the `onWrite` method with a wildcard ID:

```
exports.modifyUser = functions.firestore
        .document('users/{userID}')
        .onWrite(event => {
        var document = event.data.data();

// Update or delete the data
        var oldDocument = event.data.previous.data();

        // perform desired operations ...
        });
```

Using `event.data`, we can read the data and perform the desired action in functions. If you want to write the data with the reference of `event.data.ref`, we can achieve that.

If you want to monitor a complex document structure, you can do it with the help of wildcard values, as shown here:

```
exports.useMultipleWildcards = functions.firestore
        .document('users/{userId}/{messageCollectionId}/{messageId}')
        .onWrite((event) => {
        // If we set `/users/Vinisha/incoming_messages/167` to {body:
"Hello"} then
        event.params.userId == "Vinisha";
        event.params.messageCollectionId == "incoming_messages";
        event.params.messageId == "167";
        // ... and ...
        event.data.data() == {body: "Hello"}
        });
```

If the wildcard points to a document, the program works fine. If the wildcard is pointing to a collection, it is not valid.

Realtime Database Triggers

The Realtime Database stores and syncs data in real time across platforms and devices. To work with Function triggers for Realtime Database, you don't need to write extra code on the client side. Changes in Realtime Database can be fetched via `DeltaSnapShot`, which is an interface representing the Realtime Database. The functions for Realtime Database typically perform the following actions:

- Triggers waits for changes to be made to a particular database location
- Triggers the function when an event is fired. Also performs the task of the specific function
- Functions receive the data object with two snapshots of the data stored in Firestore, one with the old data and another with the new data

Using `functions.database`, Firebase developers can trigger a function and using one of the event handlers, the function can listen to a Realtime Database path. Functions for databases have four event handlers:

- `onWrite()`: Triggers at the time of data is created, updated, or deleted in the Realtime Database
- `onCreate(`: Triggers at the time of new data is created in the Realtime Database
- `onUpdate()`: Triggers at the time of data is updated in the Realtime Database
- `onDelete()`: Triggers at the time of data is deleted from the Realtime Database

The following code illustrates how to make use of `functions.database.ref` to pass the path and listening to the changes in the event.

```
// anticipates for change
exports.BuildUppercase =
functions.database.ref('/messages/{pushId}/original')
    .onWrite(event => {
      // fetches the data written to database
      const original = event.data.val();
      console.log('Uppercasing', event.params.pushId, original);
      const uppercase = original.toUpperCase();

      // update the data to upper case and set it.
      return event.data.ref.parent.child('uppercase').set(uppercase);
    });
```

In Realtime Database, we can also make use of wildcards for complex data structures.

Firebase Authentication Triggers

Whenever there is a new user added using Firebase Authentication, we can trigger a function to perform an action. Using the `functions.auth.user().onCreate` event handler, we can send an email or a notification, or perform some relevant operation, when new user is created:

```
exports.sendEmail = functions.auth.user().onCreate(event => {
  // ...
});
```

Functions for Authentication will trigger user creation events when:

- A user creates an account with authentic email and password
- A user signs in with an authentication provider such as Facebook, Twitter and so on
- A user logs in and with an anonymous account and creates a session for the first time

Using the `functions.auth.user().onDelete()` event, you can send *Sorry to see you go* emails and similar:

```
exports.sendEmailSorryToSeeYouGo = functions.auth.user().onDelete(event =>
{
  // ...
});
```

This code snippet triggers functions whenever the existing user gets deleted for any reason.

Analytics and Crashlytics Triggers

Analytics give a strategic understanding of how users are using the application. Cloud functions have access to conversion events that we log. Using these conversion events, we can trigger a function to perform an action.

 A conversion event in analytics or in any platform dictates the expected result of the action in comparison to the actual result. For instance, adding products to a cart is an event, but a successful purchase transaction is the conversion. At the time of writing this book, only conversion events are supported by functions.

When a user's conversion event occurs, we can use the `AnalyticsEvent` class to perform an action, such as sending a notification:

```
exports.sendCouponOnPurchase =
functions.analytics.event('in_app_purchase').onLog(event => {
  // ...
});
```

With analytics events, developers have access to every relevant parameter and user property.

Functions for crashlytics requires an `IssueBuilder` to trigger the Crashlytics function, make use of `function.crashlytics.issue()`, then call the issue generation function.

- `onNewDetected()` : When a new issue is found in the application:

```
exports.sendOnNew = functions.crashlytics.issue()
                                    .onNewDetected(event => {
// ...
});
```

- `onRegressed()`: When an issue reoccurs even after closing in Crashlytics:

```
exports.sendOnRegressed = functions.crashlytics.issue()
                                    .onRegressed(event
=> {
// ...
});
```

- `onVelocityAlert()`: When there is a crash that crossed a count of limit:

```
exports.sendOnVelocityAlert = functions.crashlytics.issue()
.onVelocityAlert(event => {
// ...
});
```

Analytics and Crashlytics can be used at the same time, since they do different jobs.

Cloud Storage Triggers

When we upload files to Cloud Storage, we can trigger functions while we are uploading, updating, or deleting files. There are different trigger functions inherited by `functions.storage` to create functions for handling cloud storage events. Targeting on specific Cloud Storage Bucket and default bucket can be done as follows:

- `function.storage.object()`: Listens to changes occurring in the default bucket
- `function.storage.bucket("Bucket name").object()`: Listens to changes occurring in a specific bucket

```
exports.thumbnail = functions.storage.object().onChange(event => {
  // ...
});
```

This code is scoped to the default bucket. Storage and also supports change events; for instance, if there are any changes, such as uploading, updating, or deleting, then functions can be triggered.

For detecting resource state, cloud function exposes most of the event attributes like timestamp and resource. The resource state attribute will have an attribute called `exist`, which denotes object creation and update, and `not_exist` for object deletion and moving. Using the meta generation attribute with the resource state attribute, we can identify whether the object has been created or not.

HTTP Triggers

Using `functions.https`, we can trigger Firebase functions. We can make use of HTTP methods such as `GET`, `POST`, `PUT`, `DELETE`, and `OPTIONS`, using the `onRequest` function and passing a request and response as a parameter, as shown here:

```
exports.date = functions.https.onRequest((req, res) => {
  // ...
});
```

The request object holds access to most of the properties send by the client. The response object sends the response back to the client.

We will use the Express Node.js Module/library to perform the HTTP requests, since Express has all the standard request templates and more.

The following example uses a complete Express application and exposes a single cloud function:

```
const app = express();

        app.use(cors({ origin: true }));

        app.use(myMiddleware);

        app.get('/:id', (req, res) =>
res.send(Widgets.getById(req.params.id)));
        app.post('/', (req, res) => res.send(Widgets.create()));
        app.put('/:id', (req, res) =>
res.send(Widgets.update(req.params.id, req.body)));
        app.delete('/:id', (req, res) =>
res.send(Widgets.delete(req.params.id)));
        app.get('/', (req, res) => res.send(Widgets.list()));

// existing express application to onRequest function
        exports.widgets = functions.https.onRequest(app);
```

HTTP triggers also support **Cross origin resource sharing (CORS)**:

```
// CORS Cross origin resource sharing
cors(req, res, () => {
  // ...
});
```

In the request, the object body is parsed based on the content type. The following table shows the different content types and their behavior:

Content Type	Request body	Behaviour
application/json	'{"name":"lalitha"}'	request.body.name equals 'John'
application/octet-stream	'Hello World'	request.body.equals '654'
text/plain	'Hello World'	request.body.equals 'Hello World'
application/x-www-form-urlencoded	'Hello World'	request.body.equals 'Hello World'

Do not forget to end an HTTP function with send(), redirect(), or end().

Cloud Pub/Sub Triggers

Cloud Pub/Sub is a message bus distributed globally. Using `function.pubsub`, we can trigger functions. Whenever a new Pub/Sub message is sent to a topic, cloud functions can trigger an event. You must define a Pub/Sub topic, and using the `onPublish()` function, we can handle the desired action:

```
exports.helloPubSub = functions.pubsub.topic('topic-name').onPublish(event
=> {
  // ...
});
```

The payload of the Pub/Sub messages can be accessed through `event.data` as a message instance.

Pub/Sub messages can be sent with attributes. Attributes are set with the `publish` command:

```
gcloud beta pubsub topics publish new_topic --attribute name=parinitha
```

And the previous attributes can be accessed like this:

```
const pubSubMessage = event.data;
// Get the `name` attribute of the message.
const name = pubSubMessage.attributes.name;
```

Now that we have seen and understood most of the triggers that Firebase functions offer, it's to explore how to write Firebase functions.

Writing Firebase functions

Firebase functions are convenient and powerful. But, sometimes you need to know the correct spells to make your magic work efficiently and effectively. Although we write all the code inside `index.js`, we have to learn many more things, and that happens only with practice. If you choose TypeScript while creating the project - if you want to explore the TypeScript way of using Firebase functions - it's almost the same, but with a few contract changes.

The file type when we choose TypeScript will be `.ts`; therefore, our `index.js` will be `index.ts`. Every time you deploy the code, you need to make sure the TypeScript code transpiled and then hosted. In case of TypeScript, we need to configure `tsconfig.json`; follow these steps to make sure of valid configurations.:

1. In `package.json`, add the `bash` command to build the TypeScript project:

```
{
        "name": "functions",
        "scripts": {
        "build": "./node_modules/.bin/tslint -p tslint.json &&
./node_modules/.bin/tsc"
        }
```

2. In `firebase.json`, add the `predeploy` hook:

```
{
        "functions": {
        "predeploy": "npm --prefix functions run build",
        }
        }
```

With this configuration, Firebase CLI builds the TypeScript project and hosts it in the Firebase cloud.

If you want to migrate JavaScript to TypeScript, follow these steps:

1. Initialize a git checkpoint and save copies of the JavaScript files
2. Redo the project initialization using the firebase init functions command and choose TypeScript as your language
3. Do not choose to overwrite `package.json`
4. You don't need `function/index.ts`, so delete it
5. In `tsconfig.json`, allow JavaScript `"allowJs": "true"`
6. Copy `package.json` into the functions directory and edit it to set the main to `lib/index.js`
7. Now, add the TypeScript build script inside `package.json`
8. Add the TypeScript dependency `npm install --save --only=dev typescript`
9. Now, do this in the project scope: run `npm install --save @types/<dependency>`

After understanding Firebase functions, let's write a simple application to fire a push notification.

Cloud Functions to fire a push notification

So far, we have explored features, functionalities, and so on. Now, it's the time to put all our learning into practice. In this example, we will use the blood bank project from Chapter 1, *Keep It Real – Firebase Realtime Database* and add the notification feature using functions. Whenever the database has a new entry, meaning whenever people add their donor details, we will get a notification of what blood group has been added.

- Go to the Realtime Database chapter code. Open it in Android Studio.
- Create the MessagingService class shown next.
- Register the service class in the manifest.
- Subscribe to the topic in the activity.

Use this code for the MessagingService class:

```
package com.ashok.packt.realtime.database;

import android.app.NotificationManager;
import android.app.PendingIntent;
import android.content.Context;
import android.content.Intent;
import android.media.RingtoneManager;
import android.net.Uri;
import android.support.v4.app.NotificationCompat;
import android.support.v4.app.NotificationManagerCompat;
import android.support.v4.app.RemoteInput;
import android.util.Log;

import com.google.firebase.messaging.FirebaseMessagingService;
import com.google.firebase.messaging.RemoteMessage;
/**
 * Created by ashok on 09/02/18.
 */

public class MessagingService extends FirebaseMessagingService {

    private static final String TAG = "MessagingService";
    public static final String EXTRA_VOICE_REPLY = "extra_voice_reply";
    public static final String REPLY_ACTION =
            "com.packt.smartcha.ACTION_MESSAGE_REPLY";
    public static final String SEND_MESSAGE_ACTION =
```

```
            "com.packt.smartchat.ACTION_SEND_MESSAGE";

    @Override
    public void onMessageReceived(RemoteMessage remoteMessage) {
        String notificationTitle = null, notificationBody = null;
        // Check if message contains a notification payload.
        if (remoteMessage.getNotification() != null) {
            Log.d(TAG, "Message Notification Body: " +
remoteMessage.getNotification().getBody());
            notificationTitle = remoteMessage.getNotification().getTitle();
            notificationBody = remoteMessage.getNotification().getBody();

            sendNotification(notificationTitle, notificationBody);

        }
    }

    // Creates an intent that will be triggered when a message is read.
    private Intent getMessageReadIntent(int id) {
        return new Intent().setAction("1").putExtra("1482", id);
    }

    // Creates an Intent that will be triggered when a reply is received.
    private Intent getMessageReplyIntent(int conversationId) {
        return new Intent().setAction(REPLY_ACTION).putExtra("1223",
conversationId);
    }

    private void sendNotification(String notificationTitle, String
notificationBody) {
        // Wear 2.0 allows for in-line actions, which will be used for
"reply".
        NotificationCompat.Action.WearableExtender inlineActionForWear2 =
                new NotificationCompat.Action.WearableExtender()
                    .setHintDisplayActionInline(true)
                    .setHintLaunchesActivity(false);

    RemoteInput remoteInput = new
RemoteInput.Builder("extra_voice_reply").build();


        // Building a Pending Intent for the reply action to trigger.
        PendingIntent replyIntent = PendingIntent.getBroadcast(
                getApplicationContext(),
                0,
                getMessageReplyIntent(1),
                PendingIntent.FLAG_UPDATE_CURRENT);
```

```
        // Add an action to allow replies.
        NotificationCompat.Action replyAction =
                new NotificationCompat.Action.Builder(
                        R.mipmap.ic_launcher_round,
                        "Notification",
                        replyIntent)

                        /// TODO: Add better wear support.
                        .addRemoteInput(remoteInput)
                        .extend(inlineActionForWear2)
                        .build();

        Intent intent = new Intent(this, MainActivity.class);
        intent.addFlags(Intent.FLAG_ACTIVITY_CLEAR_TOP);
        PendingIntent pendingIntent = PendingIntent.getActivity(this, 0,
intent,
                PendingIntent.FLAG_ONE_SHOT);

        Uri defaultSoundUri =
RingtoneManager.getDefaultUri(RingtoneManager.TYPE_NOTIFICATION);
        NotificationCompat.Builder notificationBuilder =
(NotificationCompat.Builder) new NotificationCompat.Builder(this)
                .setAutoCancel(true)    //Automatically delete the
notification
                .setSmallIcon(R.mipmap.ic_launcher) //Notification icon
                .setContentIntent(pendingIntent)
                .addAction(replyAction)
                .setContentTitle(notificationTitle)
                .setContentText(notificationBody)
                .setSound(defaultSoundUri);


        NotificationManagerCompat notificationManager =
NotificationManagerCompat.from(this);
        notificationManager.notify(0, notificationBuilder.build());
    }
}
```

Register the service class in the manifest in the application tag scope:

```
<service
    android:name=".MessagingService">
    <intent-filter>
        <action android:name="com.google.firebase.MESSAGING_EVENT"/>
    </intent-filter>
</service>
```

Subscribe to the topic in the `MainActivity` life cycle method `oncreate()`:

```
FirebaseMessaging.getInstance().subscribeToTopic("pushNotifications");
```

Now, write the following code inside the `index.js` file in the `functions` folder:

```
//import firebase functions modules
const functions = require('firebase-functions');
//import admin module
        const admin = require('firebase-admin');
        admin.initializeApp(functions.config().firebase);


// Listens for new messages added to messages/:pushId
        exports.pushNotification =
functions.database.ref('/Donor/{pushId}').onWrite( event => {

        console.log('Push notification event triggered');

        //  Grab the current value of what was written to the Realtime
Database.
        var valueObject = event.data.val();

        if(valueObject.photoUrl !== null) {
        valueObject.photoUrl= "Sent you a lot of love!";
        }

        // Create a notification
        const payload = {
        notification: {
        body: valueObject.bloodGroup,
        sound: "default"
        },
        };

        //Create an options object that contains the time to live for the
notification and the priority
        const options = {
        priority: "high",
        timeToLive: 60 * 60 * 24
        };


        return admin.messaging().sendToTopic("pushNotifications", payload,
options);
        });
```

Now, deploy the code using the `firebase deploy` command.

Whenever the user adds a donor, their blood group will be sent to the device as a notification:

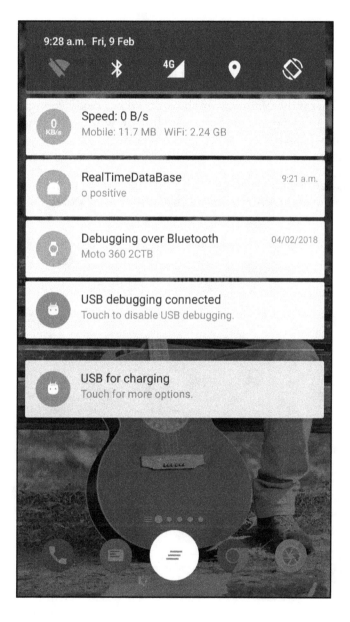

The example shows that the genie in the cloud really does a brilliant job hassle-free and convenient. If we ever wanted to configure an XMPP server and sockets to fire a notification, it would have cost time and money.

Summary

Firebase functions for Firebase tool spectrum is a really powerful and convenient tool, with just a couple of lines code. Cloud functions can be used for so many use cases and Google is continuously working on the platform, as shown by the quickly changing version numbers, with features being added. So far, we have seen how to work with cloud functions using different tools. Also, we have seen the trigger functions. The final project in the chapter is an expression of Firebase allowing FCM and Realtime database to work seamlessly.

The next chapter is about cloud storage; similar to the arsenal of arrows, whenever you need, arrows will be ready in your palm. Let's explore cloud storage in detail.

5
Arsenal for Your Files – Firebase Cloud Storage

"The more storage you have, the more stuff you accumulate."

— *Alexis Stewart*

Cloud Storage for Firebase is an intense, straightforward, and economic data storage service built at Google scale. The Firebase SDKs for Cloud Storage add Google security to file transfers and downloads for your Firebase applications, paying little respect to network quality. You can utilize SDKs to store pictures, audio, video, or other client produced content. On the server, using Google Cloud Storage, we can get access to these stored files.

Firebase Cloud Storage allows web and mobile platforms to upload and download files more elegantly and securely. Firebase SDK offers a library for Firebase Cloud Storage. Developers can write programs that can upload or download the user files. Also, Firebase SDK handles weak network connections by itself. Firebase SDK can re-initiate the process from where it stopped. It also helps developers to be less concerned about saving users time and bandwidth.

Firebase Cloud Storage is one of the most significant components in the Firebase toolchain. At the time of writing this book, Firebase Cloud Storage supports the iOS, Android, web, C++, and Unity platforms.

In this chapter, we will cover the following topics:

- Overview of Firebase Cloud Storage
- Creating references
- Uploading and downloading files
- File Metadata
- Deleting files
- Handling common errors
- Security and rules
- Extending with Cloud Functions
- Integrating with Google Cloud

Firebase a Cloud Storage

Firebase Cloud Storage service is built for scaling storage, up to exabytes, if and when it's required. Firebase also allows a smooth transition from prototype to production, using existing file storage infrastructure. Firebase Cloud Storage helps to store files inside a Google Cloud Storage Bucket. Later, the data can be accessed from Firebase and Google Cloud.

Firebase Cloud Storage permits files of any type to be stored using the Google Cloud Storage platform. All the data that we upload is saved in a Google Cloud Bucket. By default, all the data and files are stored in a single bucket, but Firebase also allows configuring multiple buckets. Firebase handles everything in the background, from resuming the upload process to retrying the loss of connectivity.

Firebase enables developers to add custom metadata to files. Similar to Real-time Database, Firebase Cloud Storage also has a set of rules and security parameters to ensure the data remains safe. Using Firebase authentication, we can make sure only authorized users are allowed to upload and download files. Also, Firebase Cloud offers robust operations, robust security, and high scalability.

The Firebase Cloud Storage filesystem is similar to a filesystem in an operating system, and Cloud Storage uses the hierarchical structure of nodes, which expresses the idea of files, directory, and subdirectories in a filesystem. Files and directories are accessed through the storage reference.

In the next section, we will understand what a storage reference is, creating a reference, accessing files through a reference, and so on.

Creating storage reference

A storage reference is like a bridge for the cloud bucket and web services to request stored files. It acts as the data communication bridge between the client and Firebase web service. All the files stored in the cloud bucket are accessible through a reference. Remarkably, references are playing a prominent role in the process of file uploads and downloads. Storage references are instances of the StorageReference class from the Firebase storage support library. Developers can get the reference by calling the getReference() method of the FirebaseStorage instance.

The quintessential process of setting up Cloud Storage is first to create a FirebaseStorage class instance:

```
FirebaseStorage storage = FirebaseStorage.getInstance();
```

For setting up reference, all we need to do is use the instance of FirebaseStorage to call the getReference() method:

```
StorageReference storageRef = storage.getReference();
```

By default, a newly obtained storage reference instance focuses on the root node of the project's default storage bucket (/). The child() method for the reference object is utilized to navigate deeper into the storage node hierarchy. The accompanying code configures a reference to point to the /pictures/photographs node of the storage bucket:

```
StorageReference imagesRef = storageRef.child("pictures");
StorageReference spaceRef =
storageRef.child("pictures/photographs/parinitha.jpg");
```

Also, using the getParent() and getRoot() methods, developers can navigate through the storage bucket. getRoot() points to the top level of storage nodes; the getParent() method returns the parent reference to the current node.

The getParent() method treats files as nodes (called name nodes). Navigating to one particular file can be done by pointing the reference to pictures/photographs/space.jpg

A client application may create as many reference objects as required, and an existing storage reference might be reused as many times as required. Once created and configured, references are used to transfer files, and delete and update documents stored using Firebase Cloud Storage. A scope of methods is additionally accessible for obtaining data about a storage reference.

`child()`, `getParent()`, and `getRoot()` can be tied together in different circumstances, as every arrival a reference. Be that as it may, calling `getRoot().getParent()` returns null:

```
StorageReference earthRef = spaceRef.getParent().child("parinitha.jpg");
```

Navigating to the files or to the right parent node is necessary to show the correct files.

Storage reference properties

The Firebase Storage support library includes three important methods in the StorageReference class that provide access to the properties of a reference:

- `getBucket()`: The `getBucket()` method returns the bucket path details to which the reference is pointing. The `getBucket()` method returns a string, for instance:

  - `<firebase-project-id>.appspot.com`

- `getPath()`: The `getPath()` method returns an analogous file path on bucket:

  - `pictures/photographs/parinitha.jpg`

- `getName()`: The `getName()` method returns the filename to which the reference is pointing:

  - `parinitha.jpg`

In the event that the final component of the path is a directory, the name of the last node is returned.

Limitations of reference

A reference path can contain a wide range of valid Unicode characters. However, Firebase imposes some restrictions:

- When we are using UTF-8 encoding standards, the total length of the reference must be between 1 and 1024 bytes
- We cannot have line feed characters or carriage returns

- We cannot use the following special characters: #, [,], *, or ? - this is because they are little troublesome for Realtime Database and gsutils.

Reference is a significant mechanism for handling Firebase storage. Check the following code that illustrate the most of reference-related operations:

```
// Points to the root reference
storageRef = storage.getReference();

// Points to "images"
imagesRef = storageRef.child("pictures");

// Points to "pictures/rafael.jpg"
// Note that you can use variables to create child values
String fileName = "rafael.jpg";
spaceRef = imagesRef.child(fileName);

// File path is "images/rafael.jpg"
String path = spaceRef.getPath();

// File name is "rafael.jpg"
String name = spaceRef.getName();

// Points to "images"
imagesRef = spaceRef.getParent();
```

After understanding the cloud reference, now it's time to look at the process of uploading and downloading files.

Uploading and downloading files

Uploading or downloading files from cloud service was aslightly troublesome, because for uploading, there exist multipart and content type upload and other different techniques, but for downloading, we need to get the file object to read the byte stream, and we can create the local replica. Firebase makes the whole process easy and efficient. Developers can upload and download files instantly. By default, Firebase Cloud Storage requires authentication to upload files, but we can change the security rules for storage to allow public access. There is also a disadvantage in changing the security parameters to public, because the default Google App Engine app and Firebase share this bucket. Public access can make newly uploaded App Engine files publicly accessible as well. Developers need to make sure to restrict access to the storage bucket again when using authentication. Now, let's see how the Firebase storage support library helps in uploading files.

Uploading files

There are three ways to upload files to Firebase Cloud Storage. The basic technique involves an event that:

- Uploads an existing file in device storage
- Uploads a file as a stream
- Uploads a file from memory

Uploading files requires managing the file uploads in case of unexpected upload failures, resuming the upload from where it stopped, or in case the user decides to cancel the upload for any reason. Apart from this, developers should be able to attach metadata about the file and customize the metadata, deleting the uploaded file and other events that happen over the time of uploading a file.

Uploading existing files

This technique uses the `putFile()` method of the storage reference instance to upload a local file. In its method parameters, we need to post the URI of the file to upload. For example, consider the following example:

```
Uri file = Uri.fromFile(new File("path/to/pictures/Ashok.jpg"));
StorageReference riversRef =
storageRef.child("pictures/"+file.getLastPathSegment());
uploadTask = riversRef.putFile(file);

uploadTask.addOnFailureListener(new OnFailureListener() {
    @Override
    public void onFailure(@NonNull Exception exception) {
        // Handle unsuccessful uploads

    }
}).addOnSuccessListener(new OnSuccessListener<UploadTask.TaskSnapshot>() {
    @Override
    public void onSuccess(UploadTask.TaskSnapshot taskSnapshot) {
        // We can use this url to fetch the file uploaded
        Uri downloadUrl = taskSnapshot.getDownloadUrl();
    }
});
```

Using the `putFile()` method, we can upload photographs and video files, and most MIME type files. In the `putFile()` method, by passing the file URI, we will return an `UploadTask`, which allows developers to manage and monitor the uploading process and its upload status.

Uploading files as a stream

Another way to upload files is as an input stream. This technique is the cleverest way to upload a file to Firebase storage. It uses a `putStream()` method, accepts `InputStream` as a parameter, and returns `UploadTask`. Using `UploadTask`, developers can manage and monitor the status of the upload:

```
InputStream stream = new FileInputStream(new
File("path/to/pictures/Ashok.jpg"));

uploadTask = mountainsRef.putStream(stream);
uploadTask.addOnFailureListener(new OnFailureListener() {
    @Override
    public void onFailure(@NonNull Exception exception) {
        // Handle unsuccessful uploads
    }
}).addOnSuccessListener(new OnSuccessListener<UploadTask.TaskSnapshot>() {
    @Override
    public void onSuccess(UploadTask.TaskSnapshot taskSnapshot) {
        // taskSnapshot.getMetadata() contains file metadata such as size,
content-type, and download URL.
        Uri downloadUrl = taskSnapshot.getDownloadUrl();
    }
});
```

Using the `UploadTask` object callbacks, we can handle the upload process.

Uploading from data in memory

In the event that the information to be contained in the file is now in the device memory, the `putBytes()` method for the storage reference will upload that data to a file in the Cloud Storage. The `putBytes()` method takes as an argument a byte array (`byte[]`). The use for this approach will be to upload a picture that is in memory, maybe inside an ImageView in a user interface. This picture can be separated from the ImageView object as a bitmap and after that, converted via byte stream to a byte array suitable for uploading to a Cloud Storage file. This method will also return `UploadTask` to manage and monitor the status of the uploading file:

```
imageView.setDrawingCacheEnabled(true);
imageView.buildDrawingCache();
Bitmap bitmap = imageView.getDrawingCache();
ByteArrayOutputStream baos = new ByteArrayOutputStream();
bitmap.compress(Bitmap.CompressFormat.JPEG, 100, baos);
byte[] data = baos.toByteArray();

UploadTask uploadTask = mountainsRef.putBytes(data);
uploadTask.addOnFailureListener(new OnFailureListener() {
    @Override
    public void onFailure(@NonNull Exception exception) {
        // Handle unsuccessful uploads
    }
}).addOnSuccessListener(new OnSuccessListener<UploadTask.TaskSnapshot>() {
    @Override
    public void onSuccess(UploadTask.TaskSnapshot taskSnapshot) {
        // use this url to download the picture to your views
        Uri downloadUrl = taskSnapshot.getDownloadUrl();
    }
});
```

This code shows how to extract data in memory and construct a file to upload to the Cloud Storage Bucket. Let's look at the process of managing and monitoring file upload.

Managing file upload

To manage the files that are uploading from the client, the device will demand certain basic operations, such as pause, resume, and cancel the uploads. These operations are carried out with the `pause()`, `resume()`, and `cancel()` methods. The `pause` and `resume` methods help in changing the progress and pause states. Canceling an upload will result in upload failure with an error indicating upload canceled. Take a look at the following code snippet that illustrates the file management scenario:

```
uploadTask = storageRef.child("images/Rafael.jpg").putFile(file);

// Pause the upload
uploadTask.pause();

// Resume the upload
uploadTask.resume();

// Cancel the upload
uploadTask.cancel();
```

Using the Upload task object, we explored how to pause, resume, and cancel the file upload. Using the `uploadTask` instance developers can observe state change events:

```
// Observe state change events like progress, pause, and resume
uploadTask.addOnProgressListener(new
OnProgressListener<UploadTask.TaskSnapshot>() {
    @Override
    public void onProgress(UploadTask.TaskSnapshot taskSnapshot) {
        double progress = (100.0 * taskSnapshot.getBytesTransferred()) /
taskSnapshot.getTotalByteCount();
        System.out.println("Upload is " + progress + "% done");
    }
}).addOnPausedListener(new OnPausedListener<UploadTask.TaskSnapshot>() {
    @Override
    public void onPaused(UploadTask.TaskSnapshot taskSnapshot) {
        System.out.println("Upload is paused");
    }
});
```

This code snippet helps the developer to display the progress state dynamically, with ratio calculated on the file size.

Monitoring file upload

One of the crucial aspects that developers need to consider is that the application should be able to re-initiate the uploading process or should let the user know on the event of upload failure. To achieve this, we need a mechanism for monitoring the file upload process. In a way, Firebase's UploadTask allows developers to attach listeners to it:

```
uploadTask.addOnFailureListener(new OnFailureListener() {
    @Override
    public void onFailure(@NonNull Exception exception) {
        // Upload failed
    }

}).addOnSuccessListener(new OnSuccessListener<UploadTask.TaskSnapshot>() {
    @Override
    public void onSuccess(UploadTask.TaskSnapshot taskSnapshot) {
        // Upload succeeded
    }
});
```

To monitor the file upload, developers can add the `onSuccess` and `onFailure` listener interfaces, which help to handle the uploading process. The `onFailure` method is triggered with the Exception instance; other listeners are called with the `TaskSnapShot` object. The `UploadTask` object returns a `TaskSnapshot` object, which has specific immutable properties:

- `getDownloadUrl`: This property is a string type and is used to download the object. This URL is a public dynamic URL; it can be shared with other clients. This value becomes active after successful file upload.
- `getError`: This property is the exception type, to return the cause of task failure.
- `getBytesTransferred`: This property is the primitive long type; this property will return the total number of bytes transferred at the time of the snapshot.
- `getTotalByteCount`: This property is the primitive long type, and denotes the total number of bytes of the file.
- `getUploadSessionUri`: This property is a String type; using this URI, a developer can continue the task from another putFile call.
- `getMetadata`: This property is a `StorageMetadata` type; before uploading, a file to server it needs to create a file header to create the file and `Metadata` denotes the file type and size and other file-related information.

- `getTask`: This property is an `UploadTask` object type; use this task object to cancel or pause, or even resume the upload.
- `getStorage`: This property is a `StorageReference` object type, which returns the UploadTask's storage reference.

In the file uploading process, managing and monitoring the upload is essential and needs to take place with all the right approaches, keeping in mind failed cases.

Beyond monitoring and managing

Software developers encounter many problems and issues in different platforms, and fixing this issues after they appear is time-consuming. Depending on the complexity of the application, it will also be a little difficult to fix them in the expected time.

For the Android platform, an Activity is a first-class citizen of the application and its views. An Activity has a life cycle, from creation state to destroyed state, and there are a couple of ways that the activity transitions during its life cycle. For example, the most basic trigger would be when the mobile phone gets rotated, the Activity will get recreated, transitioning through all its life cycles.

What if it gets recreated? Is it going to harm the application in any way? In a nutshell, when an activity gets recreated, it loses all the data it previously had. The Android SDK offers an override method to help resolve this issue.

In the Activity scope, we should subscribe all the listeners to automatically unregistering them when the activity stops and registering them when the activity restarts. Using the `getActiveUploadTasks` method, we can re-initiate the upload task from where it had stopped:

```
StorageReference mStorageReferrence;  //mStorageRef was previously used to
transfer data.

@Override
protected void onSaveInstanceState(Bundle outState) {
    super.onSaveInstanceState(outState);

    // If there's an upload in progress, save the reference so you can
query it later
    if (mStorageReferrence != null) {
        outState.putString("reference", mStorageReferrence.toString());
    }
}
```

```
@Override
protected void onRestoreInstanceState(Bundle savedInstanceState) {
    super.onRestoreInstanceState(savedInstanceState);

    final String stringRef = savedInstanceState.getString("reference");
    if (stringRef == null) {
        return;
    }
    mStorageReferrence =
FirebaseStorage.getInstance().getReferenceFromUrl(stringRef);

    // Find all UploadTasks under this StorageReference (in this example,
there should be one)
    List<UploadTask> tasks = mStorageRef.getActiveUploadTasks();
    if (tasks.size() > 0) {
        // Get the task monitoring the upload
        UploadTask task = tasks.get(0);

        task.addOnSuccessListener(this, new
OnSuccessListener<UploadTask.TaskSnapshot>() {
            @Override
            public void onSuccess(UploadTask.TaskSnapshot state) {
                processSuccess(state);
            }
        });
    }
}
```

getActiveUploadTasks returns all active upload tasks. Using this, we can continue uploading the files.

In this use case, let's assume the process shut down and the files being uploaded got terminated at 60 percent, which has used network bandwidth and time. So when the process restarts, uploading files again from the beginning will be frustrating for users. To solve this problem, we shall persist the sessionUri in SharedPreferences, or anything that is comfortable to you as a developer. In the StorageTask instance, we can call the getUploadSessionUri method to fetch the current upload session URI and use it to reinitiate the file upload from where it stopped:

```
uploadTask = mStorageRef.putFile(localFile);
uploadTask.addOnProgressListener(new
OnProgressListener<UploadTask.TaskSnapshot>() {
    @Override
    public void onProgress(UploadTask.TaskSnapshot taskSnapshot) {
        Uri sessionUri = taskSnapshot.getUploadSessionUri();
        if (sessionUri != null && !saved) {
```

```
                saved = true;
            }
        }
    });
```

By calling the `putFile` method again once the process has restarted, we will be able to start uploading the file from where it had stopped. We should pass the persisted URI in this case:

```
uploadTask = mStorageRef.putFile(localFile,
                    new StorageMetadata.Builder().build(),
savedsessionUri);
```

All these sessions have a time limit of one week. After one week, all the tasks expire and we cannot reuse them; instead, we need to create new sessions.

It's inevitable to have errors in the event of uploading files. There are numerous reasons for errors; perhaps when the application tries to upload the local file, the file may not exist, or the user might not have permission to upload data, as well as poor network connection and many other reasons. The following example helps in understanding the complete upload progress and monitoring with error handling the upload task:

```
// Blob
mfile = Uri.fromFile(new File("path/to/Rafael.jpg"));

// Creates file metadata
metadata = new StorageMetadata.Builder()
.setContentType("image/jpeg")
.build();

// Upload file and metadata to the path 'pictures/Rafael.jpg'
uploadTask =
storageRef.child("pictures/"+mfile.getLastPathSegment()).putFile(mfile,
metadata);

// monitor state changes, errors, and completion of the upload.
uploadTask.addOnProgressListener(new
OnProgressListener<UploadTask.TaskSnapshot>() {
    @Override
    public void onProgress(UploadTask.TaskSnapshot taskSnapshot) {
        double progress = (100.0 * taskSnapshot.getBytesTransferred()) /
taskSnapshot.getTotalByteCount();
        System.out.println("Upload is " + progress + "% done");
    }
}).addOnPausedListener(new OnPausedListener<UploadTask.TaskSnapshot>() {
    @Override
    public void onPaused(UploadTask.TaskSnapshot taskSnapshot) {
```

```
            System.out.println("Upload is paused");
        }
    }).addOnFailureListener(new OnFailureListener() {
        @Override
        public void onFailure(@NonNull Exception exception) {
            // unsuccessful uploads
        }
    }).addOnSuccessListener(new OnSuccessListener<UploadTask.TaskSnapshot>() {
        @Override
        public void onSuccess(UploadTask.TaskSnapshot taskSnapshot) {
            //  successful uploads on complete
            Uri downloadUrl = taskSnapshot.getMetadata().getDownloadUrl();
        }
    });
```

In Firebase storage, one of the crucial concepts is to learn how to upload files without any trouble. Now that we have explored how to upload files, let's see how to download them from the Cloud Storage Bucket.

Downloading files

The Cloud Storage administrates file saving and retrieving the files instantly and efficiently. By default, Cloud Storage requires a Firebase authentication to download files. We need to change the rules to make the download public. The primary step in downloading a file is creating a download reference.

Firebase offers FirebaseUI to download process. We have already seen that Firebase Authentication FirebaseUI is very helpful to build a common UI pattern in no time, and it is easy to customize; moreover, it is from the Firebase inhouse team, so we have less to worry, and we can start plugging the FirebaseUI library.

After creating a reference, developers can download the file using `getBytes()`, `getStream()`, and also by using `getDownloadUrl()`. Let's explore the download process in detail.

Creating a reference

The quintessential requirement for downloading a file from a storage bucket is to create a reference. In this chapter, we created a storage reference before uploading files. We can create a reference by combining child paths with the storage root, or we can create the reference from an existing URL pointing to the object in the storage bucket. The following example illustrates how to create a reference for downloading a file:

```
// Creating a storage reference
StorageReference storageRef = storage.getReference();

// Creating a reference with an initial file path and name
StorageReference pathReference = storageRef.child("pictures/Rafael.jpg");

// Create a reference to a file from a Google Cloud Storage URI
StorageReference gsReference =
storage.getReferenceFromUrl("gs://bucket/images/stars.jpg");

// Create a reference from an HTTPS URL
// Note that in the URL, characters are URL escaped!
StorageReference httpsReference =
storage.getReferenceFromUrl("https://firebasestorage.googleapis.com/b/bucke
t/o/pictures%20Rafael.jpg");
```

After creating a reference it is now the time to explore how to download the files.

Downloading into memory

As we keep learning and building software products, we try building performance-oriented mobile applications, instant reactions to user queries, and a lot more. To achieve something similar to this, sometimes we might want to download files directly to memory. If the file size is larger than the application's available memory, the application will break. The getBytes() method tries to handle this on its own, and it will set the maximum memory size to something that an app can handle. If the file size is more then the app's heap memory, then we should utilize other methods:

```
StorageReference schoolKidRef = storageRef.child("pictures/moni.jpg");

final long ONE_MEGABYTE = 1024 * 1024;
schoolKidRef.getBytes(ONE_MEGABYTE).addOnSuccessListener(new
OnSuccessListener<byte[]>() {
    @Override
    public void onSuccess(byte[] bytes) {
        // Data for "pictures/moni.jpg" will return,
    }
```

```
}).addOnFailureListener(new OnFailureListener() {
    @Override
    public void onFailure(@NonNull Exception exception) {
        // Handle any errors
    }
});
```

This method is straightforward and it loads all the content into memory instantly when it downloads the file.

Downloading into a local file

Another smart approach is to download the content into a file and create a local copy in the user's device. This will increase the application cache. We can download the file and create its replica in a some specific path. Also, whenever the file is required, it is available offline. The getFile() method returns DownloadTask, which helps in managing and monitoring the download status of the file:

```
schoolKidRef = storageRef.child("pictures/moni.jpg");

File localFile = File.createTempFile("pictures", "jpg");

schoolKidRef.getFile(localFile).addOnSuccessListener(new
OnSuccessListener<FileDownloadTask.TaskSnapshot>() {
    @Override
    public void onSuccess(FileDownloadTask.TaskSnapshot taskSnapshot) {
        // Local temp file has been created
    }
}).addOnFailureListener(new OnFailureListener() {
    @Override
    public void onFailure(@NonNull Exception exception) {
        // Handle any errors
    }
});
```

This code illustrates the process of downloading files from a storage bucket into a file.

Downloading data through a URL

The next approach is to download the content from a URL using the `getDownloadUrl()` method on the storage reference instance to download the content. If the architecture or download infrastructure of the application is based on URLs, we can continue the same technique using Firebase. The `getDownloadUrl()` method returns a downloadable URL for the files:

```
storageRef.child("users/me/rafael.png").getDownloadUrl().addOnSuccessListen
er(new OnSuccessListener<Uri>() {
    @Override
    public void onSuccess(Uri uri) {
        // Got the download URL for 'users/me/profile.png'
    }
}).addOnFailureListener(new OnFailureListener() {
    @Override
    public void onFailure(@NonNull Exception exception) {
        // Handle any errors
    }
});
```

All three methods have their own advantages and disadvantages. If you make use of these callbacks, you should know what works best for your application.

Downloading images using FirebaseUI

The FirebaseUI offers an efficient and production-ready UI, and with lesser and precise code, it looks more comprehensive. Also, it follows Google's standard best practices. Using FirebaseUI, we can download the file instantly, we can cache it, and we can also utilize a third-party library to display images and so on. In Chapter 2, *Safe and Sound – Firebase Authentication*, we explored how to make use of FirebaseUI for the many different services that Firebase authentication offers. Similarly, we have a Gradle dependency specific to storage; download the library from the Google central repository or add the following dependency to your module-level Gradle file:

```
dependencies {
    // FirebaseUI Storage only
    compile 'com.firebaseui:firebase-ui-storage:0.6.0'
}
```

Now, we can instantly download the image file from storage. The following code is a standard example of FirebaseUI using the Glide library to load the image:

```
StorageReference storageReference = ...;

// ImageView in your application
ImageView imageView = ...;

// Loading the image using Glide
Glide.with(this /* context */)
        .using(new FirebaseImageLoader())
        .load(storageReference)
        .into(imageView);
```

Now that we know how to plug a FirebaseUI into our projects, it's a very easy process to work with FirebaseUI on storage services.

Beyond downloading files

The downloading process is a network operation similar to uploading. All the problems and issues that we encounter in the uploading process are applicable to downloading as well. When a mobile device has a poor network connection and bandwidth, or when activity gets recreated - we need to handle these kinds of event. In the activity, scope lets all the listeners be subscribed; when activity stops, unregister them, and when an activity starts, register all the listeners.

Using the `getActiveDownloadTask` method, we can obtain download tasks when the activity restarts:

```
StorageReference mStorageRef;

@Override
protected void onSaveInstanceState(Bundle outState) {
    super.onSaveInstanceState(outState);
    if (mStorageRef != null) {
        outState.putString("reference", mStorageRef.toString());
    }
}

@Override
protected void onRestoreInstanceState(Bundle savedInstanceState) {
    super.onRestoreInstanceState(savedInstanceState);
    final String stringRef = savedInstanceState.getString("reference");
    if (stringRef == null) {
        return;
```

```
    }
    mStorageRef =
FirebaseStorage.getInstance().getReferenceFromUrl(stringRef);
    List<FileDownloadTask> tasks = mStorageRef.getActiveDownloadTasks();
    if (tasks.size() > 0) {

        FileDownloadTask task = tasks.get(0);
        task.addOnSuccessListener(this, new
OnSuccessListener<FileDownloadTask.TaskSnapshot>() {
            @Override
            public void onSuccess(FileDownloadTask.TaskSnapshot state) {
                handleSuccess(state); //call a user defined function to handle
the event.
            }
        });
    }
}
```

This code illustrates handling `DownloadTask` when the activity gets recreated.

As we know that errors in the network operations are inevitable; for many reasons, users have to experience app crashes and so on. Let's assume the user doesn't have file writing permission and he is trying to download a file. Similarly, in real-world scenarios, there are a lot of problems that occur, and a developer has to handle them smartly:

```
storageRef.child("users/me/profile.png").getBytes(Long.MAX_VALUE).addOnSucc
essListener(new OnSuccessListener<byte[]>() {
    @Override
    public void onSuccess(byte[] bytes) {
        // Use the bytes to display the image
    }
}).addOnFailureListener(new OnFailureListener() {
    @Override
    public void onFailure(@NonNull Exception exception) {
        // Handle any errors
    }
});
```

Using the `onSucess` and `onFailure` listeners, we can manage most of the errors encountered.

File metadata

Metadata is essential information about the file uploaded to the Cloud Storage Bucket. We can retrieve and update the metadata. For instance, we can update the content type of the file, we can update the timestamp, and so on. Firebase storage, by default, requires Firebase Authentication to retrieve and update the metadata, but developers can change this in the storage security rules.

Retrieving File Metadata

Firebase storage can store file content and file metadata, which contains properties such as the content type and timestamp of the file created in Firebase storage. Using getMetadata() on the storage reference instance, we can retrieve the metadata of the file:

```
StorageReference storageRef = storage.getReference();

StorageReference forestRef = storageRef.child("images/forest.jpg");

forestRef.getMetadata().addOnSuccessListener(new
OnSuccessListener<StorageMetadata>() {
    @Override
    public void onSuccess(StorageMetadata storageMetadata) {

    }
}).addOnFailureListener(new OnFailureListener() {
    @Override
    public void onFailure(@NonNull Exception exception) {

    }
});
```

This code retrieves the metadata of the file with success and failure callbacks to handle it properly.

Update the metadata of the file

Developers can update the metadata at any time on successful file upload. Using the updateMetadata() method with specific properties and with new metadata, we can update the metadata. For instance, consider the following code:

```
//storage reference from our app
StorageReference storageRef = storage.getReference();
```

```
//reference to the file
StorageReference forestRef = storageRef.child("images/forest.jpg");

//metadata including the content type
StorageMetadata metadata = new StorageMetadata.Builder()
        .setContentType("pictures/jpg")
        .setCustomMetadata("myCustomProperty", "myNewValue")
        .build();

// Update properties
forestRef.updateMetadata(metadata)
        .addOnSuccessListener(new OnSuccessListener<StorageMetadata>() {
            @Override
            public void onSuccess(StorageMetadata storageMetadata) {
                // Updated metadata
            }
        })
        .addOnFailureListener(new OnFailureListener() {
            @Override
            public void onFailure(@NonNull Exception exception) {
                // when error occurred!
            }
        });
```

We can delete writable properties by setting them to null, as shown here:

```
StorageMetadata metadata = new StorageMetadata.Builder()
        .setContentType(null)
        .build();

forestRef.updateMetadata(metadata)
        .addOnSuccessListener(new OnSuccessListener<StorageMetadata>() {
            @Override
            public void onSuccess(StorageMetadata storageMetadata) {
            }
        })
        .addOnFailureListener(new OnFailureListener() {
            @Override
            public void onFailure(@NonNull Exception exception) {
            }
        });
```

Some of the metadata properties for a file are listed here:

Getter property	Type	Setters
getBucket	String	NO
getGeneration	String	NO
getMetadataGeneration	String	NO
getPath	String	NO
getName	String	NO
getSizeBytes	long	NO
getCreationTimeMillis	long	NO
getUpdatedTimeMillis	long	NO
getMd5Hash	String	NO
getCacheControl	String	YES
getContentDisposition	String	YES
getContentEncoding	String	YES
getContentLanguage	String	YES
getContentType	String	YES
getDownloadUrl	Uri	NO
getDownloadUrls	List<Uri>	NO
getCustomMetadata	String	YES
getCustomMetadataKeys	Set<String>	NO

Using the properties, we can customize the metadata.

The following accessible methods are for changing a metadata property; all other `StorageMetadata` properties are used:

- setCacheControl()
- setContentType()
- setContentLanguage()
- setContentDisposition()
- setContentEncoding()
- setCustomMetadata()

`setCustomMetadata` allows us to set the custom metavalues through key-value pair information. Metadata is a very straightforward concept. Working on file storage, we will understand it more.

Deleting files

In any persistence, whether it is offline or remote storage, CRUD is the essential principle to understand. CRUD stands for Create, Read, Update, and Delete content. Now that we have explored the storage process, let's explore how to delete a file from the Firebase storage bucket. By default, the deletion process expects a Firebase Authentication, but we can change this in the storage security rules.

To delete a file, fetch the reference of the file and then simply call the `delete()` method on the reference:

```
StorageReference storageRef = storage.getReference();

StorageReference desertRef = storageRef.child("images/desert.jpg");

desertRef.delete().addOnSuccessListener(new OnSuccessListener<Void>() {
    @Override
    public void onSuccess(Void aVoid) {
    }
}).addOnFailureListener(new OnFailureListener() {
    @Override
    public void onFailure(@NonNull Exception exception) {

    }
});
```

This code deletes the file permanently.

Handling common errors

As a developer, we come across so many cases where errors occur. Storage offers `UploadTask` and `FileDownloadTask`, which can listen to the failures through onFailure listeners.

By writing our own custom `FailureListener`, we can handle the errors in a much better way. For example, consider the following class:

```
class AppFailureListener implements OnFailureListener {
  @Override
  public void onFailure(@NonNull Exception exception) {
    int errorCode = ((StorageException) exception).getErrorCode();
    String errorMessage = exception.getMessage();
  }
}
```

This code returns an error message, which is the point of common error scenarios:

Code	Reason
ERROR_UNKNOWN	When an unknown error occurred
ERROR_OBJECT_NOT_FOUND	When no object exists at the desired reference
ERROR_BUCKET_NOT_FOUND	When no bucket is configured for Cloud Storage
ERROR_PROJECT_NOT_FOUND	When no project is configured for Cloud Storage
ERROR_QUOTA_EXCEEDED	When the free quota has been exceeded
ERROR_NOT_AUTHENTICATED	When the user is unauthenticated; authenticate and try again
ERROR_NOT_AUTHORIZED	When the user doesn't have permission to perform certain operations
ERROR_RETRY_LIMIT_EXCEEDED	After many attempts of retry
ERROR_INVALID_CHECKSUM	When two files don't match the checksum of the files
ERROR_CANCELED	When the user cancels an operation

These error messages occur when exceptions and errors do.

Security and rules

The storage rules and security is the quintessential concept to understand. Firebase console provides a flexible way to manage security rules. When a mobile client requests access to create a file reference or download the uploaded file, it has to go through security rules; since Google and Firebase storage share the same storage bucket, if we make access public, it stays public in both services.

It is a very simple process to authorize users and validate requests. Storage security rules also allow path-based security, which makes managing complex requests easy. We can restrict a particular path or a person from having access to the files, or limit the file size being uploaded.

Rules are very important to the Firebase platform and give more control to developers to execute the application with elegance.

In a nutshell, Firebase auth in storage security rules plays a major role; the `request.auth` instance becomes an object that contains the user's unique ID, `request.auth.uid`, and the rest of the information in `request.auth.token`. When an unauthorized user tries to access the files request, it will become null; `request.auth` is null. The default storage security rules are shown here:

```
service firebase.storage {
  match /b/{bucket}/o {
    match /{allPaths=**} {
      allow read, write: if request.auth != null;
    }
  }
}
```

These rules allow public read but only authorized upload. Using security rules, developers can validate the data, such as determining what type of content is being uploaded, its size, and so forth:

```
service firebase.storage {
  match /b/{bucket}/o {
    match /images/{imageId} {
      allow write: if request.resource.size < 5 * 1024 * 1024
                   && request.resource.contentType.matches('image/.*');
    }
  }
}
```

Rules allow requests to be processed if the condition matches; if not, it throws an appropriate error message.

The general syntax for storage security rules

Unlike Real-time database rules, storage security rules follows a hierarchical structure. Read-write permission is usually granted to all files and directories. It allows developers to think of what rules need to be in place where and when. The rules control access to the content in the storage bucket.

There are three major keywords, `allow`, `match`, and `if`, using which we can apply rules to our storage bucket. The following rule is a typical example of how to write a condition for the path:

```
match /file/path/pattern {
    allow read, write: if <condition>;
}
```

A single match statement can have multiple allow statements; this helps in checking multiple scenario-based conditions:

```
match /file/path/pattern {
    allow read: if <condition 1>;
    allow write: if <condition 2>;
}
```

Generally, a match statement points to the path of the storage reference where rules can be applied. This example applies a rule to the files and directories in an entire storage bucket.

Using matches, developers can target specific files and directories. The following example dictates a rule specific to the path, which allows only authenticated users to read the file:

```
service firebase.storage {
    match /b/{bucket}/o {
        match /profiles/photos/rafael.png {
            allow write: if request.auth != null;
        }
    }
}
```

A match statement can also be nested to achieve complex rule conditions:

```
service firebase.storage {
    match /b/{bucket}/o {
        match /{allPaths=**} {
            allow read, write;
        }
    }
}
```

At the time of development, we can have rules be public, as shown in the previous example, but in case we need the user to authenticate, the following rules helps in that:

```
service firebase.storage {
    match /b/{bucket}/o {
        match /user/{userId}/{allPaths=**} {
            allow read, write: if request.auth.uid == userId;
        }
    }
}
```

The `allow` keyword has the capacity to set what kind of access is required for a particular match statement. Every match statement contains at least contains one allow keyword:

```
allow write: if <condition>;
```

When we do not use the `if` condition, the `allow` condition is applied to the path unconditionally.

To edit rules, Firebase offers an easy web console with all the necessary requirements. When we visit the Firebase console through the `https://console.firebase.google.com` URL, Firebase gives you the option to choose the project that you want to work with, or you can create a new one in the console. Once the project is ready, we can directly navigate to storage and we can see the console that helps to manage the storage and rules section. In the rules section, we can add any level of custom security rules, depending on the logical conclusions. By default, every user is required to be authenticated. Once we edit the rules, we will have to publish the latest changes.

Firebase console to edit and managing security rules is as shown:

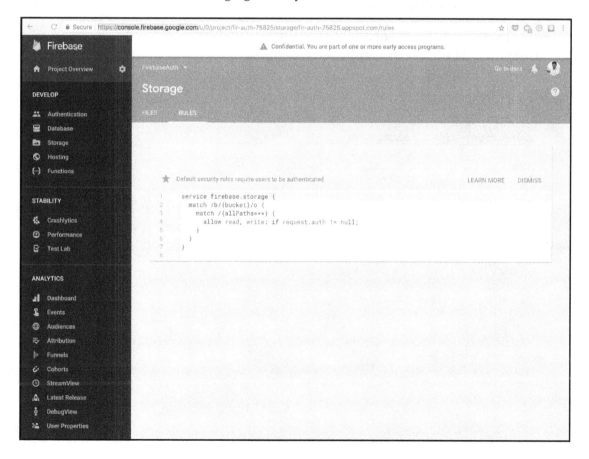

Firebase allows developers to deploy rules for multiple buckets through the `deploy targets` command.

To apply rules, we can make use of the Firebase CLI and apply the rules locally; also, developers can utilize the Firebase console and rules tab to apply the rules.

Securing user files

Firebase made it all clear: storage works on a declarative path-based security model, Firebase security rules. Firebase security rules are the most efficient and straightforward approach to secure files. As previously outlined, we have explored the general syntax and the flexibility of working with rules. It is important to make sure files that are private to a user are not accessible by other users.

Firebase security rules are essentially used to determine who has read and write access to files in storage. It also explains how files and their metadata are structured:

```
// If no condition is given, the rule evaluates to true
allow read;

// Rules can specify a condition
allow write: if <condition>;

// Rules can specify multiple request methods
allow read, write: if <condition>;
```

Storage security rules use the `match` keyword to obtain the path for files to access them from storage. These rules can match a specific path or wildcard paths and rules can also be nested. A request will be denied when there are no match rules allowing a request method:

```
// Exact match for "images/rafael.png"
match /pictures/rafael.png {
  allow write: if <condition>;
}

// Exact match for "images/sammy.png"
match /pictures/sammy.png {
  allow write: if <other_condition>;
}
```

The following example illustrates nested matches:

```
// Partial match for files that start with "images"
match /images {
  // Exact match for "images/rafael.png"
  match /rafael.png {
    allow write: if <condition>;
  }

  // Exact match for "images/sammy.png"
  match /sammy.png {
    allow write: if <other_condition>;
  }
}
```

Wildcards are variables that represent a single string with a direct filename such as rafael.png, or many path segments such as pictures/rafael.png.

Wildcards are created using curly braces around the string, such as {string}. When we have multiple wildcards, we can use =** for the wildcard name, such as {path=**}:

```
//files that start with "pictures"
match /images {
  // match for "pictures/*"
  // pictures/rafael.png is matched
  match /{imageId} {
    allow read: if <condition>;
  }

  // Exact match for "images/**"
  // pictures/rafael.png is also matched!
  match /{allImages=**}
    allow read: if <other_condition>;
  }
}
```

A wildcard can be referenced within a match keyword by providing the filename or authorization details:

```
match /pictures/{imageId} {
  allow read: if imageId == "rafael.png";
}
```

Security rules do not cascade, and rules are valid only when the request path matches a path with the condition specified. Now, applying all the security rules that we explored for protecting a file would look like this:

```
service firebase.storage {
    match /b/{bucket}/o {
        match /videos/{userId}/vinisha.mp4 {
        allow read;
        allow write: if request.auth.uid == userId;
    }
    }
}
```

Request and Resource Evaluation

In the event of file uploads, downloads and metadata alter its values or At the time of deleting the file. The request to do this processing will happen through request variable. Essentially, the request variable contains vital information about the file, such as the file path, timestamp, and HTTP headers. The request object responsibly includes the user's User ID and authentication payload in the request.auth object. The request object has a few properties, which are `auth`, `params`, `path`, `resources`, and `time`.

Security rules cater to file metadata in the resource object, which incorporates key/value pairs of the metadata constructed in the storage object. These properties can be examined in read or write requests to ensure data authenticity.

The resources object offers the following properties:

Property	Type	Description
name	string	This property is the full name of the object
bucket	string	This property is the name of the bucket a particular object resides in
generation	int	GCS object generation of a particular object
metageneration	int	GCS object metageneration of a particular object
size	int	Size of the object in bytes
timeCreated	timestamp	A timestamp that corresponds to the time the object was created
updated	timestamp	A timestamp that corresponds to the time the object was last updated
md5Hash	string	An MD5 hash of the object
crc32c	string	A crc32c hash of the object

etag	string	etag connected with this object
contentDisposition	string	Content disposition related to a particular object
contentEncoding	string	Content encoding related to a particular object
contentLanguage	string	Content language related to a particular object
contentType	string	The content type related to this object
metadata	map<string, string>	Key/value pairs, for developer-specified custom metadata

`request.resource` contains all of these properties, excluding a few timestamp properties and e-tag.

Storage and functions

We can trigger a cloud function in response to uploading, downloading or deleting files and folders in a storage bucket. To trigger a function for storage changes, developers can make use of `functions.storage` to create a function that handles storage events. Based on the use case, we can trigger cloud functions to a specific bucket or to the default bucket:

- `functions.storage.object()` to listen for object changes on the default storage
- `functions.storage.bucket('bucketName').object()` to listen for object changes on a particular bucket

For example, consider the code snippet of the functions:

```
exports.generateThumbnail = functions.storage.object().onChange((event) =>
{
  // ...
});
```

Most of the time, developers need not download or upload the files from storage. Sometimes, we might have to generate a thumbnail for the uploaded files. Cloud functions offer an efficient image processing program called *ImageMagick* that can perform most trivial image processing operations. Consider the following example for generating a thumbnail:

```
const bucket = gcs.bucket(fileBucket);
const tempFilePath = path.join(os.tmpdir(), fileName);
const metadata = {
  contentType: contentType,
};
```

```
return bucket.file(filePath).download({
  destination: tempFilePath,
}).then(() => {
  console.log('Image downloaded locally to', tempFilePath);
  // Generating a thumbnail using ImageMagick.
  return spawn('convert', [tempFilePath, '-thumbnail', '200x200>',
tempFilePath]);
}).then(() => {
  console.log('Thumbnail created at', tempFilePath);
  // adding a 'thumb_' prefix to thumbnails file name.
  const thumbFileName = `thumb_${fileName}`;
  const thumbFilePath = path.join(path.dirname(filePath), thumbFileName);
  // Uploading the thumbnail.
  return bucket.upload(tempFilePath, {
    destination: thumbFilePath,
    metadata: metadata,
  });
  // after upload delete the local file to free up disk space.
}).then(() => fs.unlinkSync(tempFilePath))
```

Firebase has bridged the functions for storage in a precise, intelligent fashion. This code snippet is a trivial use case scenario for generating thumbnails. The following example application is written in Kotlin and uploads a file to storage and retrieving it into a dynamic view, such as `RecyclerView`.

Firebase Storage in practice

After all we have explored, it is a good idea to write an Android application that covers the concepts. The complete application is written in the Kotlin language for Android:

1. Create an Android Studio project with Kotlin support enabled (it's recommended to use Android Studio V-3.0+).
2. Once the project is created with the `Hello World` boilerplate program, go to **Tools | Firebase**.
3. In the assistance window panel, connect your project to your Firebase developer account and add the dependencies. For this project, we have to add the Realtime and Storage services together:

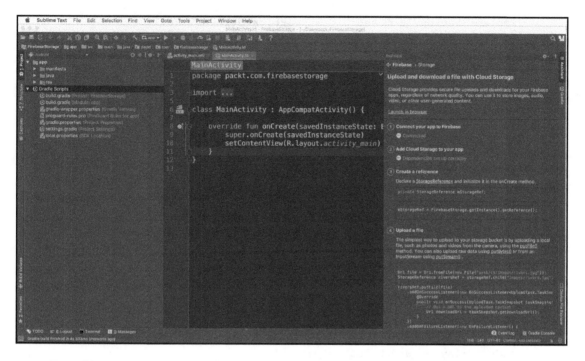

The idea of the image is to show the Firebase assistant on the right-hand side, This screenshot is not pointing any texts but it highlights the firebase assistant.

4. Once we add the dependencies for both the services we are good to deep dive into the program.

At the time of writing this book, Android Studio 3.1 had been officially released and Firebase had major updates through version 12.0.1; regardless of the 11.x.x version, you might see that you can upgrade to the latest Firebase version.

Gradle dependencies after successful connection should appear as shown here. Add the RecyclerView, CardView, and glide dependencies:

```
dependencies {
    implementation fileTree(dir: 'libs', include: ['*.jar'])
    implementation "org.jetbrains.kotlin:kotlin-stdlib-
jre7:$kotlin_version"
    implementation 'com.android.support:appcompat-v7:26.1.0'
    implementation 'com.android.support.constraint:constraint-layout:1.0.2'
    implementation 'com.google.firebase:firebase-database:11.0.4'
    implementation 'com.google.firebase:firebase-storage:11.0.4'
    implementation 'com.google.firebase:firebase-auth:11.0.4'
    implementation 'com.android.support:recyclerview-v7:26.1.0'
```

```
    implementation 'com.android.support:cardview-v7:26.1.0'

    //adding glide library
    implementation 'com.github.bumptech.glide:glide:3.7.0'
    testImplementation 'junit:junit:4.12'
    androidTestImplementation 'com.android.support.test:runner:1.0.1'
    androidTestImplementation 'com.android.support.test.espresso:espresso-
core:3.0.1'
}
```

Now, to construct our first user interface, open res/**activity_main**.xml and add the following components in a responsive layout. Since we are using a constraint layout dependency, let's use a constraint layout. For this screen, I have kept five components: EditText for file description or name, ImageView to show which file the user is choosing, and an upload button, and all of these components are wrapped inside LinearLayout and ConstraintLayout, as shown here:

```
<?xml version="1.0" encoding="utf-8"?>
<android.support.constraint.ConstraintLayout
xmlns:android="http://schemas.android.com/apk/res/android"
    xmlns:app="http://schemas.android.com/apk/res-auto"
    android:id="@+id/activity_main"
    android:layout_width="match_parent"
    android:layout_height="match_parent">

    <LinearLayout
        android:id="@+id/linearLayout"
        android:layout_width="match_parent"
        android:layout_height="wrap_content"
        android:layout_marginBottom="8dp"
        android:layout_marginEnd="8dp"
        android:layout_marginStart="8dp"
        android:layout_marginTop="8dp"
        android:orientation="horizontal"
        app:layout_constraintBottom_toBottomOf="parent"
        app:layout_constraintEnd_toEndOf="parent"
        app:layout_constraintHorizontal_bias="0.0"
        app:layout_constraintStart_toStartOf="parent"
        app:layout_constraintTop_toTopOf="parent"
        app:layout_constraintVertical_bias="0.017">

        <Button
            android:id="@+id/buttonChoose"
            android:layout_width="match_parent"
            android:layout_height="wrap_content"
            android:layout_weight=".7"
            android:text="Choose" />
```

```
    <EditText
        android:id="@+id/editText"
        android:layout_width="match_parent"
        android:layout_height="wrap_content"
        android:layout_weight=".3"
        android:hint="Enter name for image you are uploading" />

</LinearLayout>
```

The preceding code draws the design for adding the description and choosing the image from the gallery to upload.

```
    <ImageView
        android:id="@+id/imageView"
        android:layout_width="wrap_content"
        android:layout_height="wrap_content"
        android:layout_alignParentLeft="true"
        android:layout_alignParentStart="true"
        android:layout_marginBottom="8dp"
        android:layout_marginEnd="8dp"
        android:layout_marginStart="8dp"
        android:layout_marginTop="8dp"
        android:scaleType="fitCenter"
        app:layout_constraintBottom_toBottomOf="parent"
        app:layout_constraintEnd_toEndOf="parent"
        app:layout_constraintHorizontal_bias="0.5"
        app:layout_constraintStart_toStartOf="parent"
        app:layout_constraintTop_toTopOf="parent"
        app:srcCompat="@drawable/common_google_signin_btn_icon_dark" />

    <LinearLayout
        android:id="@+id/linearLayout3"
        android:layout_width="match_parent"
        android:layout_height="wrap_content"
        android:layout_alignParentBottom="true"
        android:layout_marginBottom="8dp"
        android:layout_marginEnd="8dp"
        android:layout_marginStart="8dp"
        android:orientation="vertical"
        app:layout_constraintBottom_toBottomOf="parent"
        app:layout_constraintEnd_toEndOf="parent"
        app:layout_constraintStart_toStartOf="parent">

        <Button
            android:id="@+id/buttonUpload"
            android:layout_width="match_parent"
            android:layout_height="wrap_content"
            android:layout_weight="1"
```

```
                android:text="Upload" />

        <TextView
                android:id="@+id/textViewShow"
                android:layout_width="match_parent"
                android:layout_height="wrap_content"
                android:padding="10dp"
                android:text="View Uploads"
                android:textAlignment="center"
                android:textColor="@color/colorPrimary"
                android:textStyle="bold" />
    </LinearLayout>

</android.support.constraint.ConstraintLayout>
```

Now, it's time to complete the upload process. Create a Kotlin class for the importing constants in the project:

```
class Constants {
companion object {
val STORAGE_PATH_UPLOADS = "uploads/"
        val DATABASE_PATH_UPLOADS = "uploads"
    }
}
```

The `MainActivity` for choosing a file should look like this:

```
class MainActivity : AppCompatActivity(), View.OnClickListener {

//constant to track image chooser intent
    private val PICK_IMAGE_REQUEST = 234

    //uri to store file
 private lateinit var filePath: Uri

 //firebase objects
 private var storageReference: StorageReference? = null
 private var mDatabase: DatabaseReference? = null

 override fun onCreate(savedInstanceState: Bundle?) {
super.onCreate(savedInstanceState)
 setContentView(R.layout.activity_main)
storageReference = FirebaseStorage.getInstance().reference
 mDatabase =
FirebaseDatabase.getInstance().getReference(Constants.DATABASE_PATH_UPLOADS
)

 buttonChoose.setOnClickListener(this)
```

```
buttonUpload.setOnClickListener(this);
textViewShow.setOnClickListener(this);
}

override fun onClick(view: View?) {
when (view) {
buttonChoose -> showFileChooser()
buttonUpload -> {

}
textViewShow -> {

}
}
}

private fun showFileChooser() {
val intent = Intent()
intent.type = "image/*"
intent.action = Intent.ACTION_GET_CONTENT
startActivityForResult(Intent.createChooser(intent, "Select Picture"),
PICK_IMAGE_REQUEST)
}
```

Now override the onActivity result method to set the Image on the ImageView as shown below.

```
override fun onActivityResult(requestCode: Int, resultCode: Int, data:
Intent?) {
super.onActivityResult(requestCode, resultCode, data)
if (requestCode == PICK_IMAGE_REQUEST && resultCode == Activity.RESULT_OK
&& data != null && data.data != null) {
filePath = data.data
 try {
val bitmap = MediaStore.Images.Media.getBitmap(contentResolver, filePath)
 imageView.setImageBitmap(bitmap)
 } catch (e: IOException) {
 e.printStackTrace()
 }

 }
 }

}
```

Create a class that stores image data in the Firebase Realtime Database:

```
@IgnoreExtraProperties
data class Upload( var name: String,
                   var url: String)
```

We need to add a method in `MainActivity` that retrieves the file extension:

```
fun getFileExtension(uri: Uri): String {
val cR = contentResolver
    val mime = MimeTypeMap.getSingleton()
return mime.getExtensionFromMimeType(cR.getType(uri))
}
```

Inside `MainActivity`, create another method that will upload the file:

```
private fun uploadFile() {
//checking if file is available
    if (filePath != null) {
//displaying progress dialog while image is uploading
        val progressDialog = ProgressDialog(this)
        progressDialog.setTitle("Uploading")
        progressDialog.show()

//getting the storage reference
        val sRef = storageReference?.child(Constants.STORAGE_PATH_UPLOADS +
System.currentTimeMillis() + "." + getFileExtension(filePath))

//adding the file to reference
        sRef?.putFile(filePath)
                ?.addOnSuccessListener { taskSnapshot ->
                    //dismissing the progress dialog
                    progressDialog.dismiss()

//displaying success toast
                    Toast.makeText(applicationContext, "File Uploaded ",
Toast.LENGTH_LONG).show()

//creating the upload object to store uploaded image details
                    val upload = Upload(editText.text.toString().trim(),
taskSnapshot.downloadUrl!!.toString())

//adding an upload to firebase database
                    val uploadId = mDatabase?.push()?.key
                    mDatabase?.child(uploadId)?.setValue(upload)
}
                ?.addOnFailureListener { exception ->
                    progressDialog.dismiss()
```

```
                    Toast.makeText(applicationContext, exception.message,
Toast.LENGTH_LONG).show()
}
                ?.addOnProgressListener { taskSnapshot ->
                    //displaying the upload progress
                    val progress = 100.0 * taskSnapshot.bytesTransferred /
taskSnapshot.totalByteCount
                    progressDialog.setMessage("Uploaded " +
progress.toInt() + "%...")
}
    } else {
//display an error if no file is selected
    }
}
```

Now, you can call the method in a click event:

```
override fun onClick(view: View?) {
when (view) {
        buttonChoose -> {
            showFileChooser()
        }
        buttonUpload -> {
            uploadFile()
        }
        textViewShow -> {

        }
    }
}
```

Compile the program; you will be able to see uploaded files. Storage will have created a directory name that we passed inside the program, in this case, uploads.

 If uploading fails, make sure your security rules look like this:

```
service firebase.storage {
  match /b/{bucket}/o {
    match /{allPaths=**} {
      allow read, write;
    }
  }
}
```

Firebase console is also for storage. Uploaded files can be supervised with detailed metadata:

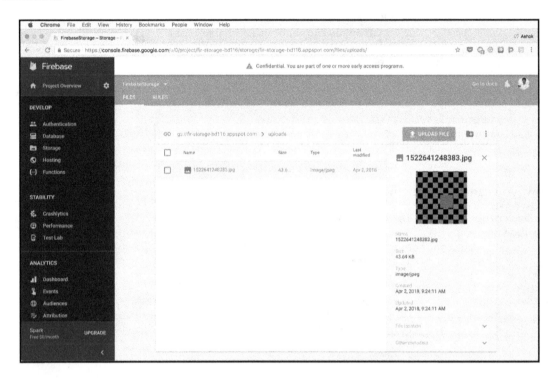

Now, for retrieving the files, we need to create an activity with a `RecyclerView`. I will call the activity `ImagesActivity`. Inside its layout, it will have a `RecyclerView` as shown here:

```xml
<?xml version="1.0" encoding="utf-8"?>
<LinearLayout xmlns:android="http://schemas.android.com/apk/res/android"
    xmlns:app="http://schemas.android.com/apk/res-auto"
    xmlns:tools="http://schemas.android.com/tools"
    android:layout_width="match_parent"
    android:layout_height="match_parent"
    android:orientation="vertical"
    tools:context="packt.com.firebasestorage.ImagesActivity">

    <android.support.v7.widget.RecyclerView
        android:id="@+id/recyclerView"
        android:layout_width="match_parent"
        android:layout_height="match_parent"/>

</LinearLayout>
```

To populate data to dynamic views such as `ListView`, `GridView`, and `RecyclerView`, which need to make use of an adapter to read the data from the array list and populate it in the dynamic views. Let's write an adapter for `RecyclerView` in Kotlin:

```kotlin
internal class ImagesAdapter(private val context: Context, private val
uploads: List<Upload>) : RecyclerView.Adapter<ImagesAdapter.ViewHolder>() {

    override fun onCreateViewHolder(parent: ViewGroup, viewType: Int):
ViewHolder {
        val v = LayoutInflater.from(parent.context)
                .inflate(R.layout.layout_images, parent, false)
        return ViewHolder(v)
    }

    override fun onBindViewHolder(holder: ViewHolder, position: Int) {
        val (name, url) = uploads[position]
        holder.itemView.textViewShow.text = name
        Glide.with(context).load(url).into(holder.itemView.imageView)
    }

    override fun getItemCount(): Int {
        return uploads.size
    }

    internal inner class ViewHolder(itemView: View) :
RecyclerView.ViewHolder(itemView) {

    }
}
```

Now, in the `ImagesActivity` that we created, add the following code:

```kotlin
class ImagesActivity : AppCompatActivity() {

    //adapter object
    private lateinit var adapter: RecyclerView.Adapter<*>
    //database reference
    private lateinit var mDatabase: DatabaseReference

    //progress dialog
    private lateinit var progressDialog: ProgressDialog

    //list to hold all the uploaded images
    private var uploads: List<Upload>? = null

    override fun onCreate(savedInstanceState: Bundle?) {
        super.onCreate(savedInstanceState)
```

```
setContentView(R.layout.activity_images)
recyclerView.setHasFixedSize(true)
recyclerView.layoutManager = LinearLayoutManager(this)
progressDialog = ProgressDialog(this)

uploads = ArrayList()
```

For fetching the images Create a simple progress dialog and then initialize the FirebaseDatabase class as shown below.

```
//displaying progress dialog while fetching images
progressDialog.setMessage("Please wait...")
progressDialog.show()
mDatabase =
FirebaseDatabase.getInstance().getReference(Constants.DATABASE_PATH_UPLOADS
)

//adding an event listener to fetch values
mDatabase.addValueEventListener(object : ValueEventListener {
    override fun onDataChange(snapshot: DataSnapshot) {
        //dismissing the progress dialog
        progressDialog.dismiss()

        //iterating through all the values in database
        for (postSnapshot in snapshot.children) {
            val upload = postSnapshot.getValue(Upload::class.java)
            upload?.let { (uploads as ArrayList<Upload>).add(it) }
        }
        //creating adapter
        adapter = ImagesAdapter(applicationContext, uploads as
ArrayList<Upload>)

        //adding adapter to recyclerview
        recyclerView.adapter = adapter
    }

    override fun onCancelled(databaseError: DatabaseError) {
        progressDialog.dismiss()
    }
})
    }
}
```

In your `MainActivity`, make sure you are launching the activity:

```
override fun onClick(view: View?) {
    when (view) {
        buttonChoose -> {
            showFileChooser()
        }
        buttonUpload -> {
            uploadFile()
        }
        textViewShow -> {
            val intent = Intent(this, ImagesActivity::class.java)
            startActivity(intent)
        }
    }
}
```

Congratulations on completing storage project. This Kotlin code is concise and does the job as expected.

Summary

The more storage you have, the more stuff you accumulate. Firebase storage is a powerful service that Firebase offers. In this chapter, we explored storage features and most importantly created a reference, without which we would not be able to proceed. Also, we understood the file upload and download processes, and had a comprehensive view of file metadata and the process of deleting the files. Firebase is network-based and a remote cloud service we will encounter, so we looked at many issues resulting in common errors that we have learned how to handle. Security rules are the most important topic of the chapter, and introduce important keywords such as allow, match, and if. We also explored the general syntax for rules.

Finally, we completed the chapter by understanding cloud functions for storage with an easy thumbnail generation code snippet. In the next chapter, we will explore another powerful tool, Firebase hosting, and we will learn more web-related activities such as deploying websites.

6
Not Just a Keeper, Firebase Hosting

"Firebase can be a host to your project, or you can be hostage to the web hosting control panels; it's your call"

— Ashok Kumar S

Firebase hosting offers instantaneous and secure static hosting solutions for your web applications. A few simple CLI commands will make your web application live instantly. In this chapter, let's learn how Firebase hosting assists developers in publishing production-grade web content. Firebase hosting deploys web applications and static content to a global CDN in a single command, which suggests that hosting a single-page website and a static web application is no hassle anymore. The Firebase hosting service can also deploy lightweight dynamic node web applications through Firebase functions.

There is only one way to approach the Firebase hosting service, which is plunging directly into practical examples and implementations. For a head-long dive as a web developer, there exists compelling and comprehensive documentation from Firebase. This chapter ensures no one is left behind without any of the information that is necessary to master this tool. It has a strong practical orientation, and there is more to it than that.

Knowing this chapter is going to be web-centric, we recommend you switch context from mobile to web. In this chapter, we'll explore the following topics:

- Overview of Firebase hosting
- Deploying a website
- Connecting a custom domain
- Connecting to Firebase cloud functions
- Customizing hosting behavior
- Reserved URLs

This chapter aims to comprehensively assist developers to become experts in these topics.

Firebase Hosting

Firebase Hosting is built for the cutting edge web developer. Static sites are more intense than ever in recent times with the ascent of frontend JavaScript frameworks such as Angular and static generator tools such as Jekyll. Regardless of whether you are deploying a basic application or a mind-boggling Progressive Web App, Hosting gives you the foundation, features, and tooling customized for publishing and managing static sites.

The Hosting service gives you a subdomain on the `firebaseapp.com` domain. With the Firebase CLI, you can publish local files from your personal computer to your Hosting server. Documents are served over an SSL connection from the nearest edge server on Firebase global CDN.

Although hosting static content, Firebase Hosting offers lightweight design alternatives for you to have the ability to construct sophisticated Progressive Web Apps. You can, without much of a stretch, modify URLs for client-side routing or set up custom headers.

Once you're prepared to take a site to production, you can connect your domain name to Firebase Hosting. Firebase outlines an SSL certificate for your domain, which helps to publish the content in a more secured manner.

Deploying a website

Deploying a website is as simple as it sounds, with three simple steps, which are install the CLI, set up a project directory, and deploy your site. Well, if you have explored Chapter 4, *Genie in the Cloud - Firebase Cloud Functions*, it explains clearly how to install a Node environment. In addition to that, it also addresses how to install Firebase tools from the CLI.

Firebase CLI is a powerful and convenient tool for developers to manage, view, and deploy hosting services. Node, a popular JavaScript framework for backends and dynamic web content, is the primary requirement for developers to install the Firebase CLI tools. Please make sure you have installed Node and npm from the following URL: https://nodejs.org/en/download/:

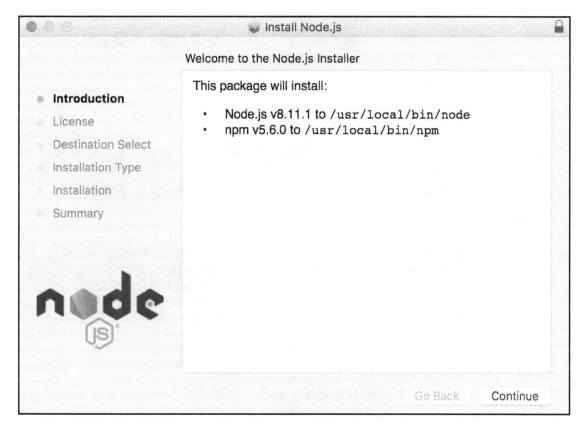

Download the node environment specific to your platform. Since node offers many binary installers, make sure you are downloading the version that suits your processor and operating system type.

To make sure you have installed the node environment, you can type `node --version` and `npm --version` in your Terminal. Node Package Manager distributes the node libraries across the platforms. npm helps us install the Firebase tools with the following command:

```
npm install -g firebase-tools
```

If you encounter any error in installing the Firebase package, please rerun the commands with superuser credentials. It should work fine. After successful installation, Firebase tools are globally available and you will be able to start Firebase commands instantly.

Before we create a project, we need to authorize the Firebase CLI with our developer gmail account or the account that we will be using to work on hosting services:

```
sh-3.2# firebase login
```

This is what we get:

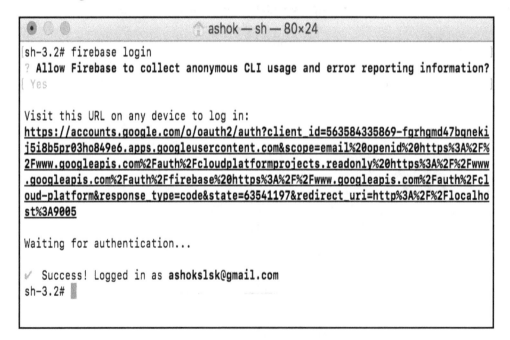

This initial setup is crucial before we start working on the actual hosting services. Several typical tasks performed by the CLI, such as deployment, require a project directory. A project directory is directory that has a `firebase.json` configuration file. Before we start initializing the project, create a directory that is helpful for you to navigate to the path on a convenient basis.

Navigate to the directory you created in the Terminal using the `cd` command. Enter the following command:

```
firebase init
```

This command gives step-by-step instructions to set up the project directory, and the `init` command can be reused to initialize the features and services at a given point in time.

CLI interface for choosing Firebase services is this:

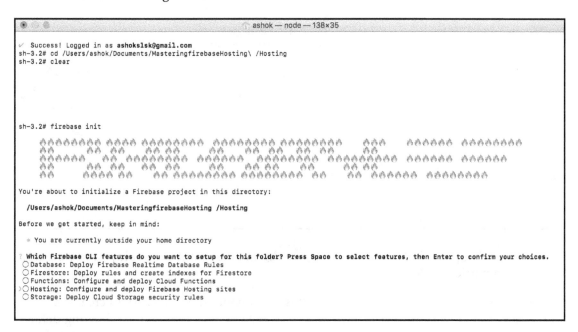

As the instruction clearly says, using the spacebar we can select which service we would like to use; choose Hosting and connect the project to Firebase by creating a new project or by using an existing one.

After successfully connecting the project, we can deploy the simple `Hello World` web project as shown here:

```
firebase deploy --only hosting
```

The following screenshot shows the hosted web app:

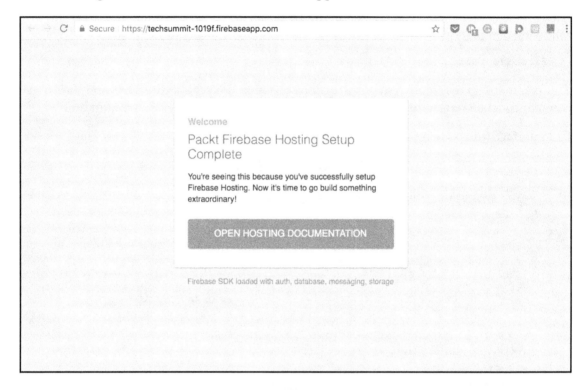

From the hosting panel in Firebase console, we can manage multiple deploys and rollbacks, and delete a particular deploy.

When we initialize the directory with a Firebase command, the Firebase CLI creates a `firebase.json` file for the service we choose. The JSON will contain the following details:

```
{
  "hosting": {
    "public": "app",
    "ignore": [
      "firebase.json",
      "**/.*",
      "**/node_modules/**"
    ]
```

```
        }
    }
```

This JSON shows how well it is organized. When we deploy Firebase, it makes sure that we are deploying static or dynamic web content.

And in the default `index.html` page, we will have the following code for the static site:

```html
<!DOCTYPE html>
<html>
  <head>
    <meta charset="utf-8">
    <meta name="viewport" content="width=device-width, initial-scale=1">
    <title>Welcome to Firebase Hosting</title>

    <!-- update the version number as needed -->
    <script defer src="/__/firebase/4.12.1/firebase-app.js"></script>
    <!-- include only the Firebase features as you need -->
    <script defer src="/__/firebase/4.12.1/firebase-auth.js"></script>
    <script defer src="/__/firebase/4.12.1/firebase-database.js"></script>
    <script defer src="/__/firebase/4.12.1/firebase-messaging.js"></script>
    <script defer src="/__/firebase/4.12.1/firebase-storage.js"></script>
    <!-- initialize the SDK after all desired features are loaded -->
    <script defer src="/__/firebase/init.js"></script>
```

In the same Index page, you can find the style code. The style defines look and feel of the page.

```css
<style media="screen">
  body { background: #ECEFF1; color: rgba(0,0,0,0.87);
         font-family: Roboto, Helvetica, Arial, sans-serif;
         margin: 0; padding: 0; }
  #message { background: white; max-width: 360px;
             margin: 100px auto 16px; padding: 32px 24px;
             border-radius: 3px; }
  #message h2 { color: #ffa100; font-weight: bold;
                font-size: 16px; margin: 0 0 8px; }
  #message h1 { font-size: 22px; font-weight: 300;
                color: rgba(0,0,0,0.6); margin: 0 0 16px;}
  #message p { line-height: 140%; margin: 16px 0 24px;
               font-size: 14px; }
  #message a { display: block; text-align: center;
               background: #039be5; text-transform: uppercase;
               text-decoration: none; color: white;
               padding: 16px; border-radius: 4px; }
  #message, #message a { box-shadow: 0 1px 3px rgba(0,0,0,0.12),
                                     0 1px 2px rgba(0,0,0,0.24); }
```

```
        #load { color: rgba(0,0,0,0.4); text-align: center;
                font-size: 13px; }
        @media (max-width: 600px) {
          body, #message { margin-top: 0; background: white;
                           box-shadow: none; }
          body { border-top: 16px solid #ffa100; }
        }
      </style>
    </head>
```

In the body tag now we can define HTML content or any exclusive scripts if we have.

```
<body>
  <div id="message">
    <h2>Welcome</h2>
    <h1>Packt Firebase Hosting Setup Complete</h1>
    <p>You're seeing this because you've successfully setup Firebase
       Hosting. Now it's time to go build something extraordinary!
    </p>
    <a target="_blank"
     href="https://firebase.google.com/docs/hosting/">Open Hosting
     Documentation</a>
  </div>
  <p id="load">Firebase SDK Loading&hellip;</p>

  <script>
    document.addEventListener('DOMContentLoaded', function() {
      try {
        let app = firebase.app();
        let features = ['auth', 'database',
                        'messaging', 'storage'].filter(feature =>
                              typeof app[feature] === 'function');
        document.getElementById('load').innerHTML = `Firebase
                        SDK loaded with ${features.join(', ')}`;
      } catch (e) {
        console.error(e);
        document.getElementById('load').innerHTML = 'Error loading
                        the Firebase SDK, check the console.';
      }
    });
  </script>
</body>
</html>
```

So as we see, the publishing site has become very straightforward. Now that we have seen how to publish a static website, let's explore how to connect to custom domains.

Connecting to custom domain

The main question we should ask ourselves after learning about Hosting a static web application is how do we associate that to our domain? So, what commands should we use in the Firebase CLI? Are commands required? What is the procedure? The answers are very simple and the process of connecting a custom domain is straightforward; it doesn't require any commands or code snippets. We need to visit `https://console.firebase.google.com/project/_/hosting/main` and if you have not hosted a static web app, you will need to click on the **Get Started** button, which allows developers to explore the additional features, including the **Connect Domain** button.

Click on the **Connect Domain** button and now enter the domain URL in the input field and click **Continue**. The process will validate that your domain is not associated with any Firebase project prior to this, and also give you the option to have a redirect mechanism point to another domain. Firebase fetches the SSL provision certificate for your current hosted web app and the domain automatically with close to a few hours of delay.

In the event that you already have a site running on another hosting provider and you need a zero-downtime migration, you can choose **Advanced Setup** from the dropdown. You will need to either update your domain's TXT records or upload a file to a specific location on your existing site to verify your domain.

We need to wait for the SSL provision certificate. Once the domain ownership is verified, Firebase automatically deploys the web application in the global CDN with the SSL certificate.

Connect the domain pop-up window for adding the custom domain URL details:

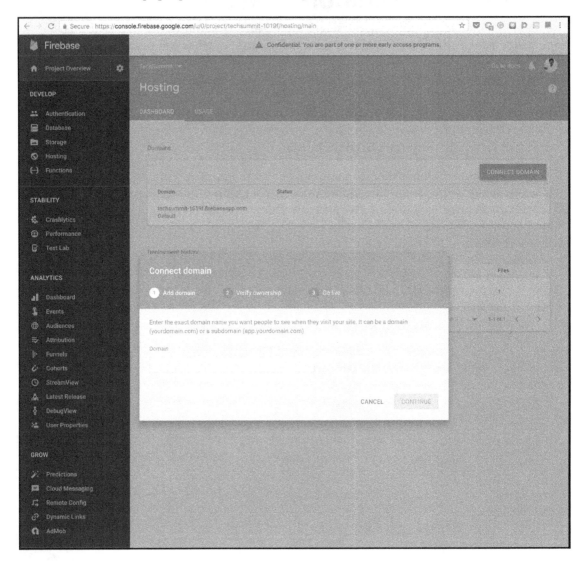

The purpose of the following window is to show the dialog for adding the domain window

So far, we have explored hosting a simple HTML web application and also connecting a custom domain, but there is more: we can use Firebase hosting for dynamic web applications using functions.

Connecting Firebase cloud functions

We will be serving dynamic content using cloud functions, which also means the website that we hosted in the Firebase hosting service is not going to be static content anymore. Let's deep dive into hosting a dynamic web application.

Create a new project and initialize Hosting and functions through the Terminal as shown here:

```
firebase init hosting
```

The following screenshot shows a successful Hosting initialization:

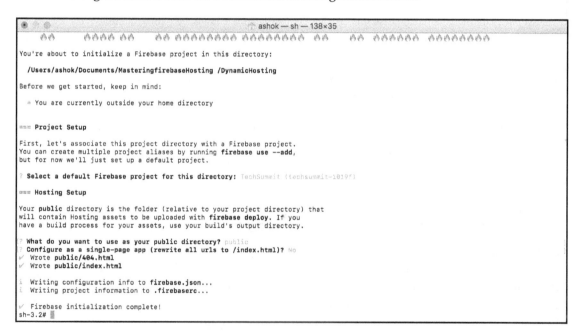

Now, initialize Firebase functions with the following command:

```
$firebase init functions
```

After successful node initialization, let's install the express server framework in the functions directory:

```
$cd functions
$npm i express --save
```

The following screenshot shows how to install additional node modules in the `functions` directory:

```
                                  ⌂ ashok — sh — 138×35
> protobufjs@6.8.6 postinstall /Users/ashok/Documents/MasteringfirebaseHosting /DynamicHosting/functions/node_modules/google-gax/node_modu
les/protobufjs
> node scripts/postinstall


> protobufjs@6.8.6 postinstall /Users/ashok/Documents/MasteringfirebaseHosting /DynamicHosting/functions/node_modules/google-proto-files/n
ode_modules/protobufjs
> node scripts/postinstall


> firebase-functions@1.0.1 postinstall /Users/ashok/Documents/MasteringfirebaseHosting /DynamicHosting/functions/node_modules/firebase-fun
ctions
> node ./upgrade-warning


======== WARNING! ========

This upgrade of firebase-functions contains breaking changes if you are upgrading from a version below v1.0.0.

To see a complete list of these breaking changes, please go to:

https://firebase.google.com/docs/functions/beta-v1-diff

npm notice created a lockfile as package-lock.json. You should commit this file.
added 646 packages in 23.2s

i  Writing configuration info to firebase.json...
i  Writing project information to .firebaserc...

✓  Firebase initialization complete!
sh-3.2# cd functions/
sh-3.2# npm i express --save
+ express@4.16.3
updated 1 package in 3.756s
sh-3.2#
```

Now, you can go to the root directory of the project and open the project in your favorite code editor. You will notice two directories: `functions` and `public`. Here, `public` is the static web application directory, whereas `functions` is the node server code. All the code you write for the server side will go inside the `functions` folder. The reason both folders are decoupled is to have better code readability and maintainability.

The following screenshot shows the first program in `functions`:

If we open `index.js`, we will see a few lines of code already written for us. Uncomment the code from exports; the require method in the code fetches the functions from the Firebase SDK, and we can use the functions instance to perform HTTP requests:

```
const functions = require('firebase-functions');

// // Create and Deploy Your First Cloud Functions
// // https://firebase.google.com/docs/functions/write-firebase-functions
//
exports.helloWorld = functions.https.onRequest((request, response) => {
  response.send("Hello from Packt-Firebase!");
});
```

Now that we know the basic structure of the node boilerplate code generated for us, let's create Express and handle the requests in other callbacks, instead of one `onRequest` callback:

```
const functions = require('firebase-functions');
const express = require('express');

const app = express();
app.get('/timestamp', (request,response) => {
  response.send('${Date.now()}');
});
// // Create and Deploy Your First Cloud Functions
```

```
// // https://firebase.google.com/docs/functions/write-firebase-functions
//
exports.app = functions.https.onRequest(app);
```

This example is very straightforward and is for displaying timestamps as a response. We have also modified the `exports.helloWorld` object to `exports.app`, which we will understand in a minute. `Date.now()` functions return the timestamp; every time we refresh the page, we will see a new timestamp.

Now, before we deploy this, we shall configure the routing mechanism. Routing will be performed in the `firebase.json` file in the root directory:

```
{
  "hosting": {
    "public": "public",
    "rewrites":[{
      "source" : "/timestamp",
      "function" : "app"
    }],
    "ignore": [
      "firebase.json",
      "**/.*",
      "**/node_modules/**"
    ]
  },
  "functions": {
    "predeploy": [
      "npm --prefix \"$RESOURCE_DIR\" run lint"
    ]
  }
}
```

Using rewrites, we can define the routing URL and the function that needs to be called. You can then emulate this in your local node server using the following command:

$firebase serve --only functions, hosting

 This is an experimental feature that is unstable, may be changed in backward-incompatible ways, and is not guaranteed to be released.

You can anyway deploy now using the Firebase deploy command; go to the route and check the expected output, which should return a UNIX timestamp format:

The example is very clear and shows how we installed another framework within a functions node environment, and also how to return simple dynamic data. Now, let's explore how can we customize the hosting behavior.

Customizing hosting behavior

Firebase hosting offers a number of customizations, including rewrites, error pages, redirects, and headers. These customizations help with how your web application is behaving at any given point. Let's explore the most important features.

Custom 404/Not Found page

As developers, we need to realise the user is not going to be tech savvy; he will run into some error scenarios, and identifying them before that happens is very helpful. If the user tries a different URL than the suggested URL, we should show an error page. The process of adding the error page is straightforward; it's just a `404.html` page inside your `public` directory and Firebase will show the page if the user tries a different URL.

Redirects

URL redirects help to avoid broken link situations and are also used for URL shortening. When a browser tries to open the shortened URL, or a URL that has moved to another destination, using redirects we can still reach the expected page. Fundamentally, redirects can be configured in the `firebase.json` file in the project setup. Consider the following example:

```
"hosting": {
  // Add the "redirects" section within "hosting"
  "redirects": [ {
    "source" : "/foo",
    "destination" : "/bar",
    "type" : 301
  }, {
    "source" : "/firebase/*",
    "destination" : "https://firebase.google.com",
    "type" : 302
  } ]
}
```

`foo` is the source, but when you use a bar as your redirected route, the browser will load the content within the bar URL. The source field is a glob pattern (`https://firebase.google.com/docs/hosting/full-config#section-glob`), which will be matched with all URL paths at the start of every request.

Rewrites

We use rewrites when we need to show the same content from multiple URLs; rewrites are very powerful in pattern matching. Using rewrites, we can support the HTML5 push state for navigation:

```
"hosting": {
  // Add the "rewrites" section within "hosting"
  "rewrites": [ {
    "source": "**",
    "destination": "/index.html"
  } ]
}
```

Headers

Headers can be custom and also file-specific. In the hosting project `firebase.json` file, will have this `headers` section:

```
"hosting": {
    // Add the "headers" section within "hosting".
    "headers": [ {
      "source" : "**/*.@(eot|otf|ttf|ttc|woff|font.css)",
      "headers" : [ {
        "key" : "Access-Control-Allow-Origin",
        "value" : "*"
    } ]
    }, {
      "source" : "**/*.@(jpg|jpeg|gif|png)",
      "headers" : [ {
      "key" : "Cache-Control",
      "value" : "max-age=7200"
      } ]
    }, {
      // Sets the cache header for 404 pages to cache for 5 minutes
      "source" : "404.html",
      "headers" : [ {
      "key" : "Cache-Control",
      "value" : "max-age=300"
      } ]
    } ]
  }
```

Hosting priorities

The different features can overlap. If there is a conflict, the response from Hosting service will resolve in priority order, from highest to lower priority in this order:

1. Reserved namespace (/__*)
2. Configured redirects: `https://firebase.google.com/docs/hosting/url-redirects-rewrites#section-redirects`
3. Exact-match static content
4. Configured rewrites: `https://firebase.google.com/docs/hosting/url-redirects-rewrites#section-rewrites`
5. Custom 404 page: `https://firebase.google.com/docs/hosting/url-redirects-rewrites#section-404`
6. Default 404 page

Reserved URLs

Firebase hosting services reserves URLs that start with /_ _ . These reserved namespaces help us to use other Firebase services with Hosting. These reserved URLs are available when we deploy the web application to hosting, and are available on the local server through the Serve command.

The Firebase SDK serves hosting over the HTTP/2 protocol when it's deployed. We can tweak the performance of file loading at the origin. Hosting serves all the SDK with the following special URL:

/__/firebase/{version}/{sdk-file}.js

The right way to import the SDK is as shown here:

```
<script src="/__/firebase/4.12.1/firebase-app.js"></script>
<script src="/__/firebase/4.12.1/firebase-auth.js"></script>
<script src="/__/firebase/4.12.1/firebase-storage.js"></script>
```

With all versions of the SDK hosted this way, it's easy to download the latest SDKs. We can also autoconfigure the SDK, as shown here:

```
fetch('/__/firebase/init.json').then(response => {
firebase.initializeApp(response.json()); });
```

This script will configure the Firebase SDK's default application. Developers can manually initialize it through JSON.

Summary

This chapter is a treat for mobile developers to get a context of publishing web applications, regardless of whether it is a static web app or a dynamic web application. Hosting is very straightforward in Firebase. In this chapter, we explored how to deploy a web application and connect it to our custom domains. Also, we saw how to connect Firebase cloud functions, explored how to customize behaviors, and learned about Firebase Reserved URLs. In the next chapter, let's switch back to mobile development and explore the Android exclusive feature called Firebase Test Lab.

7
Inspection and Evaluation – Firebase Test Lab

"A failure will not appear until a unit has passed final inspection"
– Arthur Bloch

Throughout programming history, testing has been a vital piece of the development process. With various combinations of devices and OS variants, Android presents extraordinary difficulties as far as application testing goes. It is no longer conceivable to test an application on a single device and Android version, and expect that it will keep running with unwavering quality on all other potential hardware and OS blends. Firebase Test Lab makes a huge step towards tending to this issue by giving a testing platform that permits applications to be tested using a large number of device setups.

Firebase Test Lab helps developers to test the application with a wide range of cloud-based device infrastructure. Be it Android or iOS, you can test your application with many configurations and cloud-based physical devices. And finally, we can oversee the results through logs, videos, and screenshots inside the Firebase Console.

In this chapter, we will explore Firebase Test Lab and see how it can be utilized to perform distinctive kinds of testing. The following sections cover two main testing features, Robo testing and instrumentation testing, in more detail. These topics will be covered:

- Overview of Firebase Test Lab for Android
- Testing with the Firebase Console
- Testing with CI systems
- Test Lab and Android Studio
- Robo test
- Testing with virtual devices
- Pre-launch reports and more

Firebase Test Lab

The mobile platform has evolved rapidly in the last decade, and it will continue to do so. Every year advancement in software and hardware results in so many different form factors and nuances and this causes problems when building a unified fragmented software. Also, developers are writing applications that are hardware intensive, so developers will not be able to test their application in all of the hardware. Firebase Test Lab is a cloud-based application testing service and it offers several features to test your application with a diverse range of devices and software configuration. Firebase Test Lab allows testing in Android and iOS applications seamlessly. Suppose we are writing a commercial application for both iOS and Android platforms, Firebase Test Lab will be a go-to solution.

Firebase Test Lab installs the application in a real device hosted in Google data center, so you can target a specific device and run your application to figure out the issues.

Firebase Test Lab has good workflow integration like the Firebase Console, Android Studio, and some of the IntelliJ IDEs. Also, Firebase Test Lab can be configured to CI systems such as *Buddy build*, *Bitrise*, and so on.

> You can explore these tools from the following links:
> Bitrise: www.bitrise.io
> Buddy build: www.buddybuild.com
> There are other CI and CD platforms, but they all have limitations through their pricing model.

Firebase Test Lab continuously updates the official new APIs from the platforms, and they will have customizable locale settings. This enables developers to test the application on different configurations similar to the real world.

Firebase Test Lab runs the *Espresso* UI testing framework and the *UI Automator 2.0* testing framework to test Android applications. In addition to this, Firebase Test Lab uses *XCTest framework* to test iOS applications. You can write the test code for any of these frameworks and we can execute the tests using Firebase Console and also through the cloud command line interface.

In case you are only targeting Android platforms, Test Lab creates the tests using automated Robo tests. For iOS or Android, write an instrumentation test and modify your application so that it supports a Game Loop test, or better yet let's take Robo tests assistance. We need to choose a test matrix before we continue. A test matrix includes a set of devices, OS, versions, locales, screen orientation, and other configurations.

Based on the test matrix capacity, your test might take from several minutes to hours to generate the detailed report in the console.

Test Lab for Android

Since we are focusing on the Test Lab implementation on Android platforms, we shall build some quick and easy examples of the fundamentals of testing.

As your application grows, you may think that it is important to bring information from a server, connect with the device sensors, access local storage, or render complex UIs. The flexibility of your application demands a reliable testing procedure.

When building features iteratively, you begin by either composing another test or by adding cases and assertions to a current unit test. The test fails at first, in light of the fact that the feature isn't implemented yet.

It's essential to consider the units of responsibility that develop as you design the new feature. For every unit, you write a corresponding unit test. Your unit tests ought to exhaust every single conceivable interaction with the unit, including standard cooperations, invalid sources of info, and situations where assets aren't accessible.

The following diagram shows a testing pyramid that consists of three blocks, UI Tests, Integration Tests, and Unit Tests. For convenience, we can call unit tests small tests, integration tests medium tests, and large tests are integration and UI tests put together.

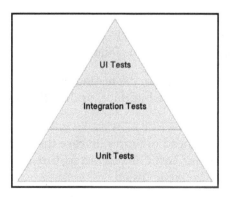

Testing pyramid of software applications

Unit tests are usually written on the business logic of the application and we should not include the system dependencies to write the unit tests.

To write small/unit tests we can make use of open source frameworks such as JUnit, Roboelectric, and so on. We can also monitor the interactions by mocking the data by using frameworks such as Mockito.

Medium tests are useful once we complete a certain programming module. Using real devices and emulators we can test the behavior of the completed module. Medium tests help in identifying the hardware dependencies. Medium tests can evaluate how your application interacts with two different modules, but they cannot be used to test the complete application. Some of the medium tests that are in practice include service tests, hermetic UI tests, and integration tests that simulate the behavior of the app dependencies. In Google IO 2017, Google acknowledged the practice of test-driven development, which includes all small, medium, and large testing practices.

Large tests are as important as the other two tests as they enable developers to test the UI, business logic, and data layer. AndroidJUnitRunner defines an instrumentation-based test runner. It permits JUnit3 and JUnit4 style testing on Android devices. Espresso is a very popular UI testing framework. Similarly, UI Automator and Android Test Orchestrator run each UI test in its own sandbox.

All these tests that developers write need an environment to test. Firebase Test Lab runs them in the test matrix. In Firebase Test Lab, Test Matrix means Test Dimensions multiplied by Test Executions.

Test dimensions are the device specifics such as device model, OS version, Locale and screen orientation, and so on. Test Executions are individual test runs with unique combinations.

Test Matrix is the test executions on the selected test dimensions. In case of any test failure, Firebase Test Lab marks the whole matrix as failed.

Developers can choose the way to initiate the testing of the application. Generally through Android Studio, gcloud command-line interface, or directly through Test Lab UI in the Firebase Console.

Developers do not need to worry, in case the application is not configured, Firebase Test Lab offers a feature called Robo test, in which even debug APK's can be tested.

We can test the app in Test Lab before publishing the application to production, we can publish it to alpha and beta channels, and Firebase assists in fetching the pre-launch reports.

Choosing the testing method

Firebase Test Lab is already a great service. Now it is developers who have to make the decisions on the way they want to test the application.

 Using Test Lab we cannot do the API stress test and Test Lab is not intended to do so.

Test Lab offers mainly three types of testing, which are enlisted as follows:

- Instrumentation tests
- Test Lab Robo test
- Game Loop test

Instrumentation tests depend on the code written for testing specific UI logic using libraries such as Espresso and UI Automator. These instrumentation tests are time consuming and it takes nearly 30 minutes in a real device and 60 minutes in virtual devices depending on the tests written.

Robo tests are similar to monkey tests offered in Android SDK. Even when you have not written code for testing, you can still perform a lot of activities and actions can be logged as a form of the report.

Developers write games in many different ways using game engines such as Unity, Unreal, and so on, and all these games need a unified way to test them. Though Firebase Test Lab is a table in every other feature, its Game Loop is a new beta support. By the time you start reading the book, I believe the Game Loop test will become stable.

Robo testing

Robo testing permits applications to be tried without writing any tests. To play out a Robo test, essentially transfer the APK file for the application and define the time for tests and the profundity inside the application to which the test ought to be performed. Robo testing works by recognizing the hierarchy of the UI and afterward, playing out a sequence of simulated user activities, (for example, button presses, user input, and screen navigation) expected to practice as a significant part of the application as conceivable. This testing will proceed until either the application crashes or the most extreme time has come to an end.

The primary motivation behind Robo testing is to rapidly and effortlessly discover bugs that cause an application to crash. Robo test has no learning about the way the application is expected to work, so it has no real way to check that any reaction from the application to a specific activity (besides a crash) was the normal reaction. This level of testing requires the utilization of instrumentation testing.

 The developer or QA Engineer can upload both the signed and unsigned APK to the Firebase Console in the **Test Lab** option.

Choosing device type and reviewing test results

Test Lab offers to test on several types and models of Android devices running in Google data center. The popular devices are listed as follows:

- Asus
- Nexus 7
- Pixel
- HTC One
- Huawei Mate 9
- Nexus 9

The popular devices support many API levels. Google also lists the deprecated devices for support, such as:

- Samsung Galaxy J5
- Nexus 5

In spite of how you initiated the tests, all your tests are managed by Test Lab and can be viewed in Firebase Console. Test results include test logs and the details of any app failure and the report includes videos and screenshots of the action.

Test Lab with Firebase Console

Firebase Console is the go-to place for most of the activities that developers perform. For Test Lab, Firebase Console has a dedicated console menu, inside which developers can choose to have a Robo test or instrumentation test.

First and foremost, create a Firebase project in the Firebase Console. You also need to be the owner of the application or you need to have edit permissions in your project.

 Using a spark or flame plan, you can have limited number of daily test executions. You can upgrade to a blaze plan if you require premium support.

Drop your APK. By default, your app is tested with a Pixel device through a Robo test.

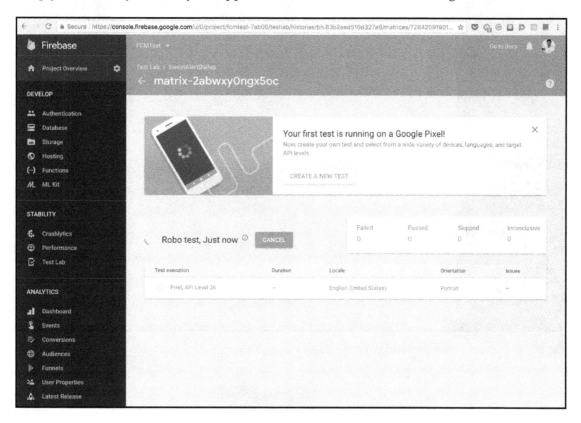

Give it some time and the Robo test will be completed with the device screenshot cluster. It will have detailed understanding of failed tests and crashes, passed actions, and so forth.

Consider the following screenshot, which is after 19 minutes, that gives the passed counts and also the test matrix details:

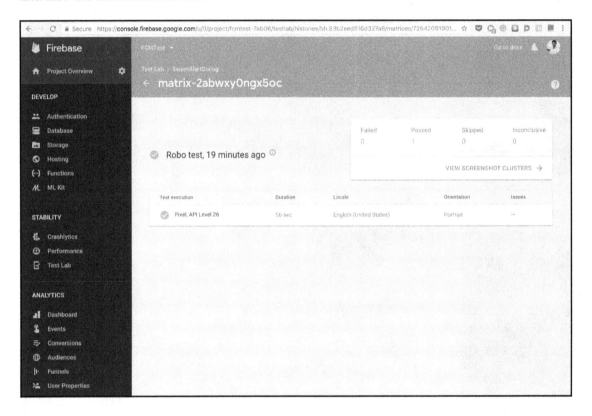

Click on **VIEW SCREENSHOT CLUSTERS** and it will show the screenshots of the application:

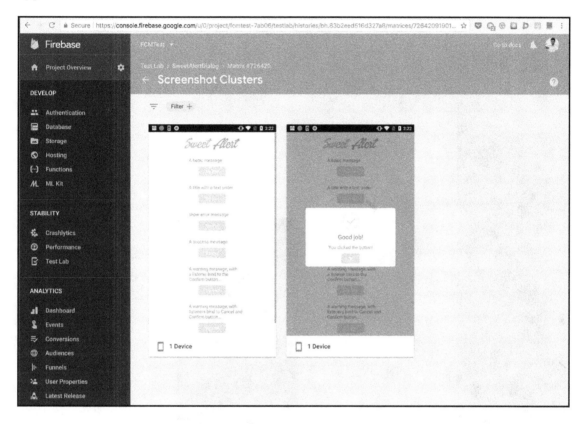

If we click on the device, Firebase Test Lab will take us to a screen with much more detailed logs and reporting mechanisms including screenshots, videos, and performance-related data:

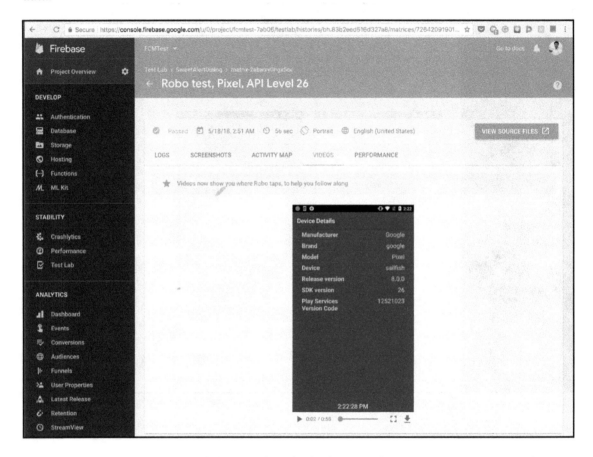

The preceding detailed report helps to identify the bugs and crashes. We can revisit the initial page and we can recreate the test on different devices depending on the available quota. Whenever we create a test we get to choose the test matrix or dimensions, as shown in the following screenshot:

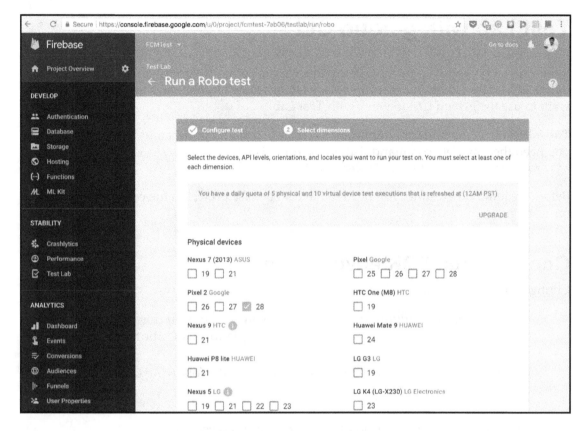

Choose the devices that you want to test the application, supervise the performance, and so on. We can also introduce a bug by writing a simple crash in the application, re-uploading it to the console, and then monitor the issues.

Similarly, you can test the instrumentation tests while creating a new test by uploading the test APK, which should have an `AndroidTestRunner` class.

Using the Test Lab console has pros and cons, which are listed as follows:

Pros:

- No shared state
- Isolated crashes

Cons:

- Longer runtime

Test Lab with gcloud CLI

Intermediate developers would already know through using one of Google's services that there exists a powerful cloud CLI. Using this we can configure pretty much most of the things in Google Cloud. For security reasons or for some implementation reason, you may want to use the gcloud CLI to work with Test Lab.

The following commands are important to create a Test Lab project and to test them. In case you need the complete command list, please use this URL `https://cloud.google.com/sdk/gcloud/reference/firebase/test/android/`

Before we jump into testing, you need to have a Firebase project in the console dedicated for testing.

Google Cloud SDK environment

Configuring Google Cloud SDK environment can be done as follows:

- To be able to configure the gcloud SDK, you need to visit this link: `https://cloud.google.com/sdk/` and download the platform-specific SDKs and install them
- Once the SDKs are up to date, you can execute the following command:

    `gcloud auth login`

- Now set the project in cloud-like, shown as follows:

    `gcloud config set project PROJECT_ID`

Now after setting the environment, we need to choose the testing configuration.

Choosing test configurations

Firebase Test Lab allows developers to use Gcloud to run and perform certain test configurations. Consider the scenario that we need to test an application using gcloud. The following steps illustrate how to run a test using the gcloud and gcloud Terminal:

- Download the application binary file, which is an Android APK file for running instrumentation tests. You can test different builds such as debug and signed builds all at once.

- After uploading the Binary file, it is time for us to explore the available devices to test. Using `MODEL_ID`, we can check for the latest API updates to the device and more. `OS_VERSION_ID` will enlist the operating systems available to the specific device. The following command helps in exploring the available devices with the OS version, model details, and much more:

  ```
  $ gcloud firebase test android models list
  ```

- Using the `describe` command, we can learn more about the specific device:

  ```
  $ gcloud firebase test android models describe Nexus5
  ```

- The following command gets the list of Android OS versions available to test:

  ```
  $ gcloud firebase test android versions list
  ```

- The following command gets the list of locales to test:

  ```
  $ gcloud firebase test android locales list
  ```

- Now after choosing all the necessary configurations in gcloud, we can start testing the app with the following command:

  ```
  $ gcloud firebase test android run
  ```

  When we run the command it will display the configuration and it will start testing according to the type:

  ```
  gcloud firebase test android run \
    --type robo \
    --app app-debug-unaligned.apk \
    --device model=Nexus6,version=21,locale=en,orientation=portrait \
    --device model=Nexus7,version=19,locale=fr,orientation=landscape \
    --timeout 90s
  ```

Scripting gcloud commands with Test Lab

We all like to automate the process of testing, gcloud allows us to use shell scripting to achieve this:

```
if gcloud firebase test android run --app packt-app.apk --test packt-
test.apk --timeout 2m
then
    echo "Test matrix for packt app successfully finished"
```

```
else
    echo "Test matrix exited abnormally with non-zero exit code: " $?
fi
```

There are a few very important scripting exit codes for Test Lab:

Exit code	Notes
0	All tests passed successfully.
1	A general failure occurred, such as filename not found, and so on.
2	Occurs when unknown commands are passed as an argument.
10	One or more test cases did not pass.

There are few more exit codes such as 15,18,19,20 addressing Firebase-related issues such as Test Lab matrix failed, not supported tests, matrix canceled by the user, and test infrastructure error occurred.

Test Lab with CI systems

Continous Integration (CI) is turning out to be a necessary tool in the development process, due to iterative development and introducing features that need to be reflected quickly in production applications. CI systems automatically build and test your application whenever you commit a code to your version control systems. There are many CI platforms for mobile apps, popular CI platforms are Jenkins, Bitrise, and Buddy build. All of these platforms offer a similar service, but ease of configuring them to your project differs.

Firebase Test Lab can be used to test the application for different scenarios when we are using CI systems to build, test, and deploy the application to Google Play Store. Consider the very popular Jenkins CI to apprehend the Test Lab along with it.

To be able to use Firebase Test Lab with Jenkins, you need to consider completing the following steps:

- Setting up gcloud: In the previous section, we learned how to configure gcloud to the project. Configure the Google Cloud SDK locally as explained in the gcloud section.

- Create a service account: Create a service account with an editor privilege in the Google Cloud platform console. This account should not be subject to spam checks or captcha prompts, which could block your CI builds.
- Enable required APIs: In the developer's console API library page, we need to enable the service that we would be using. For CI, enable the Google Cloud testing API and Cloud Tool Results API.

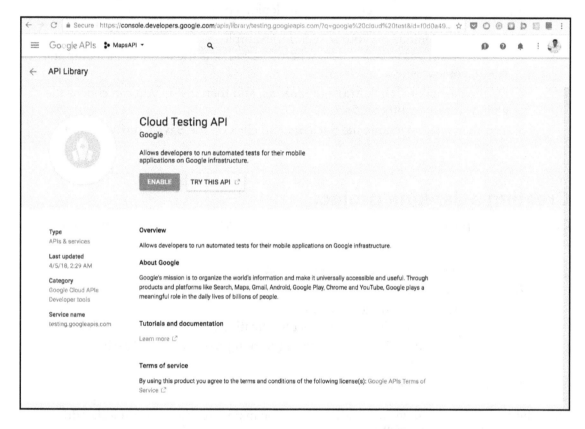

Now in your operating system, install and set up Jenkins. It is recommended to use Linux platforms to have Jenkins, but the platform also supports other popular operating systems, such as Windows.

Configuration settings for Jenkins are platform-specific, so please do read their platform-specific documentation before installing.

Jenkins also has a separate dashboard that helps in supervising the CI systems and the project-level details.

In Jenkins, it will not have the user authentication and access control in the beginning; using dashboard or command line, we need to configure the global security settings to enforce the access control and user authorization.

To configure the global security settings to your Jenkins project:

1. Navigate to Jenkins on your server, for example, `http://<servername>:8080`, where `<server>` is the name of the computer where you have installed Jenkins
2. On the dashboard, click **Manage Jenkins**, and then inside you can choose the global security configuration
3. You then need to enable the **Security** and click on the **Save Configurations** button

Creating a Jenkins project

Create a Jenkins project for CI and also integrate with Firebase Test Lab. To create a Jenkins project:

1. Go to **Dashboard** on your server.
2. Click on **New Item**.
3. Name your project in the **Item Name**:
    1. Choose a freestyle project for creating single build configurations
    2. Choose a build multi-configuration project for multiple build configurations
4. Now click on **Save** in the dashboard.

Once the project is created, your browser shows the main page for your project. Add version control and Gradle build steps.

Then using an Android Gradle build system, we can generate the APK binaries for every source code commit and check-in.

Use the following commands on your main directory:

```
./gradlew :app:assembleDebug
./gradlew :app:assembleDebugAndroidTest
```

Add Test Lab build steps to Jenkins, go to the **Dashboard** main page, and then follow these steps:

1. Click on the **Configure** button.
2. Scroll down to the **Build** section and choose **Execute shell** from the **Add build** step.
3. In the Jenkins shell command window, enter the following command:

```
$ gcloud firebase test android run --app
<local_server_path>/<app_apk>.apk --test
<local_server_path>/<app_test_apk>.apk
```

Once the test is completely executed, we can go to Firebase Console for the data and reports, which are also inside Google Cloud storage in your project. To go to your project from GCP (Google Cloud Platform), use the Google Terminal gsutil command with the shell command shown previously and you can retrieve all the data to your local computer.

There are CI systems that allow Test Lab to work seamlessly, such as Circle CI.

Test Lab with Android Studio

Android Studio is a powerful IDE built for developing JVM applications. Firebase Test Lab integration is completely straightforward using Android Studio. All the tests such as instrumentation and UI can be performed.

In this section, we will learn how to modify the instrumented tests in Android Studio for using cloud-based infrastructure through Test Lab. Once we have a Blaze plan for Firebase billing, we can create a test configuration and run tests:

1. Create a new configuration by clicking on **Run** and edit configurations within Android Studio.
2. Add a new configuration and select **Android Tests**.
3. Inside the **Android Test Configuration** dialog:
    - Enter your test details such as name, module type, and test classes
    - In the **Target** dropdown, choose **Deployment Target** options and select **Firebase Test Lab Device Matrix**
    - Your Android Studio should be connected with your Firebase account or Google Developer account

4. Configure a test matrix:
    - In the **Matrix Configuration** dropdown, click **Open Dialog**
    - Add a new configuration
    - Name your configuration and select the devices and Android versions, locales and screen orientation, and so on
5. Save the configuration, now you are going to compile the project.

Firebase Test Lab captures screenshot and records videos. To capture the screenshots, we need to add test Gradle dependency, as shown in the following code:

```
repositories {
    jcenter()
    flatDir {
        dirs '../aars'
    }
}
```

In your module level dependency, add the following dependency:

```
dependencies {
    // Cloud testing
    androidTestCompile (name:'cloudtestingscreenshotter_lib', ext:'aar')
    }
```

We need to ensure that we have added internet and file writing permission inside the manifest file of the application:

```
<uses-permission android:name="android.permission.WRITE_EXTERNAL_STORAGE"/>
<uses-permission android:name="android.permission.INTERNET"/>
```

To capture the screenshot of the application, we can write a snippet at any point in your test where you can take a screenshot:

```
ScreenShotter.takeScreenshot("main_screen_2", getActivity());
```

All the screenshots taken will be organized as a tree structure and we can check them when we need to.

The powerful Espresso is a UI testing framework that generates clicks and touches and gestures programmatically, so we need a way to record the interactions on a device and add assertions to verify that the UI elements are showing the valid data and has the valid input action.

Espresso test recorder records all the action and data activities and saves it in the machine at a specific path. Espresso test recorder also generates a corresponding Espresso UI test that can be used in Test Lab.

To modify the instrumented test behavior for Test Lab, we need to use the system property and set a `testLabSetting` string to `true`:

```
String testLabSetting =
    Settings.System.getString(context.getContentResolver(),
"firebase.test.lab");
    if ("true".equals(testLabSetting)) {
        // Do something when running in Test Lab
    }
```

Firebase Test Lab results

There are a number of ways to run tests in Firebase Test Lab, including CLI, Android Studio, Test Lab Console, and so on. However, all the tests and their results will be stored in the Firebase Console in a specific project that you have chosen to integrate with the Firebase Test Lab.

To apprehend the result report in the Firebase Console, we need to explore the key concepts used by Test Lab. Visit the Firebase Console and choose **Test Lab** in the navigation panel. This page displays all the controls required for you to plunge into testing your application.

We have understood that **Test Dimensions × Test Executions = Test Matrix**, where Test Dimensions are device-specific configurations and Test Executions are individual test runs. Each test is unique with the test dimensions that are selected.

In Test Lab, the console shows the most recent five results, if we need to understand the previous results we can click on the test matrices and a complete test list will be available for reference.

Generally, in the test matrix, we can run the test on different devices and each test result can have a different outcome, the possible outcomes would include the following:

- Passed: No failures were encountered
- Failed: At least one test has failed
- Inconclusive test passed: Inconclusive due to Test Lab error
- Skipped test passed: A selected device for testing the application is incompatible, for instance, you cannot test an Android TV App feature on a wearable watch device

Robo test results will also include almost similar data and can also show the touches that Robo has simulated. Robo test will also record a video to understand the actions it has taken to perform the tests.

A single test would return the logs, screenshots, and videos as in a Robo test result matrix, but specific to a particular test execution.

Test Lab performance metrics talk about required device configuration for app startup time and CPU usage, memory usage, network activity, frames per second and graphics stats, and more. Also, all these reports will be kept in Test Lab for 90 days after we run a test.

Available devices in Test Lab

Test Lab offers a great contract of devices including popular manufacturers, high-performance devices, and mid-range devices too.

The following list is the available device list from Firebase:

Manufacturer	Model	Type	Android version
Asus	Nexus 7 (2012)	Virtual	19, 21, 22
Asus	Nexus 7 (2013)	Physical	19, 21
Google	Nexus 6P	Virtual	23, 24, 25, 26
Google	Pixel	Physical	25, 26
HTC	Nexus 9	Virtual	21, 22, 23, 24, 25
HTC	HTC One (M8)	Physical	19
Huawei	Huawei Mate 9	Physical	24
Huawei	Huawei P8 lite	Physical	21
LG	Nexus 4	Virtual	19, 21, 22
LG	Nexus 5	Virtual	19, 21, 22, 23
LG	Nexus 5	Physical	21, 23
LG	Nexus 5X	Virtual	23, 24, 25, 26
LG	LG G3	Physical	19
LG	LG G6	Physical	24
Motorola	Nexus 6	Virtual	21, 22, 23, 24, 25
Motorola	Nexus 6	Physical	21, 22, 23
Motorola	Moto G4 Plus	Physical	23
Motorola	Moto G4	Physical	23
Motorola	Moto G Play	Physical	23
Motorola	Moto X	Physical	19

More devices are being included continuously. At the time of reading, you can expect the latest Pixel 2 and 3 devices to be added. Similarly, to be able to provide good service, Firebase also deprecates devices. The following devices are no longer supported:

Manufacturer	Model	Type	Device/Version	Removing on
Samsung	Galaxy J5	Physical	Device	2018-05-04
LG	Nexus 5	Physical	Versions 19, 22	2018-06-01
Motorola	Moto G (Gen 3)	Physical	Device	2018-06-01
HTC	Nexus 9	Physical	Version 21	2018-06-01
Samsung	Galaxy Note 4	Physical	Device	2018-06-01
Samsung	Galaxy S4 mini	Physical	Device	2018-06-01

The preceding available devices can be used to perform Robo tests and instrumentation tests.

Firebase Test Lab Game Loop testing

Games and game development is one of the fastest growing software industries. There are numerous types of game development processes and types of games, including 3D games, network games, and mobile games. With the rate of growth, it also leads to the problem of automation and testing. Firebase Test Lab offers beta support for game testing. Using logical labels, you can run the related loops.

When carrying out a Game Loop test in Test Lab, you need to modify your game as follows:

1. Launch the loop
2. Run the loop
3. Close the game

To launch the loop, there is a specific intent filter that we need to use inside manifest, as shown in the following code:

```
<activity android:name=".MyActivity">
    <intent-filter>
        <action android:name="com.google.intent.action.TEST_LOOP"/>
        <category android:name="android.intent.category.DEFAULT"/>
        <data android:mimeType="application/javascript"/>
    </intent-filter>
    <intent-filter>
        ... (other intent filters here)
    </intent-filter>
</activity>
```

Game intent filters are supposed to be used in games exclusively instead of for any other purpose.

To run the loop when an activity is launched, we need to check whether the intent is launched by the specified activity. If so, we can handle the game loop as follows:

```
launchIntent = getIntent();
if(launchIntent.getAction().equals("com.google.intent.action.TEST_LOOP")) {
    int scenario = launchIntent.getIntExtra("scenario", 0);
    // Code to handle your game loop here
}
```

It is recommended to run the code in an `onCreate` method, but you can run it with any other Android context-based logic.

Test Loop Manager

To ensure that the game loop is integrated into your local devices, Test Loop Manager offers to make the process easy. It is also completely open source and if you have any contribution to game testing through programming you can introduce it to Test Loop Manager.

To use Test Loop Manager:

1. Download Test Loop Manager.
2. Install Test Loop Manager on your device by using the following command:

   ```
   adb install testloopmanager.apk
   ```

3. You can now start the Test Loop Manager app on your phone or tablet. The app can check the game loop-based applications and it will enlist them on its homepage.
4. Select **Game app** and **Run Test**.

In the end, you can close your activity by using the `finish()` method in one of the life cycle methods.

Game loop in Test Lab

In the Firebase Console, we can choose or create a project for the game loop test. We have already learned that Firebase has testing quota limits in spark plan; depending on how complex the game is, you can change the quota by paying some extra premiums.

 It is not recommended to use virtual devices for game loop tests.

In the Firebase Console, follow these steps to run a game loop:

- In the Firebase Console, choose **Test Lab**
- Run your first test
- Choose **Game Loop** as the **Test Type** and click **Continue**
- Browse the game application binary APK file
- Click on **Continue** and choose the test matrix
- Now you are all set to click on **Start tests**

You can write the output data to a file using the following code snippet:

```
Uri logFile = launchIntent.getData();
int fd = -1;
if (logFile != null) {
    Log.i(TAG, &quot;Log file &quot; + logFile.getEncodedPath());
    try {
        fd = getContentResolver()
                .openAssetFileDescriptor(logFile, &quot;w&quot;)
                .getParcelFileDescriptor()
                .getFd();
    } catch (FileNotFoundException e) {
        e.printStackTrace();
        fd = -1;
    } catch (NullPointerException e) {
        e.printStackTrace();
        fd = -1;
    }
}
native_function(fd);  // C++ code invoked here.
```

If you want to do multiple game loops, you can pass the value in the `meta-data` tag, as shown in the following code:

```
<application>
    ...
  <meta-data android:name="com.google.test.loops" android:value="5" />
    ...
</application>
```

This will execute five game loops in your application.

Prelaunch reports

Firebase Test Lab offers a service to upload and publish your application to alpha or beta channels in the Google Play console. The prelaunch report is enabled by Robo test. You can Robo test an application for target-specific devices, locales, or different versions of Android. Robo tests can be more customizable than the prelaunch report.

Robo test is preferred for testing APKs. If you are using Test Lab for a large application, it might be a good idea to upgrade the plan to support the application. You can use CI as described in previous sections to make use of build deploy automation and testing.

Summary

Firebase Test Lab is a brilliant service that offers a cloud-based testing environment. As well as all the unique services it offers, it helps to speed up the development process without worrying about device-level testing.

Firebase Test Lab offers integration through the Firebase Console, Android Studio, and gcloud. We have explored all of them. We have learned how to analyze the test results and so forth. Game loop testing is another brilliant support that is in beta and I hope that at the time of reading it will be stable and in production.

In the next chapter, we will look at the performance of applications using performance monitoring services.

8
A Smart Watchdog – Firebase Performance Monitoring

"The accurate measure of any great software product is its PERFORMANCE."

– Unknown

The name of this tool clearly indicates that it is a service for monitoring the performance of an application. It gives a comprehensive insight into the performance characteristics of your iOS and Android apps. Firebase offers an SDK to help in capturing the data of an application. Later, developers can review and analyze this data in the Firebase Console. Performance Monitoring also assists in improving performance based on the data captured and by fixing issues which result in poor performance.

The Performance Monitoring tool is in the beta stage, in spite of the fact its beta Performance Monitoring delivers excellent features for improving application performance. In this chapter, we will explore the following aspects of Performance Monitoring:

- An overview of Firebase Performance Monitoring
- Automatic traces
- Disabling Performance Monitoring
- Keeping your app fast and responsive
- Network behavior
- Understanding the origin of an issue

Firebase Performance Monitoring

Performance Monitoring is a savior service when an application is experiencing crashes due to memory issues at the time of network calls, or even if the app is not fluid and is experiencing glitches in graphical redraw processes, and so on. There are two circumstances where developers have to write this application. The first one is when lower memory devices install the app and the second one is regarding lower bandwidth and network attenuation situations, and the application needs to behave based on network and memory adaptivity. To identify this on a wide variety of devices is practically impossible, so here we plug the Performance Monitoring SDK into iOS or Android applications to monitor traces and HTTP/s network requests from the app. The SDK will keep track of startup time and background activities. Performance Monitoring key capabilities include automatically monitoring app performance and network behaviors. Performance Monitoring assists developers by giving them insight into where app performance can be improved, and developers can also customize Performance Monitoring in regards to the app.

Performance Monitoring relies on data called traces. Traces are data that has been captured between two points in time within the execution cycle of your application.

Extending on automatic traces, Performance Monitoring also allows you to have room for custom traces through code snippets initialized inside the application. The custom traces also enables Performance Monitoring to start and stop capturing data of the application to evaluate a specific functionality. Custom traces can be added to particular functions by merely adding a single annotation to function declarations within the source code of the app.

Concerning the data involved in Performance Monitoring, this incorporates app version, country, device, operating system, radio, and carrier information. For HTTP/S network requests, the response time, payload size, and success rate are also captured. The results of Performance Monitoring are viewed within the Performance Monitoring section of the Firebase Console.

 Performance Monitoring will not collect user data by itself such as name, email, and so on by itself. Only by using custom attribute developers can it collect such data. Even after collecting user data, it will be subject to deletion without notice.

Performance Monitoring for Android

Adding Performance Monitoring to your Android project will be straightforward and it will be a similar process for other Firebase tools with small changes. You can implement the Performance Monitoring SDK with your project, as it can go with any other Firebase tools without any difficulty. Performance Monitoring starts capturing data automatically and you can also define custom traces and counters to measure specific aspects of application performance. Later, you can start using this data to analyze the performance of the application in the Firebase Console. The Firebase Console also allows developers to filter the data through different demographics like app version, OS, country, device, and so on.

Let's create a project in Android Studio to exclusively explore the Performance Monitoring service:

1. **Create a project in Android Studio:** Create an Android Kotlin Supported Project and call it `PerfMoni`. Choose all default templates including an empty activity.

2. **Integrate Firebase SDK to the project:** You can do so by going to the **Tools | Firebase** menu option, and when the Firebase window panel pops up, simply choose the service you wish to connect to and click on **Connect to Firebase**. In recent versions of Android Studio, Performance Monitoring is not included by default. In that case, just add any service, for example, cloud messaging or analytics:

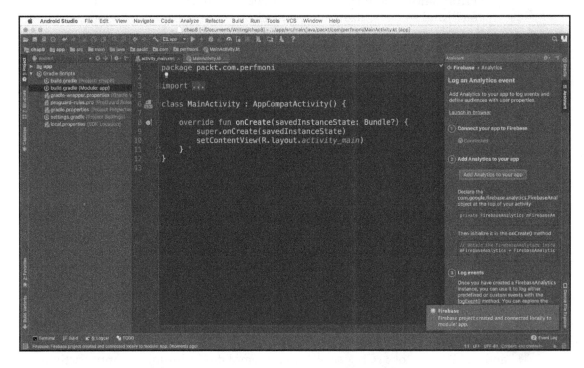

The purpose of the following image is to show that reader can connect to analytics from the firebase tools in the android studio

3. After connecting to Firebase, it is time to add the Performance Monitoring. Open the project scope `build.gradle` file and add the following dependency:

```
//Recommended for Android Studio version 3.X
classpath 'com.google.firebase:firebase-plugins:1.1.5'

//Recommended for Android Studio version 2.Xclasspath
'com.google.firebase:firebase-plugins:1.1.1'
```

4. Open the App level `build.gradle` file, apply the Firebase plugin, and add the dependency as follows:

```
apply plugin: 'com.google.firebase.firebase-perf'

// Add the following under dependency section
/* You can use compile keyword depending on the Android Studio
version you would be using.*/
implementation 'com.google.firebase:firebase-perf:15.0.0'
```

5. Compile the project now and run the application: you are all set to use Performance Monitoring.

Now, we are ready to explore its performance. Compile and rebuild the application and Firebase will automatically start monitoring the following details after successful configuration.

Automatic traces

A trace is a performance report captured between two points in time within an app. Performance Monitoring uses methods to identify whether automatic traces have started or stopped. The definitions for the automatic trace are as follows:

- **App Startup**: When the application is launched, it goes through a certain life cycle and it will also rasterize the graphical UI elements to be responsive to the user. This internal process basically covers the application's lifecycle.
- **App Background**: Performance Monitoring captures the data while the app goes into the background. Performance Monitoring starts the trace from the point when the application goes to the `onStop()` callback till the app goes to the `onResume()` callback. Performance Monitoring automatically stops the data capture.
- **App Foreground**: These are traces from Performance Monitoring of the application when the app is in the foreground. Data capturing will start when the application goes to the `onResume()` callback of the launcher activity and it will stop capturing data at the `onStop()` callback.
- **Network Requests**: Performance Monitoring traces all network requests being fired from the application and it will also look for whether network responses have been received. This includes response time, the size of the payload, and a percentile of successful requests.

Custom trace and counters

A custom trace is performance data that has been captured on specific start and end points through the code. We can have any number of custom traces and all of them can run in parallel without affecting the actual code's performance.

Each and every custom trace can have one or more counters for helping in capturing performance-related data, and all the counters are mapped to the traces that create them.

You can start working on the custom trace straight away by using the following classes:

```
import com.google.firebase.perf.FirebasePerformance
import com.google.firebase.perf.metrics.AddTrace
import com.google.firebase.perf.metrics.Trace
```

To create your first custom trace, create an instance of the `Trace` class, which needs to be created via a call to the `newTrace()` method of the `FirebasePerformance` instance. You can pass any name so that you can identify the trace. The trace is started with a call to the `start()` method:

```
myTrace = FirebasePerformance.getInstance().newTrace("packt_trace")
myTrace?.start()
```

To end the trace, we can utilize the `stop()` method to trace the object, as follows:

```
myTrace?.stop()
```

You can add a custom trace within one method for some specific operation. Now, in the following example, I am firing an analytics event and I am checking the performance trace, as can be seen in the following code:

```
myTrace = FirebasePerformance.getInstance().newTrace("packt_trace")
myTrace?.start()
val bundle = Bundle()
bundle.putString("oncreate", "created")
mFirebaseAnalytics?.logEvent(FirebaseAnalytics.Event.SELECT_CONTENT,
bundle)
myTrace?.stop()
```

You can also use a dedicated annotation for methods to cover a complete method and the operations inside of it. Th `@AddTrace` annotation in the following example of an `onCreate` method covers the complete `onCreate` method and its functionalities:

```
@AddTrace(name = "onCreateTrace", enabled = true)
    override fun onCreate(savedInstanceState: Bundle?) {
        super.onCreate(savedInstanceState)
```

```
        setContentView(R.layout.activity_main)
        val bundle = Bundle()
        bundle.putString("oncreate", "created")
mFirebaseAnalytics?.logEvent(FirebaseAnalytics.Event.SELECT_CONTENT,
bundle)
    }
```

To add the trace counters, we can call the `incrementCounter()` method to the trace object, passing a name to the counter for contextual reference. Like in the following code, increment the counter whenever the `onCreate` method is called:

```
myTrace?.incrementCounter("onCreatedCounter")
```

You can increment this before stopping the trace object.

Performance Monitoring for Android performance

The Google Play console offers the Android Vitals dashboard for improving the performance of your application. We know that Performance Monitoring plays a major role when we cannot identify performance flaws. Consider the example of custom view components being used in an application, and it is taking some time to render the view. By using Performance Monitoring, we can identify the reason for UI flaws and so forth. We can identify the flaw easily through the following steps in the devices by running an API at level 24 or higher:

- Start the custom trace, which is `myTrace.start()`
- You can call the `FrameMetricAggregator` object to understand the view rendering delay
- Before stopping, the trace stops `FrameMetricAggregator`
- In the console, you can check the detailed report for the view rendering issue

 Sometimes, Performance Monitoring data will take 12 hours or longer to reflect in the Firebase Console, so you need to wait patiently.

Monitoring for specific network requests

As we have already learned, Performance Monitoring captures network data automatically. When your application has too many network calls and you want to monitor a specific network, call the following code snippet, as it explains how to achieve this:

```
HttpMetric metric =
FirebasePerformance.getInstance().newHttpMetric("https://www.google.com",
    HttpMethod.GET);
final URL url = new URL("https://www.google.com");
metric.start();
HTTPURLConnection conn = (HttpURLConnection) url.openConnection();
conn.setDoOutput(true);
conn.setRequestProperty("Content-Type", "application/json");
try {
  DataOutputStream outputStream = new
DataOutputStream(conn.getOutputStream());
  outputStream.write(data);
} catch (IOException e) { }
metric.setRequestPayloadSize(data.length);
metric.setHttpResponseCode(conn.getResponseCode());
printStreamContent(conn.getInputStream());

conn.disconnect();
metric.stop();
```

The preceding code captured the specific network-related metrics and also automatically captured data. We can see this in the performance console.

 There are some known issues with Firebase plugin 1.1.0, which Google is already aware of, and they are working on fixing these known issues. We hope that by the time you read this book, Post-Google IO 2018 issues will have been resolved.

Monitoring custom attributes

Sometimes, in real-world use cases, we need to monitor different data segments and focus on application performance. Performance Monitoring offers a variety of attributes out of the box such as the operating system, location, device, app versions, and so on.

In addition, we can also create custom attributes to break down your application in a more detailed manner. For example, in commerce applications, shopping can be done through different categories.

Performance Monitoring will not collect personal data, unless we are creating an attribute with user data, and then it is subject to deletion without notice:

```
trace.putAttribute("email", user.getEmailAddress());
```

Instead, we can set a generic type of user to attributes, as follows:

```
trace.putAttribute("experiment", "A");
```

Like every data or file management system ever invented, Firebase offers a CRUD method for creating custom attributes, reading them, updating them, and deleting them. This will happen through the use of the following code snippet:

```
val myTrace = FirebasePerformance.getInstance().newTrace("test_trace")

// Update scenario.
    myTrace.putAttribute("experiment", "A")

// Reading scenario.
    val experimentValue = myTrace.getAttribute("experiment")

// Delete scenario.
    myTrace.removeAttribute("experiment")

// Read attributes.
    val traceAttributes = myTrace.getAttributes()
```

In the Performance Monitoring console, we can monitor all our custom attributes, and Firebase will create the card with all the data for that segment. You can also filter the data from custom attributes.

Enabling Logcat output

The latency of 12 hours is a big drawback to Performance Monitoring to test whether Performance Monitoring is working or not. We don't need to wait for 12 hours; we can simply enable the Logcat output and we can locally confirm that data is being sent to Firebase, what information is being sent, and so on. To enable Logcat, we need to add a metadata tag inside the application tag within the manifest file as follows:

```
<application
    android:allowBackup="true"
    android:icon="@mipmap/ic_launcher"
    android:label="@string/app_name"
    android:roundIcon="@mipmap/ic_launcher_round"
    android:supportsRtl="true"
```

```
        android:theme="@style/AppTheme">
        <meta-data android:name="firebase_performance_logcat_enabled"
android:value="true" />
        <activity android:name=".MainActivity">
            <intent-filter>
                <action android:name="android.intent.action.MAIN" />

                <category android:name="android.intent.category.LAUNCHER" />
            </intent-filter>
        </activity>
    </application>
```

Now, we need to compile and run the application, and you can check the Logcat string `FirebasePerformance` for filtering the logs specific to Firebase Performance Monitoring:

The following image shows the Logcat window of the Android Studio, the picture is not pointing to any text. So this should not be an issue.

If you can see the logs in **Logcat**, then in 12 hours time, this data will be reflected in the Firebase Console.

You can disable Performance Monitoring at build-time by changing the metadata value to false as follows:

```
<application>
    ...
<meta-data android:name="firebase_performance_collection_enabled"
android:value="false" />
    ...
</application>
```

We can also disable Performance Monitoring at runtime-based conditions. We can also use `remote config` to turn off Performance Monitoring. Consider the following example:

```
//Setup remote config
final FirebaseRemoteConfig mFirebaseRemoteConfig =
FirebaseRemoteConfig.getInstance();
// You can uncomment the following two statements to permit more fetches
when
```

```
// validating your app, but you should comment out or delete these lines
before
// distributing your app in production.
// FirebaseRemoteConfigSettings configSettings = new
FirebaseRemoteConfigSettings.Builder()
//        .setDeveloperModeEnabled(BuildConfig.DEBUG)
//        .build();
// mFirebaseRemoteConfig.setConfigSettings(configSettings);
// Load in-app defaults from an XML file that sets perf_disable to false
until you update
// values in the Firebase Console
mFirebaseRemoteConfig.setDefaults(R.xml.remote_config_defaults);
//Observe the remote config parameter "perf_disable" and disable
Performance Monitoring if true
if (mFirebaseRemoteConfig.getBoolean("perf_disable")) {
FirebasePerformance.getInstance().setPerformanceCollectionEnabled(false);
} else {
    FirebasePerformance.getInstance().setPerformanceCollectionEnabled(true);
}
```

Now, based on what configuration is activated in remote config, Performance Monitoring will continue to work. Once remote config has fetched data activates and the condition is set to perf_disable, Firebase Performance Monitoring will be turned off at runtime:

```
//Remote Config fetches and activates parameter values from the service
mFirebaseRemoteConfig.fetch(3600)
    .addOnCompleteListener(this, new OnCompleteListener() {
        @Override
        public void onComplete(@NonNull Task task) {
            if (task.isSuccessful()) {
                mFirebaseRemoteConfig.activateFetched();
            } else {
            }
        }
    });
```

Firebase Console for Performance Monitoring

Though latency is a big downside of the Firebase Console, it offers great analytical cohorts and graphs for Performance Monitoring with precise details. This is one of the reasons for latency. In the **Performance** option of the Firebase Console, choose the package address you created for Performance Monitoring. If you see a message to install the SDK, it may take a while to see the data in the console.

Once Firebase has the data, it shows a quick overview of the data that's been captured:

Firebase Performance Console

The screen also includes tabs or links so that you can access detailed information on traces and network-related data. The screen provides options to filter the results, specify the date range, and so on. The overview includes the following data:

- **Traces by frequency**: This shows the traces that were most frequently over the selected time
- **Network success rate**: This shows the percentage of successful HTTP/S network requests made by the app over time
- **Network response latency**: This shows the median network latency for HTTP/S network requests from your app across various locations
- **Network response MIME types**: This shows network traffic broken down by the MIME type
- **App start trace: Median duration**: This shows the median app start time for the most widely used versions of your app

Through the filters and screens, we can aggregate the data and identify problems, if they exist, and we can find solutions for them.

Summary

Firebase Performance Monitoring offers a straightforward approach to monitoring the performance of an app. Performance is monitored using traces that measure app performance at certain periods of execution. Once the Performance Monitoring library has been added to an app, a number of trace metrics are monitored automatically. Custom traces can be created by making trace start and stop calls within the app. Once performance data has been captured, the data is analyzed within the Performance Monitoring section of the Firebase Console. We have explored how to enable and disable the Logcat and build time, and we have also explored disabling runtime through the support of Firebase Remote Config. We now have a fairly good understanding of the Firebase Console for Performance Monitoring.

In the next chapter, we will deep dive into Firebase Analytics and Cloud Messaging for Android.

9
Application Usage Measuring and Notification, Firebase Analytics, and Cloud Messaging

"Not everything that can be counted counts, and not everything that counts can be counted."

– Albert Einstein, Physicist

Firebase Analytics offers an approach to find out about the user base of an application, and to examine and track the manner by which those users are drawn in and connect with the application.

This chapter will provide an overview of Firebase Analytics and present the highlights of this service. The chapter will start by outlining the distinctive features of Firebase Analytics including events, user parameters, and audiences.

The subsequent sections will help us explore the different screens that make up the analytics area of the Firebase console before working through a tutorial exercise including the aforementioned events.

Also in this chapter, we will be exploring **Firebase Cloud Messaging** (**FCM**), which is a cross-platform messaging solution that allows delivery of the messages.

In this chapter, let's explore the following topics:

- Overview of Firebase Analytics and push notifications
- Setting log events
- Setting user properties
- Implementing analytics in WebView on Android
- Setting up an Android client
- Sending the first message
- Sending messages to multiple devices
- Receiving messages
- Sending messages to topics, device groups, and messages through the Firebase console

Firebase Analytics

With Firebase Analytics, application developers can capture and analyze information about users and the manner in which they interact with an application. Firebase Analytics is comprised of a library that is incorporated with the application combined with a set screen inside the Firebase console, resulting in effectively justifiable visual representations of the gathered information in graphs, charts, and tables.

Without the need to include a single line of code in an application project, Firebase Analytics will give statistical information about an application's user base, including age, gender, and geographical locations. Likewise, various events are caught, consequently counting the first run through user's App launch, Google Play in-application buys, user engagement with the application, application crashes, and the receipt and opening of Firebase notification messages are collected.

With the option of a couple of lines of code, application engineers can add custom events to track pretty much any sort of user association inside an application, thus permitting the analytics information captured to be adapted to the particular prerequisites of the application.

Firebase Analytics likewise enables custom groups of users to be characterized, enabling users to be assembled together based on behavioral patterns. Once created, groups of users can be utilized inside other Firebase features, for example, Notifications and Remote Config. The four key components of Firebase Analytics are: objects, events, user properties, and audiences. Each component will be covered in detail in the rest of this chapter.

Firebase Analytics for Android

Powered by Google Analytics, Firebase offers easy integration and plenty of analytical features, including unlimited reporting for 500 distinct events. These reports help us to understand how users interact with the application.

Firebase Analytics can be integrated with the following services:

- BigQuery
- Firebase Crash Reporting
- FCM
- Firebase Remote config
- Google Tag Manager

Firebase Analytics follows a similar process to other Firebase tools for integration. Connect your application to Firebase, add the updated dependency, and log the custom data, shown as follows:

```
implementation 'com.google.firebase:firebase-core:15.0.0'
```

To start logging activities, we can use the `FirebaseAnalytics` object in the `onCreate()` method:

```
mFirebaseAnalytics = FirebaseAnalytics.getInstance(this);
```

If you want to log custom events, use the `logEvent` method as follows:

```
Bundle bundle = new Bundle();
bundle.putString(FirebaseAnalytics.Param.ITEM_ID, id);
bundle.putString(FirebaseAnalytics.Param.ITEM_NAME, name);
bundle.putString(FirebaseAnalytics.Param.CONTENT_TYPE, "image");
mFirebaseAnalytics.logEvent(FirebaseAnalytics.Event.SELECT_CONTENT,
bundle);
```

We can check whether events are being logged by enabling verbose logging, as shown here:

```
adb shell setprop log.tag.FA VERBOSE
adb shell setprop log.tag.FA-SVC VERBOSE
adb logcat -v time -s FA FA-SVC
```

Setting user properties

User properties are attributes that identify the user in a more precise fashion. In the event of a crash for a particular user, we can send them notifications using FCM. Analytics automatically logs some of the user properties.

User properties are case sensitive; to log a user property, use case-sensitive keys.

The following method attaches the user property to the events:

```
mFirebaseAnalytics.setUserProperty("favorite_food", mFavoriteFood);
```

Analytics in a WebView

WebView-based applications still solve some unique problems. Most banking applications are hybrid and WebView-based. Before `WebView` sends anything to Firebase, it needs to send the native code. The following JavaScript code shows how to handle analytics on both platforms:

```
function logEvent(name, params) {
  if (!name) {
    return;
  }

  if (window.AnalyticsWebInterface) {
    // Call Android interface
    window.AnalyticsWebInterface.logEvent(name, JSON.stringify(params));
  } else if (window.webkit
      && window.webkit.messageHandlers
      && window.webkit.messageHandlers.firebase) {
    // Call iOS interface
    var message = {
      command: 'logEvent',
      name: name,
      parameters: params
    };
    window.webkit.messageHandlers.firebase.postMessage(message);
  } else {
    // No Android or iOS interface found
    console.log("No native APIs found.");
  }
}

function setUserProperty(name, value) {
  if (!name || !value) {
```

```
      return;
    }

  if (window.AnalyticsWebInterface) {
    // Call Android interface
    window.AnalyticsWebInterface.setUserProperty(name, value);
  } else if (window.webkit
      && window.webkit.messageHandlers
      && window.webkit.messageHandlers.firebase) {
    // Call iOS interface
    var message = {
      command: 'setUserProperty',
      name: name,
      value: value
    };
    window.webkit.messageHandlers.firebase.postMessage(message);
  } else {
    // No Android or iOS interface found
    console.log("No native APIs found.");
  }
}
```

Now, we need a native code implementation for the preceding code, shown as follows:

```
public class AnalyticsWebInterface {

    public static final String TAG = "AnalyticsWebInterface";
    private FirebaseAnalytics mAnalytics;

    public AnalyticsWebInterface(Context context) {
        mAnalytics = FirebaseAnalytics.getInstance(context);
    }

    @JavascriptInterface
    public void logEvent(String name, String jsonParams) {
        LOGD("logEvent:" + name);
        mAnalytics.logEvent(name, bundleFromJson(jsonParams));
    }

    @JavascriptInterface
    public void setUserProperty(String name, String value) {
        LOGD("setUserProperty:" + name);
        mAnalytics.setUserProperty(name, value);
    }

    private void LOGD(String message) {
        // Only log on debug builds, for privacy
        if (BuildConfig.DEBUG) {
```

```
            Log.d(TAG, message);
        }
    }

    private Bundle bundleFromJson(String json) {
        // ...
    }

}
```

In your `WebView`, you can register the interface so that analytics starts working.

```
if (Build.VERSION.SDK_INT >= Build.VERSION_CODES.JELLY_BEAN_MR1) {
    mWebView.addJavascriptInterface(
            new AnalyticsWebInterface(this), AnalyticsWebInterface.TAG);
} else {
    Log.w(TAG, "Not adding JavaScriptInterface, API Version: " +
Build.VERSION.SDK_INT);
}
```

The preceding code snippet fetches the click and other actions from the `WebView` and logs them in Firebase Analytics.

Debugging events

Firebase offers a feature for debugging events. In the Firebase console, **DebugView** enables you to see the events data logged by the debug application in real time. This is very useful for validating custom events and other data.

To enable the debug mode, you can enter the following CLI command in Terminal:

```
adb shell setprop debug.firebase.analytics.app <package_name>
```

By default, every 60 seconds, the command fires the event to Firebase. There is also a device selector feature, in case we are looking for any specific data. Use **DebugView** for test events fired from the test device, as shown in the following screenshot:

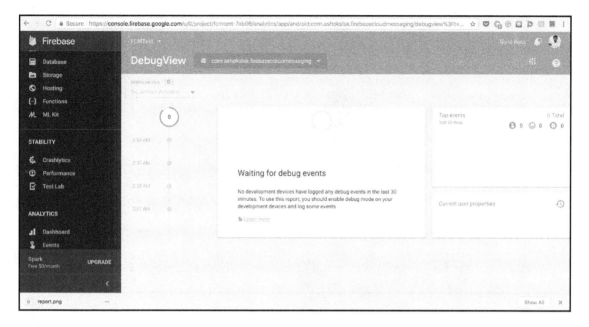

In **DebugView**, we can see the current events associated with the user properties. Also, we can track the screens using the following code:

```
mFirebaseAnalytics.setCurrentScreen(this, screenName, null /* class
override */);
```

The preceding code fires the screen details in which users would be switching screens and so on.

Firebase Analytics and functions

Functions can be triggered when a particular custom event is fired. For example, if your application user purchases something, and you make revenue through that, you can fire a thank-you notification and mail inside the following code snippet:

```
exports.sendCouponOnPurchase =
functions.analytics.event('in_app_purchase').onLog((event) => {
  // ...
});
```

If you want to access event properties, do that through the following code snippet:

```
exports.sendCouponOnPurchase =
functions.analytics.event('in_app_purchase').onLog((event) => {
  const user = event.user;
  const uid = user.userId; // The user ID set via the setUserId API.
  const purchaseValue = event.valueInUSD; // Amount of the purchase in USD.
  const userLanguage = user.deviceInfo.userDefaultLanguage; // The user
language in language-country format.

  // For purchases above 500 USD, we send a coupon of higher value.
  if (purchaseValue > 500) {
    return sendHighValueCouponViaFCM(uid, userLanguage);
  }
  return sendCouponViaFCM(uid, userLanguage);
});
```

The preceding code fires a coupon through email or a notification when a specific event occurs.

Cloud Messaging

Firebase Cloud Messaging (FCM) is a messaging service that offers a cross-platform messaging solution. FCM can be used to notify when there is new data available to sync. Using FCM, we engage the user and increase the chance of user retention. FCM allows up to 4 KB of payload transfer. The legacy way to send messages and notifications was the now-deprecated GCM. Google officially recommends using FCM for notifications and data messages.

There are some outstanding key capabilities, such as versatile message targeting, which allows device-specific messaging and the grouping of devices, including those subscribed to topics, and the sending of messages from user apps that can send acknowledgments, chats, and other messages from FCM.

FCM essentially includes two components: sender and receiver. The sender can be the application backend server or trusted services such as Firebase functions. Receivers are mobile and web platforms such as iOS and Android devices.

Messages can be fired using the Admin SDK or HTTP and XMPP APIs. To test notifications, Firebase Console also offers **Notification Composer**. Implementing FCM is similar to implementing other services that need to have the connected Firebase in the project. Then, it is just a matter of connecting the right SDK.

Since Firebase follows the rules of semantic versioning from May 2018, the library versions will differ with each tool starting from version 15.0.0. If you run into system errors because of these changes, you need not worry about it, just update the right version number.

FCM fires the messages in two types: notification messages handled by FCM SDK and data messages handled by the client application.

Notification messages will have the following payload signature:

```
{
  "message":{
    "token":"bk3RNwTe3H0:CI2k_HHwgIpoDKCIZvvDMExUdFQ3P1...",
    "notification":{
      "title":"Packt JUNIT 5",
      "body":"A brilliant testing book go ahead click here to read more"
    }
  }
}
```

Data messages will have data objects, shown as follows:

```
{
  "message":{
    "token":"bk3RNwTe3H0:CI2k_HHwgIpoDKCIZvvDMExUdFQ3P1...",
    "data":{
      "Nick" : "Mario",
      "body" : "great match!",
      "Room" : "PortugalVSDenmark"
    }
  }
}
```

The data field is processed and parsed by applications. To handle this onMessageRecieved() in Android and didReceiveRemoteNotification on iOS, onMessage in web applications as well.

In Android, there is both normal and high priority for sending notifications based on allotted priority to downstream messages. Normal priority messages are usually delivered immediately. If the device is in Doze mode, delivery may be delayed to save the battery. Use Firebase Job Scheduler Dispatch or JobIntentService to handle the notification or background data.

High priority messages attempt to deliver the message immediately, even if there are messages in the stack. High priority messages will be fired first.

A typical priority-based notification payload will look as follows:

```
{
  "message":{
    "topic":"subscriber-updates",
    "notification":{
      "body" : "Packts new book is available in",
      "title" : "packtpub.com",
    },
    "data" : {
      "volume" : "3.21.15",
      "contents" : "http://www.pactpub.com/"
    },
    "android":{
      "priority":"normal"
    },
    "apns":{
      "headers":{
        "apns-priority":"5"
      }
    },
    "webpush": {
      "headers": {
        "Urgency": "high"
      }
    }
  }
}
```

Every message that we fire will have a flag called `time_to_live` and the default timeout is four weeks.

Firebase Cloud Messaging in Android

Firebase Cloud Messaging for Android expects some basic features such as the FirebaseMessaging class and Android Studio 1.4 and above with Gradle. The next step assumes that you have a Firebase connected project and we are trying to accelerate the FCM implementation in Android.

Add the following dependency to your app-level Gradle file:

```
implementation 'com.google.firebase:firebase-messaging:15.0.2'
```

Add the following to the applications manifest file. This is a service class that extends to `FirebaseMessagingService`. It is required for handling messages, sending upstream messages, and so forth:

```
<service
    android:name=".MyFirebaseMessagingService">
    <intent-filter>
        <action android:name="com.google.firebase.MESSAGING_EVENT"/>
    </intent-filter>
</service>
```

A service that extends to `FirebaseInstanceIdService` to handle the push token registration is shown as follows:

```
<service
    android:name=".MyFirebaseInstanceIDService">
    <intent-filter>
        <action android:name="com.google.firebase.INSTANCE_ID_EVENT"/>
    </intent-filter>
</service>
```

Optionally, we can also add the metadata tags for handling notification icons, shown as follows:

```
<meta-data
  android:name="com.google.firebase.messaging.default_notification_icon"
    android:resource="@drawable/ic_stat_ic_notification" />


<meta-data
  android:name="com.google.firebase.messaging.default_notification_color"
    android:resource="@color/colorAccent" />
```

Accessing the device registration token

On application startup, developers can generate a push token using FCM SDK. If we need to target a single device, we need to have a reference to push the token in our backend to associate it with the user Auth details.

Generally, push tokens are accessed using `FirebaseInstanceIdService` and are unique to devices and applications.

Push tokens may change or update their key in the following scenarios:

- The application deletes the instance ID
- The application is restored on a new device
- User uninstalls/reinstalls the application
- The user clears application data

The following code snippet obtains the push token:

```
@Override
public void onTokenRefresh() {
    // Get updated InstanceID token.
    String refreshedToken = FirebaseInstanceId.getInstance().getToken();
    Log.d(TAG, "Refreshed token: " + refreshedToken);

    sendRegistrationToServer(refreshedToken);
}
```

Firebase also generates the instance ID automatically. We can prevent this by adding a `false` value in the following metadata:

```
<?xml version="1.0" encoding="utf-8"?>
<application>
  <meta-data android:name="firebase_messaging_auto_init_enabled"
             android:value="false" />
  <meta-data android:name="firebase_analytics_collection_enabled"
             android:value="false" />
</application>
```

If you want to use the service again, we can enable it at runtime using the following code snippet:

```
FirebaseMessaging.getInstance().setAutoInitEnabled(true);
```

Now we have explored the configuration part of the FCM, it's time to explore the process of sending and receiving notifications.

Cloud Messaging explained

The configuration of Firebase Cloud Messaging is straightforward, as explained in the previous section. In this section, we will see how to send the first notification and how to receive it in the mobile application. Also, let's explore the other brilliant features that FCM offers.

Sending the first notification

Create an Android Studio project and connect it with Firebase and the configurations discussed previously. Go to **Tools** and choose **Firebase**, and in the Firebase window panel, choose to **Connect to Firebase**. If your project exists, choose it, and if not, create a new project. After connecting, add the FCM dependencies, as shown in the following snippet:

```
implementation 'com.google.firebase:firebase-messaging:15.0.2'
```

Now create a new Android Studio project and add the following code snippets to generate push tokens.

Create a class called `MyFirebaseInstanceIDService` and add the following code:

```
class MyFirebaseInstanceIDService : FirebaseInstanceIdService() {

    override fun onTokenRefresh() {

        //Fetch the push token
        val refreshedToken = FirebaseInstanceId.getInstance().token
        Log.d(TAG, "Refreshed token: " + refreshedToken!!)

    }

    private fun sendRegistrationToServer(token: String) {

        }

    companion object {
        private const val TAG = "MyFirebaseIIDService"
    }
}
```

Now we need a service class to process the notification received. I will be using the notification `Builder` class to construct the notification.

Receiving the notification on a mobile end requires the service callback method `onMessageRecieved`, shown as follows:

```
class MyFirebaseMessagingService : FirebaseMessagingService() {

    override fun onMessageReceived(remoteMessage: RemoteMessage?) {
        Log.d(TAG, "From: " + remoteMessage!!.from!!)
        Log.d(TAG, "Notification Message Body: " +
remoteMessage.notification!!.body!!)
        processNotification(remoteMessage.notification!!.body)
    }


    private fun processNotification(messageBody: String?) {
        val intent = Intent(this, MainActivity::class.java)
        intent.addFlags(Intent.FLAG_ACTIVITY_CLEAR_TOP)
        val pendingIntent = PendingIntent.getActivity(this, 0, intent,
                PendingIntent.FLAG_ONE_SHOT)

        val defaultSoundUri =
RingtoneManager.getDefaultUri(RingtoneManager.TYPE_NOTIFICATION)
        val notificationBuilder = NotificationCompat.Builder(this)
                .setSmallIcon(R.mipmap.ic_launcher)
                .setContentTitle("Firebase Push Notification")
                .setContentText(messageBody)
                .setAutoCancel(true)
                .setSound(defaultSoundUri)
                .setContentIntent(pendingIntent)

        val notificationManager =
getSystemService(Context.NOTIFICATION_SERVICE) as NotificationManager

        notificationManager.notify(0, notificationBuilder.build())
    }

    companion object {

        private const val TAG = "MyFirebaseMsgService"
    }
}
```

Now, after writing these two classes, add the service tag in the manifest. Make sure that this service class is within the application tag scope, shown as follows:

```
<application> ..
<service
 android:name=".MyFirebaseMessagingService">
 <intent-filter>
 <action android:name="com.google.firebase.MESSAGING_EVENT"/>
 </intent-filter>
 </service>

<service
 android:name=".MyFirebaseInstanceIDService">
 <intent-filter>
 <action android:name="com.google.firebase.INSTANCE_ID_EVENT"/>
 </intent-filter>
 </service>
</application>
```

Now you are all set to receive your first Firebase push notification. Compile the project and get the device push token.

It is recommended to use a real device for push notifications. You can also use the latest emulators with the Play services.

The push token will look as shown in the following screenshot:

Now, copy the single device push token, go to the Firebase console, choose **Cloud Messaging**, and click on **Compose new message**.

Now, in **Target**, choose the **Single device** option and add the copied push token. Compose the message and click on **SEND MESSAGE**:

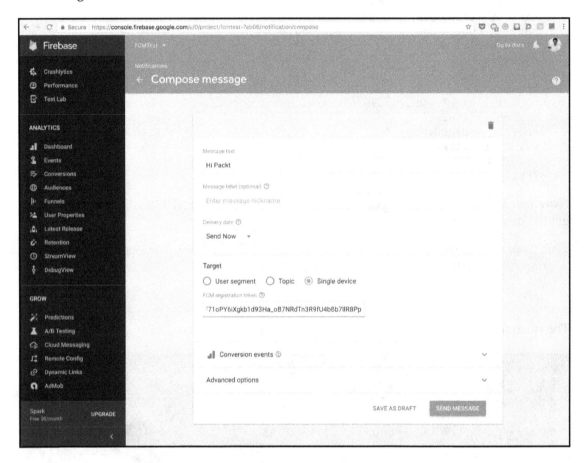

After a successful fire, we will receive a notification on the phone with processed info that will look as follows:

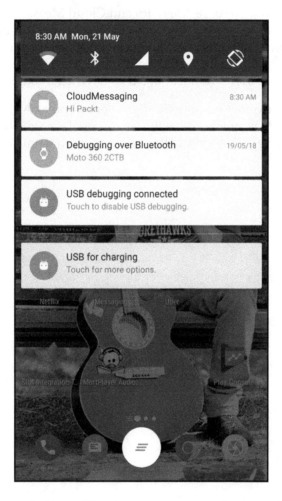

Similarly, if we want to send the notification to a group, perhaps to all of the application's users, we choose **User Segment** and package address, and fire the notification. For topic-based notifications, we will choose the topic and fire the notification with the topic title. In the notification payload, we can also send sound information and vibration pattern information.

Summary

In this chapter, we explored Firebase Analytics and Cloud Messaging. We also learned how to set up analytics. In addition to this, we learned about the default data being logged in the analytics console, and how to write a custom event, attach a custom screen, and so on. We also explored Cloud Messaging and how to construct a notification builder for the received notification as well as how to fire notifications through the Firebase console.

In the next chapter, let's explore Remote Config, a very popular A/B testing and remote service for managing data remotely. We will also discuss Dynamic Links, which constructs dynamic links for mobile applications. Let's explore them in detail.

10
Changing Your App – Firebase Remote Config and Dynamic Links

"Art of changing the look and feel"

– Unknown

Firebase Remote Config is one of the most talked about concepts in recent times; it's a tool that offers support for A/B testing and other significant features, such as the customization of an application. When it was announced at Google I/O 2016, Remote Config created a huge buzz in the developer community. Before then, there was not an easy way to change simple functionality or even the appearance of an application published on the Play Store. Developers were having to use a separate production app even for the simplest of changes. Since the release of Remote Config, rolling out updates without needing to install an app is now straightforward, and the dynamic changes implemented can be released to users through the Firebase console. In this chapter, we are going to explore Remote Config in detail.

In addition, Dynamic Links helps new users to install an application from the Play Store, whether via the web, the app itself, or a specific screen within the app. In this chapter, we will look at the comprehensive features available in Dynamic Links, as well as some examples.

In this chapter, we will cover the following topics:

- An overview of Firebase Remote Config and Dynamic Links
- Setting up Remote Config on Android
- Parameters and conditions in Remote Config
- Remote Config analytics
- How to convert web users to app users with referrals
- Viewing analytics data
- Debugging Dynamic Links

Firebase Remote Config

Before Firebase Remote Config, there was no simple method for rolling out unique improvements to an application's look or functions without issuing an update to existing users. There was, likewise, no real way to control which users got the update, making the rolling out of changes, performing A/B testing, or targeting particular user demographics difficult.

Firebase Remote Config solves this issue by giving developers a simple way to roll out remote configurations to an application and then target a particular group of users who will receive those changes. As with most other Firebase services, Remote Config starts by integrating a library into the project. Inside the application, an arrangement of parameters are then defined either in a Map object or an XML resource file.

These parameters appear as key-value pairs that are utilized to control the default design of the application. The code of the application is implemented with the end goal that these parameters are checked at predefined interims and are utilized as part of the rationale of the running application. An in-app parameter could, for instance, be proclaimed with a default setting to design an orange background or to show a specific welcome message.

These default in-application parameters may then be overridden on every parameter using a set of corresponding server-side parameters, the values of which are controlled from inside the Firebase console.

The choice of whether a server-side parameter will override the corresponding in-app parameter or not may be made conditional on the basis of certain variables, for example, user location, device operating system, and the user's language and region settings.

Parameters may likewise be focused to randomized rates of the user base, or in conjunction with an audience that has been characterized using Firebase Analytics. Once a server-side parameter has been configured, it is distributed and prepared to be fetched by the application. Once fetched, the parameters should then be activated before they can be used to override the corresponding in-app parameters.

Setting up Remote Config on Android

Setting up Firebase Remote Config on Android is very straightforward. Despite the platform's continuous evolution, Remote Config follows a similar setup to other Firebase services. The steps to set up your Firebase Remote Config are as follows:

1. Add Firebase to your app
2. Get the Remote Config singleton object
3. Set the in-app default parameter values
4. Get parameter values to use in your app
5. Set the parameter values in the Remote Config service as needed
6. Fetch and activate values from the Remote Config service as needed

We have explored how to connect the Android Studio project with Firebase in all of our previous chapters. Click on **Open Tools** | **Firebase** | **Remote Config** and then click **Connect**. Follow the steps onscreen to add the latest dependency in your build-level app. Make sure that you have everything ready before writing any code:

```
compile 'com.google.firebase:firebase-config:15.0.0'
```

The previous dependency fetches the necessary SDK from Google Repositories and adds it to the library of your project.

Remote Config's singleton object

The primary object responsible for Remote Config support within an Android app is the `FirebaseRemoteConfig` object. The first step in implementing Remote Config support within an application is to initialize and obtain a reference to that object, as follows:

```
FirebaseRemoteConfig fbRemoteConfig = FirebaseRemoteConfig.getInstance();
```

The previous instance of `FirebaseRemoteConfig` is accountable for storing the local parameters within the app. It also fetches the server-side parameters and oversees them when they are activated for use within the application.

In-app parameters

To define a set of key-value parameters along with a few default parameter values, you need to use a Map object or an XML asset file that is stored in your application's `res/XML` directory. Make sure you sync the following values to the Remote Config object using `setDefaults()`:

```
firebaseRemoteConfig.setDefaults(R.xml.remote_config_params);
```

The XML resources should look like the following snippet:

```xml
<?xml version="1.0" encoding="utf-8"?>
<defaultsMap>
    <entry>
        <key>welcome_text</key>
        <value>Welcome to Packt Remote Config</value>
    </entry>
    <entry>
        <key>main_background_color</key>
        <value>#42f486</value>
    </entry>
</defaultsMap>
```

Default in-app parameters can be declared inside XML assets bundled with the application or contained inside a Java Map object. Remember that when using XML assets, the file must be placed inside the `res/XML` directory of the application. The previous code contains a basic Remote Config parameter file containing the app's background color and even welcome message values.

Instead of using an XML resource file, the same result can be achieved using a `HashMap`, as shown in the following snippet:

```java
HashMap<String, Object> config_params = new HashMap<>();

//Key value pairs
config_params.put("welcome_text", "Welcome to Remote Config");
config_params.put("main_background_color", "#42f486");
fbRemoteConfig.setDefaults(config_params);
```

The previous code should be self-explanatory.

Accessing the Remote Config parameters

Once the in-app parameters have been connected to the FirebaseRemoteConfig object, the code should have the capacity to obtain the values, while keeping in mind that its end goal is to make use of them when configuring the application's appearance and behavior.

This is accomplished by calling one of a number of get methods on the FirebaseRemoteConfig instance as an argument – the key for which is the comparing value. The right get method to call will rely upon the kind of the value associated with the parameter; the methods available are as follows:

- getBoolean()
- getByteArray()
- getDouble()
- getLong()
- getString()

We can fetch the values using those methods, as shown in the following examples:

```
String color = fbRemoteConfig.getString("background_color");
layout.setBackgroundColor(Color.parseColor(color));
```

The background_color is a key parameter that we have set either in an XML resource file or from the server side with the Firebase Remote Config console. This particular instance will fetch the color value and set it as the layout's background.

Server-side parameters

Remote Config by definition allows developers to change the application to cater to their needs, including changing its behavior and functionality remotely. Now that we have configured the application to work with Firebase Remote Config, the next step is to understand the process of overriding the in-app parameter with server-side parameters. Server-side parameters are declared through the Firebase Console.

To enable server-side parameters, visit the console at the following address: `https://console.firebase.google.com`. Then, choose your project if you already have one, or create one exclusively for Remote Config, as shown in the following screenshot:

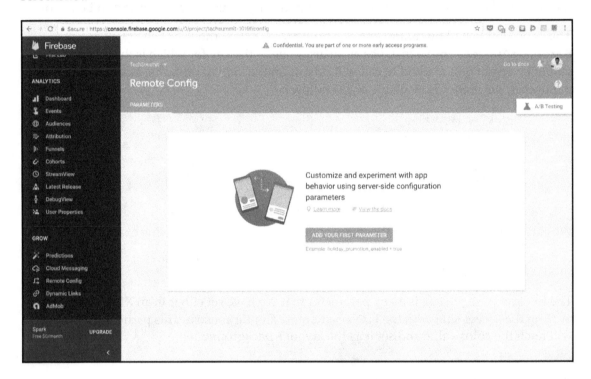

As you can see in the previous screenshot, clicking on the **Add Your First Parameter** button will prompt a dialog, inside which the key and value for the parameter can be entered. While including server-side parameters, the key must match that of the in-application parameter that is being overridden, shown as follows:

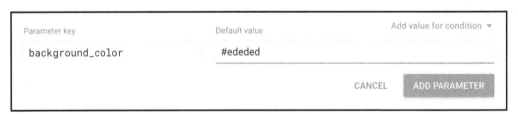

After adding it, the value will be added to the parameter list. Any changes can be made via the edit icon next to the list, and once everything has been finalized, the changes can be published by pressing the **Publish Changes** button, as shown in the following screenshot:

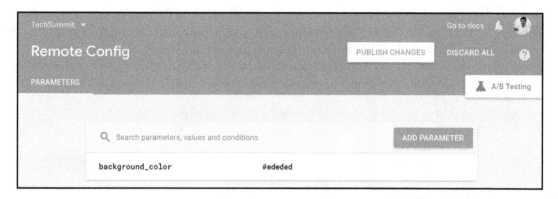

If you want to add another parameter, use the **Add Parameter** button at the bottom of the screen.

Fetching the parameters

Even if your server-side parameters have been proclaimed and distributed, nothing will change on the client's application unless the parameters have been fetched and activated. The fetching task is initiated through a call to the `fetch()` method in the `FirebaseRemoteConfig` object.

When the parameters are received, they are saved inside the cache of the `FirebaseRemoteConfig` object. As a matter of course, the cache will consider these parameters to be legitimate for 12 hours after being fetched. Any following `fetch` calls within that time period will keep on using the cached parameters. After the first 12 hours, the following fetch method call will download the parameters from the server:

```
fbRemoteConfig.fetch();
```

A shorter cache expiration length can be indicated by passing through the number of seconds desired as an argument to the `fetch()` method. We have set the cache to terminate after 60 minutes in the following example:

```
fbRemoteConfig.fetch(3600);
```

Practically speaking, the expiration time ought not to be set too low, as the demands of Remote Config's fetch method are vulnerable to throttling by the Firebase server. If an application makes too many fetch requests, future requests will be denied until a timeout period has passed.

When testing Remote Config during development, we recommend setting the cache timeout to zero with the idea that any changes can be tested instantly. To avoid server request rejections while testing the application, use the setConfigSettings() method of the FirebaseRemoteConfig object to enable the developer mode, shown as follows:

```
fbRemoteConfig.setConfigSettings(new FirebaseRemoteConfigSettings.Builder()
.setDeveloperModeEnabled(true)
.build());

fbRemoteConfig.fetch(0);
```

Note that the developer mode must be disabled before the application is distributed to clients.

The fetch task is an asynchronous call, so we need to add the completion listener in order to be notified when the task is complete. The following code illustrates this:

```
fbRemoteConfig.fetch(0).addOnCompleteListener(this, new
OnCompleteListener<Void>() {

@Override
open void onComplete(@NonNull Task<Void> assignment) {
if (task.isSuccessful())
{
//Fetch succeeded
} else {
//fetch failed
}
}
}
);
```

Now that we have received values for the application, we need to activate them.

Activating parameters

On successful fetching, we then need to activate the parameters before other methods access the values. To do this, we will add the call inside the `onComplete()` method, shown as follows:

```
public void onComplete(@NonNull Task<Void> task) {
        if (task.isSuccessful()) {
            fbRemoteConfig.activateFetched();
        } else {
// Fetch failed
        }
    }
```

Conditions, rules, and values

Condition and rules are used to target a specific set of users or app instances. Conditions are made up of one or multiple rules, which need to be true for all of the conditions in a particular app instance. If the value is not defined, the rule will be false by default:

We can define our new condition by clicking on **Add value for condition**, as seen in the previous screenshot. Note that we can also perform an A/B test with the old reference value and the new value:

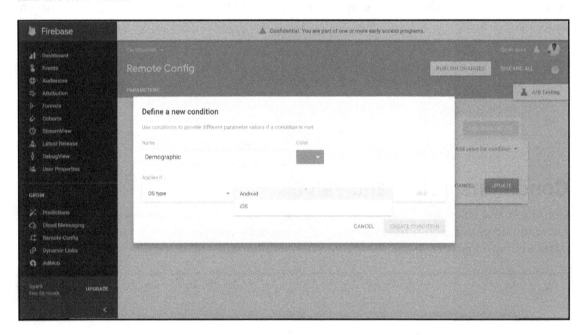

Some of the default and essential rules are as follows:

- **App ID** – This is the Android package name for the app
- **App version** – This is the app version as in the manifest
- **OS type** – This is a device's operating system, for example, Android or iOS
- **User in random percentile** – This targets a random sample of users up to a specified percentage of the overall user base and is helpful when implementing A/B testing to gauge users' reaction to any changes
- **User in audience** – This is a selection of user groups as defined by the Analytics feature in Firebase
- **Device in country/region** – These are users in one or more specific geographic regions
- **Device language** – This is the locale and language configured on a user's device
- **User property** – This targets users based on user properties configured by Firebase Analytics

By using the previous conditions, we can set the criteria for application behavior and changes.

Remote Config and Google Analytics

Remote Config is a one-of-a-kind tool, so when developers integrate Firebase with a project they can easily bridge the gap between Google Analytics and other Google services. Using Analytics with Remote Config has numerous benefits, such as being able to understand the application's users better and responding to their needs directly. Google Analytics allows developers, using user properties, to customize an app conveniently and accurately.

We have already explored Google Analytics in Chapter 9, *Application Usage Measuring and Notification, Firebase Analytics and Cloud Messaging.* We also have learned that Remote Config enables the use of user properties from Analytics to create conditions, allowing developers to customize the app more precisely than ever before.

Note that there are limitations in using Analytics with Remote Config, for example, user properties are permanent once assigned. However, we can also customize the following properties so that they are temporary:

- Countdown_timer
- Alarm_time
- Snooze_timing

These properties can be reevaluated according to the platform being used, the region, and any customization that has already been configured.

To set the user properties for Remote Config, we need to add the FirebaseAnalytics object instance, shown as follows:

```
private FirebaseAnalytics mFirebaseAnalytics;

// Obtain the FirebaseAnalytics instance.
mFirebaseAnalytics = FirebaseAnalytics.getInstance(this);
```

The previous code helps Google Analytics to start collecting the data.

A/B Testing with Remote Config

The following tutorial illustrates how Remote Config can help to change the UI and behavior of an application, as well as with A/B testing. A/B testing has enabled developers to understand how a user reacts to new features and which feature works best for them.

A/B testing presents an essentially infinite list of possible rules, implementations, and so on. In this example, we will aim to understand the basic ideology of A/B testing in Remote Config. To get started, complete the following steps:

1. Create a directory in your `res` folder and call it as an XML document.
2. Create a `remote_config.xml` file for adding the parameters
3. Configure the Firebase project and install the Remote Config library
4. Finally, use Kotlin to create the project

Make sure that you have added the latest Firebase dependency before following the previous steps, shown as follows:

```
implementation 'com.google.firebase:firebase-config:15.0.0'
```

Next, inside the `remote_config.xml` file, add the following code:

```xml
<?xml version="1.0" encoding="utf-8"?>
<defaultsMap>
    <entry>
        <key>onboarding</key>
        <value>None</value>
    </entry>
</defaultsMap>
```

Once finished, you can begin adding UI elements to the layout, as shown in the following example:

```xml
<?xml version="1.0" encoding="utf-8"?>
<RelativeLayout
    xmlns:android="http://schemas.android.com/apk/res/android"
    xmlns:tools="http://schemas.android.com/tools"
    android:layout_width="match_parent"
    android:layout_height="match_parent">

    <TextView
        android:id="@+id/bubble_top"
        android:layout_alignParentTop="true"
        android:visibility="invisible"
        android:text="TOP"
```

```
        android:textColor="@color/colorAccent"
        android:layout_height="wrap_content"
        android:layout_width="wrap_content"/>

    <TextView
        android:id="@+id/bubble_bottom"
        android:layout_alignParentBottom="true"
        android:visibility="invisible"
        android:text="BOTTOM"
        android:textColor="@color/colorAccent"
        android:layout_height="wrap_content"
        android:layout_width="wrap_content"/>


</RelativeLayout>
```

By default, both the buttons created using the previous code are invisible. Fetching the correct Remote Config value will make the buttons visible. Note that here we are also performing A/B testing on the same application.

Now, in your `Activity` code, you can enable the developer mode and start fetching the server-side values, as follows:

```
class MainActivity : AppCompatActivity() {

    private var mFirebaseAnalytics: FirebaseAnalytics? = null
    private var mFirebaseRemoteConfig: FirebaseRemoteConfig? = null
    private var experiment1_variant: String? = null


    override fun onCreate(savedInstanceState: Bundle?) {
        super.onCreate(savedInstanceState)
        setContentView(R.layout.activity_main)
        mFirebaseAnalytics = FirebaseAnalytics.getInstance(this);
        mFirebaseRemoteConfig = FirebaseRemoteConfig.getInstance();

        val configSettings = FirebaseRemoteConfigSettings.Builder()
            .setDeveloperModeEnabled(BuildConfig.DEBUG)
            .build()
        mFirebaseRemoteConfig?.setConfigSettings(configSettings)
        mFirebaseRemoteConfig?.setDefaults(R.xml.remoteconfig)
        fetchData()
    }


    private fun fetchData() {
        var cacheExpiration: Long = 3600 // 1 hour in seconds.
        if
```

```
(mFirebaseRemoteConfig?.info?.configSettings?.isDeveloperModeEnabled ==
true) {
        cacheExpiration = 0
    }
    Log.d("IID_TOKEN", FirebaseInstanceId.getInstance().token);
    mFirebaseRemoteConfig?.fetch(cacheExpiration)?.addOnCompleteListener
{ task ->
        if (task.isSuccessful) {
            mFirebaseRemoteConfig?.activateFetched()
            experiment1_variant =
mFirebaseRemoteConfig?.getString("onboarding")
            Log.d("welcome",""+experiment1_variant)
            mFirebaseAnalytics?.setUserProperty("MyExperiment",
experiment1_variant)
            if (experiment1_variant?.toLowerCase()?.contentEquals("top") ==
false) {
                bubble_top?.visibility = View.VISIBLE
                Toast.makeText(this,
""+experiment1_variant,Toast.LENGTH_LONG).show()
            } else {
                Toast.makeText(this,
""+experiment1_variant,Toast.LENGTH_LONG).show()
                bubble_bottom?.visibility = View.VISIBLE
            }
        }
    }
}
```

Once we have successfully compiled the program, and depending on Remote Config's value, the view in the console should look like the following screenshot:

As you can see, when the value is `top`, the `TextView` at the top is visible.

As you can see in the preceding screenshot, when the value is `bottom`, the text is visible at the bottom of the page.

So far, we have looked at how to fetch values from Remote Config with two different configurations. Now it's time to explore a more advanced feature offered by Remote Config, and that is A/B testing. Though the feature is still very much in development, it is stable enough to have in production applications.

Click on the **A/B Testing** button, as shown in the following screenshot. If you don't have an experiment available, you can create a new one by clicking on **Create experiment** and selecting the appropriate data metrics:

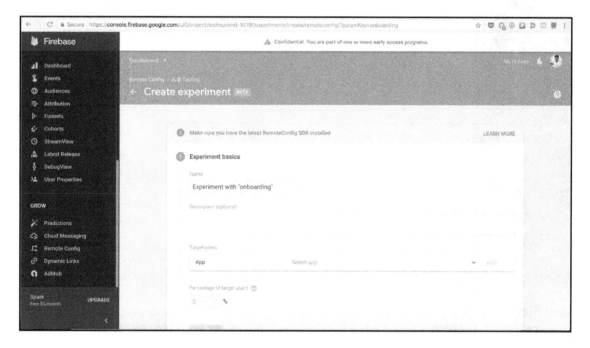

Enter the description of the experiment and select the target audience. Use the **AND** button to keep adding filters if you need to. Then, add the variants and their experimental values, as shown in the following screenshot:

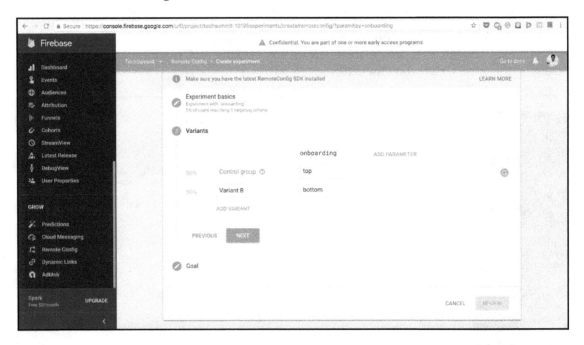

Last but not least, we need to select the resulting metric, which is very important when an application's success rate is defined by user engagement. Before starting an experiment, note that we can review it and also add a testing device. Once we have successfully added an experiment, we have to wait a few days to find the leader with two variants.

Firebase Dynamic Links

Firebase Dynamic Links helps us to create URL links that allow new users to install an application or enables deep linking within the application itself. In this chapter, we have already explored Remote Config and its customization tools. Now it's time to look at Dynamic Links so that your users can visit a particular page by simply clicking on a URL.

Social media or promotional campaigns use something similar to a URL, which is analyzed by the marketing team to check installs or page visits from potential users. There are many use cases available in Dynamic Links that will allow you to make the most of your application.

In addition, Dynamic Links can also prompt users to install an application if it is not already installed. (Dynamic Links supports iOS and Android at the time of writing.)

The main purpose of Dynamic Links is to permit application developers to create a URL that, when clicked, will either take the client to a particular location in an application or, if the application isn't yet installed, opens the relevant Google Play Store page so that it can be installed and launched. A site may, for instance, incorporate a **Download App in the Google Play Store** button, which utilizes a Dynamic Link.

Dynamic Links can also be utilized for sharing references to content inside an application itself. An application may, for instance, enable users to recommend to others specific content inside the app. When a user follows such a link, the application will open and utilize the Dynamic Link to display the relevant content.

Dynamic Links may likewise be configured with a fallback URL, which will open an assigned web page if launching or opening an application isn't possible. Dynamic connections are cross-platform and can be implemented on Android and iOS applications, or even utilized solely for online content.

In this section, we will explore all the things that are related to Dynamic Links.

To create a Dynamic Link, one can either use the Firebase console, the REST API, the iOS or Android Builder API, or construct the URL by adding link parameters to a domain specific to your app. Implementing Dynamic Links in Android is completely straightforward.

To configure Dynamic Links within your Android project, make sure you have connected your project to Firebase and have added the Dynamic Link SDK. Then, using the Firebase console or programmatically, Dynamic Links can be created.

After creating the Dynamic Link, you need to handle the link programmatically. Remember that you can also track the performance of a new Dynamic Link with analytics data.

Dynamic Links use cases

Web applications are great but mobile devices are becoming more popular and more trusted among users, as well as more familiar. Mobile phones are no longer used just for communication.

There are three convincing use cases of Dynamic Links. The first one is converting web users to app users. If a user opens a URL that isn't a Dynamic Link and then installs the application, they will simply be navigated to the launch activity. If the user has the Dynamic Link SDK, however, they can go to a specific screen that will provide developers with analytical information.

The second use case involves campaigns. Social media, email, and SMS campaigns are easy to publish to a specific set of users or even a single user. If your application has enough users and you monetize your app through ad services, you can also send offers through to specific users.

The third use case involves real-world app promotions.

Converting mobile web users to native app users

Converting mobile web users to native application users has become a necessity because of the performance anomaly of mobile web applications, where the user experience is less than desirable. Even if you have built a groundbreaking mobile web application, your conversion rate will be higher if you allow users to download the native mobile application.

Mobile-responsive web applications should navigate to the Play Store with a direct download link on your application. This will give developers a higher conversion rate – and users a better experience.

Dynamic Links make the process of implementing an action from a click much easier for developers. Some of the key advantages of Dynamic Links are as follows:

- It can turn mobile web users into native app users
- It allows users to open the app, which has the same content as the web application
- It enables simple integration

Dynamic Links also helps to make your application's content deep-linkable. If we just promote the native application, users may not install it. Consider the application Quora, for example, a blogging platform where people share knowledge about different areas. When a mobile web user clicks on a particular link, Quora opens the same content in the native application rather than using the web. This feature soon turned most of Quora's mobile web users into daily, active native application users.

This feature can be implemented in iOS using universal links and in Android using Android App links. Configure the Dynamic Link's SDK to your project and add open in-app links to your web pages with the following code:

```
implementation 'com.google.firebase:firebase-invites:15.0.1'
```

Add the previous dependency in the build-level Gradle file. The following code illustrates opening a specific screen:

```
<a
href="https://abc123.app.goo.gl/?link=https://example.com/content?item%3D12
34&apn=com.example.android&ibi=com.example.ios">Open this web page in your
app!</a>
```

To open the previous link within an Android application, we can use the `getInvitation()` and `getDeepLink()` methods, shown as follows:

```
AppInvite.AppInviteApi.getInvitation(mGoogleApiClient, this,
false).setResultCallback(/* ... */);

String link = AppInviteReferral.getDeepLink(intent);
```

We can also retrieve content through the `getDeepLink` method. As you can see from the previous examples, with just a few lines of code we can convert mobile web users to native application users.

Sharing content between users

Word of mouth is a great way to get publicity, and sharing content is just another way of doing that. Here, we ask users to share an application with their friends either for referral points or because they believe the app is genuinely useful.

With Dynamic Links, we can create a great user-to-user sharing experience – when users receive a link from friend, they can directly land on the content page. This happens even if the user is a new user or is installing the application for the first time.

There are some key benefits of using Firebase Dynamic Links in this way, and they are as follows:

- It offers a great sharing experience and allows users to connect with each other in the application
- The first run experience for users can be customized

- It makes the sharing of content between users and their family and friends easy across multiple platforms

In Android, we can add a share button with the material design guidelines and ask existing users to share the application, as shown in the following code:

```
Intent sendIntent = new Intent(); String msg = "Hey, check this out: " +
myDynamicLink; sendIntent.setAction(Intent.ACTION_SEND);
sendIntent.putExtra(Intent.EXTRA_TEXT, msg);
sendIntent.setType("text/plain"); startActivity(sendIntent);
```

The previous code generates shareable dialog.

We can retrieve this using the following two methods:

```
AppInvite.AppInviteApi.getInvitation(mGoogleApiClient, this,
false).setResultCallback(/* ... */);

String link = AppInviteReferral.getDeepLink(intent);
```

It's important that we have a good content sharing experience because of how quickly data grows. Sharing experience should be easy and rewarding.

Rewarding referrals using Firebase

We all like to be rewarded. Recent research has shown that people play games to increase their score even if that score has no monetary value. Reward points are therefore an effective way of attracting new users. For instance, the Google Tez application utilized referral points and a cashback initiative for those who installed the application. Using Firebase Realtime Database and functions, we can automate this referral process.

The benefits of implementing a referral process are as follows:

- The growth rate of an application will increase with a reward scheme
- Invitation links work across all platforms
- New users will receive a customized first run experience; they are also able to connect with the friend who invited them
- Delaying rewards can also be implemented based on certain conditions, such as completing the sign-up process

We can create an invitation link with the following code:

```
FirebaseUser user = FirebaseAuth.getInstance().getCurrentUser();
String uid = user.getUid();
String link = "https://mygame.example.com/?invitedby=" + uid;
FirebaseDynamicLinks.getInstance().createDynamicLink()
.setLink(Uri.parse(link))
.setDynamicLinkDomain("abc123.app.goo.gl")
.setAndroidParameters(
new DynamicLink.AndroidParameters.Builder("com.example.android")
.setMinimumVersion(125)
.build())
.setIosParameters(
new DynamicLink.IosParameters.Builder("com.example.ios")
.setAppStoreId("123456789")
.setMinimumVersion("1.0.1")
.build())
.buildShortDynamicLink()
.addOnSuccessListener(new OnSuccessListener<ShortDynamicLink>() {
@Override
public void onSuccess(ShortDynamicLink shortDynamicLink) {
mInvitationUrl = shortDynamicLink.getShortLink();
}
});
```

To send invitations, we can use the following intent mechanism:

```
String referringUserName =
FirebaseAuth.getInstance().getCurrentUser().getDisplayName();
String subject = String.format("%s wants you to Read this Packt Book",
referringUserName);
String invitationLink = mInvitationUrl.toString();
String msg = "Let's play MyExampleGame together! Use my referrer link: "
+ invitationLink;
String msgHtml = String.format("<p>Let's read the packt junit5 book"
+ "<a href=\"%s\">referrer link</a>!</p>", invitationLink);Intent intent =
new Intent(Intent.ACTION_SENDTO);
intent.setData(Uri.parse("mailto:")); // only email apps should handle this
intent.putExtra(Intent.EXTRA_SUBJECT, subject);
intent.putExtra(Intent.EXTRA_TEXT, msg);
intent.putExtra(Intent.EXTRA_HTML_TEXT, msgHtml);
if (intent.resolveActivity(getPackageManager()) != null) {
startActivity(intent);
}
```

To retrieve the referral information regarding your application, use the following code:

```
@Override
protected void onCreate(Bundle savedInstanceState) {
FirebaseDynamicLinks.getInstance()
.getDynamicLink(getIntent())
.addOnSuccessListener(this, new OnSuccessListener<PendingDynamicLinkData>()
{
@Override
public void onSuccess(PendingDynamicLinkData pendingDynamicLinkData) {
Uri deepLink = null;
if (pendingDynamicLinkData != null) {
deepLink = pendingDynamicLinkData.getLink();
}
FirebaseUser user = FirebaseAuth.getInstance().getCurrentUser();
if (user == null
&& deepLink != null
&& deepLink.getBooleanQueryParameter("invitedby")) {
String referrerUid = deepLink.getQueryParameter("invitedby");
createAnonymousAccountWithReferrerInfo(referrerUid);
}
}
});
}

private void createAnonymousAccountWithReferrerInfo(final String
referrerUid) {
FirebaseAuth.getInstance()
.signInAnonymously()
.addOnSuccessListener(new OnSuccessListener<AuthResult>() {
@Override
public void onSuccess(AuthResult authResult) {
FirebaseUser user = FirebaseAuth.getInstance().getCurrentUser();
DatabaseReference userRecord =
FirebaseDatabase.getInstance().getReference()
.child("users")
.child(user.getUid());
userRecord.child("referred_by").setValue(referrerUid);
}
});
}
```

Once a user's account has been authorized, we can use the `AuthCredential` object to register them, shown as follows:

```
AuthCredential credential = EmailAuthProvider.getCredential(email,
password);
```

We can also link accounts to the Firebase anonymous account using the following code:

```
FirebaseAuth.getInstance().getCurrentUser()
.linkWithCredential(credential)
.addOnSuccessListener(new OnSuccessListener<AuthResult>() {
@Override
public void onSuccess(AuthResult authResult) {

}
});
```

Once the relevant app-level configuration is complete, we need to have a system that actually grants the rewards to the referrer and the recipient. For that, we will make use of some Javascript code with Node.JS running in Firebase, as follows:

```
const functions = require('firebase-functions');
const admin = require('firebase-admin');
admin.initializeApp(functions.config().firebase);

exports.grantSignupReward =
functions.database.ref('/users/{uid}/last_signin_at')
.onCreate(event => {
var uid = event.params.uid;
admin.database().ref(`users/${uid}/referred_by`)
.once('value').then(function(data) {
var referred_by_somebody = data.val();
if (referred_by_somebody) {
var moneyRef = admin.database()
.ref(`/users/${uid}/inventory/pieces_of_eight`);
moneyRef.transaction(function (current_value) {
return (current_value || 0) + 50;
});
}
});
});
```

After the successful callback of a Realtime Database, trigger the function `linkWithCredential` success listener, as follows:

```
FirebaseAuth.getInstance().getCurrentUser()
.linkWithCredential(credential)
.addOnSuccessListener(new OnSuccessListener<AuthResult>() {
@Override
public void onSuccess(AuthResult authResult) {
FirebaseUser user = FirebaseAuth.getInstance().getCurrentUser();
DatabaseReference userRecord =
FirebaseDatabase.getInstance().getReference()
```

```
.child("users")
.child(user.getUid());
userRecord.child("last_signin_at").setValue(ServerValue.TIMESTAMP);
}
});
```

Using the Firebase service, we can automate a fully-fledged referral backend and application business logic.

The anatomy of Dynamic Links

Dynamic Links can be used with both short and long-form URLs that can later hide the URL content.

A typical example of a dynamic URL is as follows:

```
http://<appCode>.app.goo.gl/?apn=<packageName>&link=
<deeplinkUrl>&ad=<value>&afl=<fallbackUrl>&amv=
<version>&utm_source=<utmSource>&utm_medium=
<utmMedium>&utm_campaign=<utmCampaign>&utm_term=
<utmTerm>&utm_content=<utmContent>?st=<title>?sd=<description>?si=
<imageink>
```

In a dynamic URL, the tags will be replaced by the following values:

- `<appcode>`: This is a unique code that identifies the Firebase project
- `<packageName>`: This is the package name of the application
- `<deeplinkUrl>`: This is the URL passed to the application for deep-linking a specific page
- `<ad>`: This tag can be used to advertise certain campaigns
- `<fallbackURL>`: This applies when a clicked URL fails to launch or install an application
- `<version>`: This is the minimum version of the application
- `<utmSource>`: This is used in promotional and ad campaigns

There are also other tags that can construct a dynamic URL, including `<st>`,`<sd>`, and `<si>`.

Creating Dynamic Links

Developers can create Dynamic Links using Dynamic Links Builder API. This API can accept any form of Dynamic Link.

To create a Dynamic Link, use the `buildDynamicLink` or `buildShortDynamicLink` methods of the Builder API, shown as follows:

```
DynamicLink dynamicLink =
FirebaseDynamicLinks.getInstance().createDynamicLink()
.setLink(Uri.parse("https://packt.com/"))
.setDynamicLinkDomain("com.firebase.mastering.in")
.setAndroidParameters(new DynamicLink.AndroidParameters.Builder().build())
.setIosParameters(new
DynamicLink.IosParameters.Builder("com.firebase.mastering.in").build())
.buildDynamicLink();

Uri dynamicLinkUri = dynamicLink.getUri();
```

The previous code illustrates how to create a dynamic URL programmatically and also how to handle a dynamic URL on both an iOS and Android platform.

To create a short URL, use the `ShortDynamicLink` class as follows:

```
Task<ShortDynamicLink> shortLinkTask =
FirebaseDynamicLinks.getInstance().createDynamicLink()
```

Now, we can start constructing the data using setter methods.

The following code will create a link with several common elements of data:

```
DynamicLink dynamicLink =
FirebaseDynamicLinks.getInstance().createDynamicLink()
.setLink(Uri.parse("https://example.com/"))
.setDynamicLinkDomain("abc123.app.goo.gl")
.setAndroidParameters(
new DynamicLink.AndroidParameters.Builder("com.example.android")
.setMinimumVersion(125)
.build())
.setIosParameters(
new DynamicLink.IosParameters.Builder("com.example.ios")
.setAppStoreId("123456789")
.setMinimumVersion("1.0.1")
.build())
.setGoogleAnalyticsParameters(
new DynamicLink.GoogleAnalyticsParameters.Builder()
.setSource("orkut")
```

```
.setMedium("social")
.setCampaign("example-promo")
.build())
.setItunesConnectAnalyticsParameters(
new DynamicLink.ItunesConnectAnalyticsParameters.Builder()
.setProviderToken("123456")
.setCampaignToken("example-promo")
.build())
.setSocialMetaTagParameters(
new DynamicLink.SocialMetaTagParameters.Builder()
.setTitle("Example of a Dynamic Link")
.setDescription("This link works whether the app is installed or not!")
.build())
.buildDynamicLink(); // Or buildShortDynamicLink()
```

After creating the URL, it's now time to make it elegant. In the next section, we will explore how to read a received link.

Receiving Dynamic Links

Once we receive Dynamic Links, we can process them through the simple intent filter, shown as follows:

```
<intent-filter>
    <action android:name="android.intent.action.VIEW"/>
    <category android:name="android.intent.category.DEFAULT"/>
    <category android:name="android.intent.category.BROWSABLE"/>
    <data android:host="yoursite.example.com" android:scheme="http"/>
    <data android:host="yoursite.example.com" android:scheme="https"/>
</intent-filter>
```

We can also handle deep links by calling the `getDynamicLink` method as follows:

```
FirebaseDynamicLinks.getInstance()
        .getDynamicLink(getIntent())
        .addOnSuccessListener(this, new
OnSuccessListener<PendingDynamicLinkData>() {
            @Override
            public void onSuccess(PendingDynamicLinkData
pendingDynamicLinkData) {
                // Get deep link from result (may be null if no link is
found)
                Uri deepLink = null;
                if (pendingDynamicLinkData != null) {
                    deepLink = pendingDynamicLinkData.getLink();
                }
```

```
            }
    })
    .addOnFailureListener(this, new OnFailureListener() {
        @Override
        public void onFailure(@NonNull Exception e) {
            Log.w(TAG, "getDynamicLink:onFailure", e);
        }
    });
```

We can record analytics automatically when we use Dynamic Links. To help us to measure the effectiveness of Dynamic Links, their details will be logged in the Firebase console. This includes events tracked, data access, and campaign attributions.

Firebase Dynamic Links' analytics keep track of clicks, redirects, installs, first-opens, and much more.

Summary

Remote Config and Dynamic Links are very powerful tools. In this chapter, we have explored how to set parameter values in the Firebase console for Remote Config and also how to retrieve it on the application side. We also looked at A/B testing in Remote Config. With Dynamic Links, we have looked at its use cases and learned how to create and receive Dynamic Links. You should now have a good idea of how to share data using Dynamic Links.

In the next chapter, we will expand on what we've learned in this chapter and look at Firebase app invites and application indexing.

11
Bringing Everyone on the Same Page, Firebase Invites, and Firebase App Indexing

"Promotions cannot happen when you cross your fingers, you need to put in a decent amount of effort."

— Unknown

Firebase Invites offers a way for users to promote the application to other potential users. Firebase Invites is a unique service for application referrals and sharing by means of email, SMS, or any means of communication developers intend. To make the invite user experience easier and more helpful or to produce links programmatically, we can utilize Firebase Dynamic Links. Word of mouth is a great medium for promoting products.

In a recent study on 1,000 smartphone users, researchers found that the primary reason why people installed the certain app is due to the fact that it was recommended by a friend or colleague. Firebase Invites is a straightforward solution to make your existing users into your applications strongest advocates.

Firebase Invites can be integrated easily and also can be achieved programmatically in very few lines of code. When the user chooses to refer your app to someone else, Firebase handles all aspects of the invitation process, including presenting an invitation dialog from which recipients may be selected and transmitting the messages to the chosen recipients.

The invitation takes the form of an email or SMS message containing a Firebase Dynamic Link URL which, when clicked, takes the user to the page within the Google Play Store from which the app can be installed. Once the app has been installed, the dynamic link is passed to the app when it is launched, allowing the custom behavior to be implemented using the steps outlined in the previous chapter. In this chapter, we will explore two popular Firebase tools and their concepts, as listed here:

- Overview of Firebase Invites and Firebase App Indexing
- Sending and receiving invites from Android applications
- Enabling public content indexing
- Enabling personal content indexing
- Logging user actions
- Testing your implementations
- Enhancing search performance and migrating to the latest API

Firebase Invites

The title of the tool clearly implies something about inviting. Perhaps this is the time to explore what Firebase offers as a platform to recommend your application to a user's friends, colleagues, and so on. If you think you have built a perfect and great application and you don't know how to reach a vast amount of users, think of the old saying "word of mouth is the best way to reach people". Here in Firebase Invites, we will integrate a rich sharing mechanism and if your existing users like the product, they do not have to write a big email and don't have to undertake any kind of trouble since Firebase helps in simplifying the whole process of recommending your application.

In `Chapter 10`, *Firebase Remote Config and Dynamic Links,* we explored dynamic links, which actually play a great role in inviting users. To implement an easy sharing experience, Firebase handles the invitation flow for you, this helps you to focus on some of the unfinished features of your application without spending much time on the inviting process.

Since the invitation is built on top of dynamic links, invitations work across the Play Store installation process and also ensure that the user will get the referral code or shared content. Firebase Invites combines the most common sharing channels in the platform, including iOS and Android. It also offers a merged contacts selector that populates the user contacts on a share screen from the user's Google contacts and the contacts stored on their phone.

Firebase manages to identify wise recommendations on the contacts that the user communicates with more often. Application developers and marketing teams always want to customize the invitation message for a number of reasons and Firebase Invites allows us to customize a message that can have both defaults and allows to edit the invite content. Android users can also invite without signing in to the application.

Firebase Invites smartly takes the users to the App Store or Play Store depending on the invites dynamic link, if it is a web user they will be directed to the specific page. Also since Firebase Invites uses dynamic links, this makes sure that the link contained in the invitation doesn't get lost.

The whole process of inviting triggers from a share button click event that usually shows a popup for sharing through SMS and email. The user will choose contacts and they can email or send SMS with the dynamic link to the application. Handling links in Android is straightforward using intent-filters. Identify a good UX for the share button inside your application. Set up the Firebase invite SDK to set up sharing the screen.

Sending and receiving invites from Android applications

Firebase Invites integration is similar to the process we followed for other Firebase tools. Connect your application to Firebase and add the tools dependency, that's all it takes to integrate them. Before you integrate the invite, please make sure you have enabled the dynamic links and you enable it from Firebase console too. At the time of writing, Firebase's latest release was 15.0.1, the dependency is shown as follows:

```
implementation 'com.google.firebase:firebase-invites:15.0.1'
```

Add this to your `build.gradle` app-level dependency and download the repository by clicking on **Sync now**.

Sending invitations usually starts from an intent with the `AppInviteInvitation.IntentBuilder` class. When users click on the **Share** button, this class handles the smart sharing mechanism. Consider the following code:

```
private void onInviteClicked() {
    Intent intent = new
AppInviteInvitation.IntentBuilder(getString(R.string.invitation_title))
            .setMessage(getString(R.string.invitation_message))
.setDeepLink(Uri.parse(getString(R.string.invitation_deep_link)))
.setCustomImage(Uri.parse(getString(R.string.invitation_custom_image)))
            .setCallToActionText(getString(R.string.invitation_cta))
```

```
                .build();
        startActivityForResult(intent, REQUEST_INVITE);
}
```

When a user clicks on the **Share** button, it shows a share intent with the App icon, an integrated deep link, and also `CallToActionText`. A number of methods are available for customizing the intent, including the following:

- `setMessage()` – Used to declare a default message to be included with the invitation. This default text can be modified by the user within the invitation dialog before the message is sent.

- `setDeepLink()` – The deep link URL that is to be embedded into the dynamic link sent with the message. This can be used to pass information to the app when it is installed and launched by the message recipient.

- `setCustomImage()` – Allows an image to be included in the message. The image can be up to 4000x4000 pixels in size, though 600x600 pixels is the recommended size.

- `setCallToActionText()` – The text that is to appear on the **Install** button included within email messages. The text is limited to 32 characters.

- `setEmailHtmlContent()` – Allows HTML content to be defined for email-based invitations. The dynamic link URL should be substituted by the `%%APPINVITE_LINK_PLACEHOLDER%%` string. This method must be used in conjunction with the `setEmailSubject()` method. When using HTML content, the `setMessage()`, `setCustomImage()`, and `setCallToActionText()` methods are redundant.

- `setEmailSubject()` – Used to set the email subject line when using HTML content.

- `setGoogleAnalyticsTrackingId()` – Allows a Google Analytics tracking ID to be specified to track the performance of the invitation. The following code fragment shows an example invitation that makes use of HTML content:

```
var intent = AppInviteInvitation.IntentBuilder("My Invitation")
        .setDeepLink(Uri.parse("http://www.mackt.com/"))
        .setEmailSubject("I recommend this app")
        .setEmailHtmlContent("<body><p>I've been using this app." +
            ".<p>You should try it. " +
            "You can use this " +
            "<a href=\"%%APPINVITE_LINK_PLACEHOLDER%%\">link</a>" +
            " to install it on your Android device.</p></body>")
        .build()
startActivityForResult(intent, INVITE_REQUEST);
```

Handling the activity result took place through the onActivityResult override method, as follows:

```
override protected fun onActivityResult(requestCode: Int, resultCode: Int,
data: Intent) {
    super.onActivityResult(requestCode, resultCode, data)
    Log.d(TAG, "onActivityResult: requestCode=$requestCode,
resultCode=$resultCode")

    if (requestCode == REQUEST_INVITE) {
        if (resultCode == RESULT_OK) {
            // Get the invitation IDs of all sent messages
            val ids = AppInviteInvitation.getInvitationIds(resultCode,
data)
            for (id in ids) {
                Log.d(TAG, "onActivityResult: sent invitation $id")
            }
        } else {
            // Sending failed or it was canceled, show failure message to
the user
            // ...
        }
    }
}
```

When a user receives an invitation, if the user has not yet installed the application they can choose to install the app from Google Play Store. After the application installation at the event of application start, it will receive the URL content if you have sent the exclusive content. To handle this use case, dynamic link offers a method called getDynamicLink, illustrated as follows:

```
override fun onCreate(savedInstanceState: Bundle?) {
    // ...

    // Check for App Invite invitations and launch deep-link activity if
possible.
    // Requires that an Activity is registered in AndroidManifest.xml to
handle
    // deep-link URLs.
    FirebaseDynamicLinks.getInstance().getDynamicLink(intent)
            .addOnSuccessListener(this, object :
OnSuccessListener<PendingDynamicLinkData>() {
                fun onSuccess(data: PendingDynamicLinkData?) {
                    if (data == null) {
                        Log.d(FragmentActivity.TAG, "getInvitation: no
data")
                        return
```

```
            }

            // Get the deep link
            val deepLink = data!!.getLink()

            // Extract invite
            val invite = FirebaseAppInvite.getInvitation(data)
            if (invite != null) {
                val invitationId = invite!!.getInvitationId()
            }

            // Handle the deep link
            // ...
        }
    })
    .addOnFailureListener(this, object : OnFailureListener() {
        fun onFailure(e: Exception) {
            Log.w(FragmentActivity.TAG, "getDynamicLink:onFailure",
e)
        }
    })
}
```

You should call `getDynamicLink()` in each action that may be opened by the link, despite the fact that the link may be accessible from the intent using `getIntent().getData()`. Calling `getDynamicLink()` recovers the link and invite ID, and clears that information so it is just handled once by your application.

There are some best practices that we need to follow if we are using the Firebase Invite and Dynamic links:

- Make sure the share button is easy to notice. You can place it inside the navigation drawer or some prominent place, but not hidden inside such as in a settings menu or about app section.
- Try building a custom share sheet.
- Offer incentives for those who are clicking on the link.
- Customize invites to emphasize the purpose of the application.

Firebase also has some case studies posted in the documentation for two applications, you should check them out. Now let's explore App Indexing our Android mobile application.

 Case studies can be found at the following link:
https://firebase.google.com/docs/invites/case-studies

Firebase App Indexing

Search engine optimization, also known as SEO, allows the content of a web application to be discoverable in search engines such as Google, Bing, and so on. App Indexing is a similar technique for allowing in-app content to be discoverable in mobile or web search results.

It increases the user base and also user engagement. If the user has already installed the app they can directly go to the content-specific screen. App Indexing establishes a good amount of engagement with your app users by finding both public and personal content on the device. It also helps in the process of search autocompletion to help the users. If the user doesn't have the app, search results will show a card to the user that helps them to install the application.

One of the difficulties confronting application developers today is figuring out how to encourage users to use an application once it has been installed on a device. While some applications such as news or informal community applications tend to encounter visits, numerous applications will stay unused in the wake of being installed on the user's device. One answer for this includes giving the client notifications that endeavor to give them the motivation to open the application. Another choice is to make use of App Indexing. With application ordering, when a client has an application installed and performs an important search either on the web or device, the coordinating content inside the application will show up inside the query items. At the point when the result is clicked, the application will launch and exhibit the content to the user.

Application Indexing may likewise be utilized to log the activities performed by users inside the application in relation to the content. These activities are then used to enhance the positioning of your content when the user performs a content-related Google search and furthermore to give autocomplete proposals while the user is entering a search inquiry.

Firebase App Indexing categorizes application content as either public or personal. The public content is content related to the application that is visible to all application users. This can appear as content given by the application, or content included by users with the understanding that it will be made visible to every single other user. Personal content, then again, is content that is included by users exclusively for their own personal use. While actualizing application ordering, it is vital to separate the public and personal content and activities with the goal that a user privacy of the data is ensured.

What feature works for your application?

App Indexing offers an improvement to the public content indexing and logging for user actions with both public and personal content of the application. Depending on your app's use cases, the following glance guide helps you to choose what to index from your app:

App content type	Public content indexing (Android and iOS)	Personal content indexing (Android only)	Log user actions (Android only)
Public content only Users don't create personal content in these apps, for example, Article post on Quora.	Yes		Yes
Personal content only The content in these apps is almost exclusively tied to a specific user, for example, a messaging app such as Gmail or a productivity app such as Keep.		Yes	Yes
Both public and personal content These are the apps that have both in app-generated public content and user-generated personal content.	Yes	Yes	Yes

There are so many use case studies that Firebase offers on the App Indexing subject. You can find them at the following link: `https://firebase.google.com/docs/app-indexing/`.

To implement App Indexing, the first and primary action is to associate your website with the mobile application and later associate your app to parse the HTTP URLs that match links to your website and the application. Within the device, enable the personal content that populated search results in the Google app on Android. For many use cases, you can log the user actions so that Firebase can suggest the pages they have visited. You can test your implementation using the search preview tool to validate that your App Indexing operates as expected. Developers can also analyze the impact quality of the content using the search console.

Enabling public content indexing

Before we jump into understanding public content indexing, let's get our development environment for Firebase Invite ready. Similar to how we followed the Firebase configuration in other Firebase services, we need to connect the application to Firebase before adding the tool dependency, and then later just add the following dependency to your app-level `build.gradle` script:

```
implementation 'com.google.firebase:firebase-appindexing:15.0.0'
```

Now right after configuring `firebase-appindexing` into your project, you are all set to understand indexing. Before we continue exploring indexing, Firebase has mentioned a few necessary things on indexing such as structuring the website and application in similar visual patterns. So the URLs that redirect us to particular pages will also take us to a particular screen in your Android application.

Google search fetches the data through its search engine mechanism for the links, and later it uses it to send users to your application directly.

Public content indexing incorporates links to application content inside Google search query items, despite whether the search inquiry is performed on the Google search site or using the Google application on the device. On the off chance that the client has the application installed and application indexing has been implemented, the user can tap the link to launch the application and get to the content. As will be exhibited in a later section, the search query items on the device show up on the **Apps** page of the Google search page.

Public content indexing involves indexing content that is thought to be accessible to all users and must be implemented if the content inside the application specifically corresponds to the content structure of a website. Deep Link URLs that launch the right content inside the application must match the URL to achieve similar content inside the website. Consider, for instance, a site that contains portrayals of painting frames. The URLs for some pages may be organized as follows:

```
http://www.packtpaintings.com/paints/monalisa
```

```
http://www.packtpaintings.com/paints/picasso
```

```
http://www.packtpaintings.com/paints/Davinci
```

Unmistakably, entering one of the preceding URLs into a browser's search bar would stack the website page for the relative paintings. We can expect that the site likewise has a companion Android application containing the same content. Keeping in mind the end goal to have the support for application indexing, the application must acknowledge similar URLs as Deep Links and show similar content.

In a normal situation, the user may install the application, view data about the Davinci, and then proceed to close the application. Sooner or later the same user may perform a Google search for the Da Vinci paintings using the Chrome program or Google application.

Firebase App Indexing will perceive that the search inquiry identifies with content that the client already saw within the application and give a link to the application-based content inside the indexed lists. Choosing the connection will dispatch the application and shows the Da Vinci painting related content to the user. When content has been publicly indexed, it can possibly show up in list items for users that have yet to install the application. In this circumstance, an install button will show up alongside the search query item, giving a helpful installation path for new users.

As mentioned in this chapter, public content indexing requires coordinating website and application content, both accessible using the same URL structure. Accepting that this necessity has been met, public content indexing is essentially a matter of connecting the website with the application. This is accomplished by placing a JSON config file on the website containing data about the companion application as a digital resource file.

The JSON file must be named `assetlinks.json` and must be situated in the well known directory of the site. A digital resource link contains a relation proclamation conceding authorization for a target application to be launched using the site's link URLs and an objective proclamation pronouncing the partner application package name and SHA-256 finger print. An ordinary resource link file may, for instance, read as follows:

```
[{
    "relation": ["delegate_permission/common.handle_all_urls"],
    "target" : { "namespace": "android_app",
        "package_name": "<app package name here>",
        "sha256_cert_fingerprints": ["<app certificate here>"] }
}]
```

The asset `links.json` document can contain various digital resource links, conceivably permitting a single website to be related within excess of one companion application. At the point when the application is launched as the result of a link click, the Android application link mechanism is used to launch the application and go through the URL. Much like Firebase Dynamic Links, the target application must be set up to deal with the application intent. The initial step involves adding an intent-filter channel for the target activity inside the project `AndroidManifest.xml` file:

```
<activity android:name=".PaintingHomeActivity">
<intent-filter>
<action android:name="android.intent.action.MAIN" />
<action android:name="android.intent.action.VIEW" />
<category android:name="android.intent.category.DEFAULT" />
<category android:name="android.intent.category.BROWSABLE" />
<data
android:host="packtpaintings.com"
android:pathPrefix="/paintings"
android:scheme="http" />
</intent-filter>
</activity>
```

When the application is launched, intent needs to be handled, as follows:

```
Intent intent = getIntent();
String action = intent.getAction();
String data = intent.getDataString(); // Get the URL
if (Intent.ACTION_VIEW.equals(action) && data != null) {
  // Code here to parse URL and display content
}
```

Developers can exclude screen by adding it into the metadata through an XML resource file. Using the `<noindex>` tag we can tell indexing to not index some of the data. Add the following lines of codes into a projects `xml` folder and name it `noindex.xml`:

```
<?xml version="1.0" encoding="utf-8"?>
<search-engine xmlns:android="http://schemas.android.com/apk/res/android">
<noindex android:value="notification"/>
<noindex uri="http://packtpaintings.com/paintings/personal-data"/>
<noindex uriPrefix="http://packtpaintings.com/paintings/personal_prefix"/>
</search-engine>
```

Add `noindex.xml` to the `application` tag within the `manifest` file as follows:

```
<manifest xmlns:android="http://schemas.android.com/apk/res/android"
package="com.recipe_app">
<application>
```

```
<activity android:name=".art.GalleryActivity" ...>
...
</activity>
<meta-data android:name="search-engine" android:resource="@xml/noindex"/>
</application>
...
</manifest>
```

After doing all this, we need to check the public content in our search queries. Unfortunately, we don't have any console to check for more details on the setup we have accomplished, but we can test our implementation, which we will explore in a later section. Now let's look at how to enable personal content indexing.

Enabling personal content indexing

Personal content is user-produced content that is not expected to be seen by different users. The case vintage PC application may, for instance, give the choice for users to include notes about the cost and condition of a computer they are thinking about purchasing. Notes, for example, would be indexed as personal content.

Personal content indexes are stored locally on the device and appear just inside searches performed using the Google application and just when the owner signed into the device. Unlike public content indexing, personal content indexing does not require that the content additionally exists on a companion website.

Personal content indexing is achieved by making calls to the Firebase indexing API Content attached or added to the index on the device in the form of indexable objects that are formed using either indexable, builder, or one of the builders offered by Firebase indexing APIs. The following code creates a recipe note indexable object:

```
Indexable noteToIndex = Indexables.noteDigitalDocumentBuilder()
                .setName(recipe.getTitle() + " Note")
                .setText(note.getText())
                .setUrl(recipe.getNoteUrl())
                .build();
```

It is also good practice as a developer to make sure that the indexing happens on the background thread. If we want to achieve multiple indexing on a similar use case, consider going through the following code:

```
public class AppIndexingUpdateService extends JobIntentService {
    // Job-ID must be unique across your whole app.
    private static final int UNIQUE_JOB_ID = 42;
```

```java
public static void enqueueWork(Context context) {
    enqueueWork(context, AppIndexingUpdateService.class, UNIQUE_JOB_ID, new
Intent());
  }

  @Override
  protected void onHandleWork(@NonNull Intent intent) {
    // TODO Insert your Indexable objects — for example, the recipe notes
look as follows:

    ArrayList<Indexable> indexableNotes = new ArrayList<>();

    for (Recipe recipe : getAllRecipes()) {
        Note note = recipe.getNote();
        if (note != null) {
            Indexable noteToIndex = Indexables.noteDigitalDocumentBuilder()
                    .setName(recipe.getTitle() + " Note")
                    .setText(note.getText())
                    .setUrl(recipe.getNoteUrl())
                    .build();

            indexableNotes.add(noteToIndex);
        }
    }

    if (indexableNotes.size() > 0) {
        Indexable[] notesArr = new Indexable[indexableNotes.size()];
        notesArr = indexableNotes.toArray(notesArr);

        // batch insert indexable notes into index
        FirebaseAppIndex.getInstance().update(notesArr);
    }
  }
}
```

The preceding code indexes the details on `JobIntentService` from the Android SDK.

Another builder that is a convenient builder to add the indexable object to Firebase is `noteDigitalDocumentBuilder()`:

```java
var indexableNote = Indexables.noteDigitalDocumentBuilder()
        .setUrl("http://www.packtpainting.com/computers/atarist/comment")
        .setName("Davinci painting notes")
        .setText("Three in good condition on eBay")
        .setImage("http://www.packtpainting.com/paints/davinci.png")
        .setDateCreated(creationDate)
        .build()
```

After creating the indexable object, it needs to be added to the device. This use case needs a reference to the `firebaseAppindex` instance and we need to call its `update` method. Consider the following example:

```
Task<Void> task = FirebaseAppIndex.getInstance().update(indexableComputer);
task.addOnSuccessListener(new OnSuccessListener<Void>() {
    @Override
    public void onSuccess(Void aVoid) {
        // Content added to index
    }
});
task.addOnFailureListener(new OnFailureListener() {
    @Override
    public void onFailure(@NonNull Exception exception) {
        // Failed to add content to index
    }
});
```

This `Task` object returns the locally added personal content.

Through a broadcast receiver `AppIndexingUpdateService` class, whenever there is an update sent by Google Play Services it will update the on-device index:

```
class AppIndexingUpdateReceiver : BroadcastReceiver() {

    fun onReceive(context: Context, intent: Intent?) {
        if (intent != null &&
FirebaseAppIndex.ACTION_UPDATE_INDEX.equals(intent.action)) {
            // Schedule the job to be run in the background.
            AppIndexingUpdateService.enqueueWork(context)
        }
    }
}
```

Add the receiver in your projects manifest as follows:

```
<receiver android:name=".AppIndexingUpdateReceiver"
        android:exported="true"
android:permission="com.google.android.gms.permission.APPINDEXING">
    <intent-filter>
        <action android:name="com.google.firebase.appindexing.UPDATE_INDEX"
/>
    </intent-filter>
</receiver>
```

It also requires the wakelock permission with the service also registering inside manifest, as follows:

```
<uses-permission android:name="android.permission.WAKE_LOCK" />
<service android:name=".AppIndexingUpdateService"
        android:permission="android.permission.BIND_JOB_SERVICE" />
```

Users can update a personal index there. For this we can use the `update` method and update the indexes:

```
private void indexNote() {
        Note note = mRecipe.getNote();
        Indexable noteToIndex = Indexables.noteDigitalDocumentBuilder()
                .setName(mRecipe.getTitle())
                .setText(note.getText())
                .setUrl(mRecipe.getNoteUrl())
                .build();

        Task<Void> task =
FirebaseAppIndex.getInstance().update(noteToIndex);
        ...
    }
```

If a user logs out of the device and some other user logs into the application, we can delete the indexes by using the following method:

```
FirebaseAppIndex.getInstance().removeAll();
```

The preceding method will remove all the indexes from the device.

Logging user actions

Google search queries utilize the data relating to the actions of users on public content and personal content to improve the ranking for search results and suggestions. There are limitations and restrictions on what kind of data you can log. Firebase documentation mentions the following as guidelines to follow:

- Log user interactions like viewing content: New content created, sharing content
- Only log actions that users take on content: Not background actions such as incoming texts, and so on
- Do not log actions: Do not log actions for each item of interactions, for instance, transition of screens and button tap events

Through URL and the appropriate action type, one can create an action object. By using the `start()` and `end()` methods, one can log the actions:

```
FirebaseUserActions.getInstance().start(getRecipeViewAction());
```

To constrict actions we can use the `Action` class and add the necessary information to the object. Consider the following example:

```
// This is just to build the knowledge but this method is legacy way
setting action.
var action = Action.Builder(Action.Builder.VIEW_ACTION)
        .setObject("Davinici",
"http://www.packtpaintings.com/paints/davinci")
        .build()
```

In addition to the preceding method, the `Action` object can be created using the `newView()` method as follows:

```
var action = Actions.newView("davinci",
"http://www.packtpaintings.com/paints/davinci")
```

Before action can be logged, content needs to be indexed. To end the user action logs you can make use of the following code:

```
FirebaseUserActions.getInstance().end(action); // action ends
```

Testing your implementation

Now let us identify the ways to test applications and App Indexing mechanisms in debug mode and also in production applications. Testing the URL's is one of the primary activities that we need to do. To test the URL we can make use of Android Studio Lint 2.x, which identifies the syntax errors and flags them for you in intent-filters. It automatically scans the manifest and raised errors in your manifest directly.

Another way is to analyze the syntax manually, to do this go to the **Analyze | Inspect code** option of Android Studio. HTTP URL errors are identified by the red underlines. Now you can also test your URLs through Android Debug Bridge or the URL QR code testing tool.

Using ADB we can test the URLs as follows:

```
adb shell am start -a android.intent.action.VIEW -d "{URL}" {package name}
```

To check the public and personal content logging, you can enable and view the logs by using the following two lines:

```
adb shell setprop log.tag.FirebaseUserActions VERBOSE
adb logcat -v time -s FirebaseUserActions:V
```

Android Studio and tools such as ADB offer a great way to test implementations. Before you take your application to production, please log and test them.

Search performance and latest APIs

To enhance your application search we have done necessary integration (App Indexing), so now the question is how do we analyze it to get a rationale on the past and present of the application status? The answer is by integrating all the necessary tools for App Indexing. Firebase analytics offers Search Analytics with the detailed and straightforward report for the application search performance.

You can also analyze the search referrals from the links and its click events. To understand this use case comprehensively, Firebase also offers tailored app and document material at the following link https://codelabs.developers.google.com/codelabs/deeplink-referrer/#0

The ADB shell command helps by showing logs in local for the analysis. The command to achieve that is as follows:

```
adb shell am start
-a android.intent.action.VIEW
-c android.intent.category.BROWSABLE
-e android.intent.extra.REFERRER_NAME android-
app://com.google.android.googlequicksearchbox/https/www.packtpaintings.com
-d http://examplepetstore.com/host_path com.packt.android
```

Extracting referrer information happens through a Firebase SDK class called `AndroidAppUri` and it helps with extracting the referrer URIs. If the app is opened from another app, this indicates to the referrer that we can fetch the details as follows:

```
AndroidAppUri appUri = AndroidAppUri.newAndroidAppUri(referrer);
            String referrerPackage = appUri.getPackageName();
```

Having tools like this in Android prime time, we should start building good web and mobile content.

Migrating the `Appindex` API is very simple to make sure that you are using the latest version of the dependency:

```
dependencies {
    ...
    implementation 'com.google.firebase:firebase-appindexing:15.0.0'
    ...
}
```

Update the SDK imports if you are using the following classes:

```
// Before
    import com.google.android.gms.appindexing.Action;
    import com.google.android.gms.appindexing.AppIndex;
    import com.google.android.gms.common.api.GoogleApiClient;

    // After
    import com.google.firebase.appindexing.Action;
    import com.google.firebase.appindexing.FirebaseUserActions;
    import com.google.firebase.appindexing.Indexable;
    import com.google.firebase.appindexing.builders.Actions;
```

There is no need for the Google API anymore, so you can remove it:

```
    // Delete this
    mClient = new GoogleApiClient.Builder(this)
        .addApi(AppIndex.API)
        .build();
      ...
    }
```

As we said earlier, action builders now use the `newView` method instead of builders:

```
//Before
    public Action getAction() {
      Thing object = new Thing.Builder()
        .setName(mText)
        .setUrl(mUrl)
        .build();


      return new Action.Builder(Action.TYPE_VIEW)
        .setObject(object)
        .build();
    }
```

```
    // After
    public Action getAction() {
        return Actions.newView(mText, mUrl);
    }
```

Update the user action calls to something like the following:

```
//Before

@Override
protected void onStart() {
    super.onStart();
    mClient.connect();
    AppIndex.AppIndexApi.start(mClient, getAction());
}

@Override
protected void onStop() {
    AppIndex.AppIndexApi.end(mClient, getAction());
    mClient.disconnect();
    super.onStop();
}


// After

@Override
protected void onStart() {
    super.onStart();
    FirebaseAppIndex.getInstance().update(getIndexable());
    FirebaseUserActions.getInstance().start(getAction());
}

@Override
protected void onStop() {
    FirebaseUserActions.getInstance().end(getAction());
    super.onStop();
}
```

These are the latest API changes for App Indexing. If you are starting the indexing from scratch, then this is not for you.

Summary

The objective of this chapter was to have a detailed look at app invites and also App Indexing on search engines. We have looked at all the combinations of activities that we can perform in Firebase Invites and App Indexing. We have also explored public content indexing, personal content indexing, and logging user actions. We have understood application invite sharing using Firebase Invites.

Now let's explore how to make a monetary impact using the application we have built. In the next chapter, we will explore the two major advertisement and promotion tools offered by Firebase, which are AdWords and AdMob.

12
Making a Monetary Impact and Firebase AdMob and AdWords

"Creative without strategy is called Art, Creative with strategy is called Advertising."

- Prof. Jef I Richards

Firebase offers two more services, namely AdWords and AdMob. These tools are exclusively dedicated to application promotions and advertisements. AdWords help in getting more users to install the application, understanding the insights about users, and converting users into active users. AdWords can run targeted ad campaigns based on the Google Analytics data. AdWords can also make use of Firebase Analytics to create an audience for specific campaigns to engage the user base. After connecting AdWords to Firebase, developers or the digital marketing team get the powerful utilities that assist in AdWords investment for installs and in-app purchase actions.

AdMob helps in generating the revenue from your applications. AdMob can also be integrated with Firebase Analytics for more insights. AdMob allows developers to create different types of ad banners to display ads.

Let's plunge into assisting your fellow digital marketing friend or learn how to generate revenue from the mobile application you have developed. In this chapter, we will explore the following topics:

- Overview of Firebase AdWords and AdMob
- Creating banner ads
- Creating fullscreen ads
- Best practices for monetizing your app
- Creating ad campaigns and more

Firebase AdWords

Firebase AdWords is the service that helps to marketize your application for online users. Marketizing is all about taking the product you have built for potential customers, which leads to app installs, ad conversions, and targeted ad campaigns with user engagement plans.

When we connect or link Firebase with AdWords, we will have access to powerful tools that help in supervising AdWords investments, app installs, and in-app actions. Firebase and AdWords can export user lists, import the analytics, and much more. Some of the outstanding key features include:

- Audience segmentation based on the analytics data
- Exporting the audience list to AdWords
- Importing the events from analytics to AdWords

When we integrate AdWords to the Firebase project, we can create a mobile application marketing list based on the analytics users. By default, it includes the purchasers and all users of the application.

We also can create custom segmentation in Firebase using any combination of events, user attributes, and user properties. With such categorized users, we can target ad campaigns. For instance, we can create an audience segment based on their region: "Mapt subscribers who live in Germany", and then we can run targeted ad campaigns to those users.

Analytics data that is of the list data structure can only be used for network campaigns.

To make sure that AdWords is up and running for your project, you need to have an AdWords account. If you do not, please create one. After creating the account, configure Firebase Analytics for your Android project. Connect your AdWords account to your Firebase project.

To add or to know more about the analytics of your project, please read Chapter 9, *Application Usage Measuring and Notification, Firebase Analytics and Cloud Messaging*.

Creating an AdWords account

To create the account for AdWords, please visit the URL, `https://adwords.google.com/home/`, which redirects you to the AdWord home page. If you have an account already, please log in. If not, sign up using your Gmail email address.

After a successful account creation, you can create multiple dashboards, and you get access to all the other features of AdWords.

AdWords also provides a decent amount of comprehensive documentation in the previous link if you are completely new to AdWords. You can visit the **How it works** option to understand more. In the process of creating ad campaigns, AdWords offers powerful tools such as Keyword Planner, AdWords Editor, Manager Accounts, and so on.

Using Manager Accounts, we can manage all the activities of AdWords from a single dashboard, such as consolidated billing, cross-account campaign management, reporting, access control, and much more. Filling out a simple form enables the Manager Account. You can easily monitor what's working out for your product and what's not.

The keyword for ad campaigns plays a crucial role. Reaching the right customer with the right keyword will help the product to trend in searches and can help users to see only relevant advertisements.

AdWords Editor is a free application that helps to manage a large AdWords account. In case you want to download and understand the features of AdWords Editor, please download it from the following link: `https://www.google.com/intl/en/adwordseditor/thankyou.html`

AdWords Editor offers features such as uploading changes to all campaigns, managing your ads, downloading all the campaigns or selected campaigns, and so on.

The following screenshot shows AdWords Editor for performing larger campaigns:

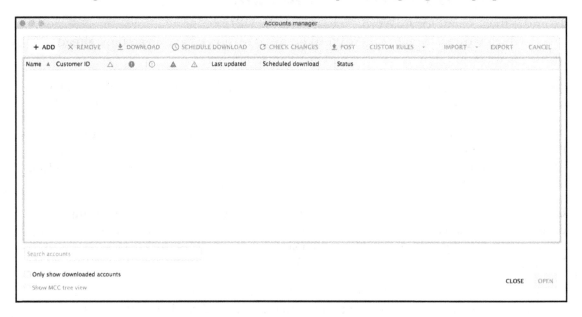

Now that we have a fair idea on what AdWords is and its offerings, it is time to learn how to link AdWords to Firebase.

Linking AdWords to Firebase

The process of linking AdWords to Firebase helps to share the analytics events from Firebase to AdWords and share the audience to AdWords. Before we proceed further, here are some of the rules that we need to follow before we link AdWords to Firebase:

- Your account should be the owner of the project that you want to link
- The same account should have administrative access

If you have a Manager Account, any data that you import from Firebase will be available to all of your client accounts on successful linking of AdWords. We can selectively import the Firebase conversion events to AdWords. The audience created in Firebase Analytics is also shared to AdWord accounts.

To link AdWords to a Firebase project, follow these steps:

1. Sign in to Firebase.

2. Click on the **Project settings** icon in the top left-hand corner.
3. Click on the **Integrations** tab.
4. With the **AdWords** card you have the option to share the audience automatically with linked AdWords accounts.
5. Click on the **Link** button:

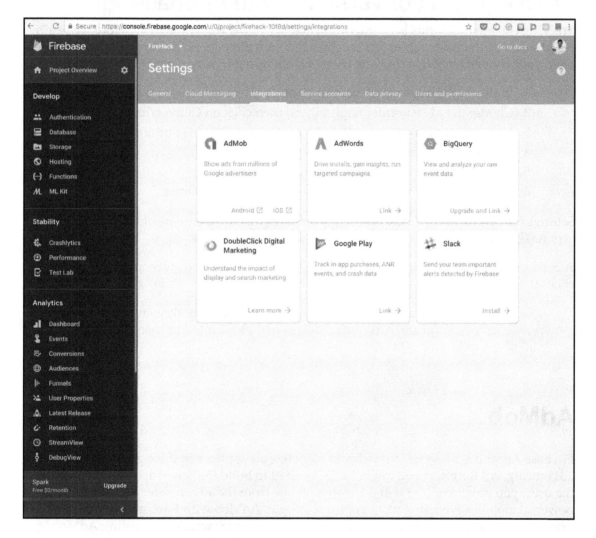

6. Choose the correct AdWords account, and click on **Add Account**.

We have successfully linked AdWords and Firebase. To unlink AdWords from Firebase, click on the **Integration** tab and choose the **AdWords** card, click on the **Manage link** and unlink the accounts, and then confirm the unlink.

Tracking app conversions with Firebase

Tracking conversion events is an important activity of the AdWords tool. Before we begin, make sure that the Android project is connected with Firebase SDK. Through the Analytics plan, your conversion events may be users' first in-app purchase event:

1. In the AdWords account, visit the tools icon.
2. Choose the **Measurement** option, and then click on **Conversions**.
3. Now add the conversion events by clicking on the plus button.
4. Choose your application from the conversion types.
5. Click the button for Firebase, and click **Continue**.
6. Select the events you would like to import and click **Done**.

Settings for automatically tracked in-app purchases include the name of the conversion action. The count will show one or every conversion per ad click.

A conversion window is the time duration of how long to track conversions after someone clicks the ad.

 AdWords is a powerful tool, but Google recommends using Firebase. In the near future, AdWords features will blend into Firebase tools.

AdMob

Firebase AdMob is a service that helps to monetize an application through in-app advertising. All the effort you might have invested to build that great application and all the users you have acquired will generate revenue from the advertisements. AdMob is a powerful mobile advertising platform from Google. AdMob with Firebase provides an extensive data and analytics capabilities. Firebase integrates with your existing AdMob configurations too. Some of the key capabilities are earning through in-app advertisement, improving user experience, quick scaling capabilities, accessing monetization reports, and much more.

AdMob offers different types of ads such as banner ads, interstitial ads, video ads, or native ads. These components are added to the native UI components. Additionally, AdMob also offers in-app purchase advertisements, which allow users to buy an advertised product within the application. AdMob uses the Google Mobile Ads SDK. The SDK also helps developers to fetch more data about the purchase and maximizes ad revenue. By default, SDK collects information such as device information, publisher-provided location information, and purchase currency.

To configure AdMob into your project, you need to connect the application to Firebase SDK. You can read about the procedure to connect Firebase SDK in Chapter 1, *Keep It Real – Firebase Realtime Database*. Add the AdMob dependency after connecting Firebase SDK. Now you can use the banner ad or the ad that you wanted to add to your application. In order to monetize with ads, we need to have the unique ad unit IDs.

The latest Gradle dependency is as follows:

```
implementation 'com.google.firebase:firebase-ads:15.0.1'
```

Add the dependency before you attach further dependencies.

AdMob can be used without Firebase, but Firebase linking is recommended. It follows a similar procedure to AdWords, but when you go to the Firebase console, click on the link that says **Link your apps in AdMob**.

The following screenshot illustrates the process of linking the app:

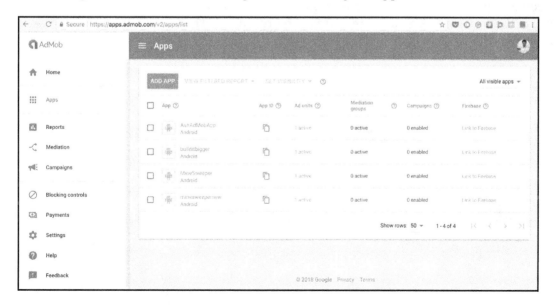

If your app is not available, click on the **Add app** button in the top-right corner. Then create the new app and ad unit ID.

The following screenshot illustrates the process of creating an ad unit ID:

Keep the ad unit ID safe. Before creating the screen, AdMob asks for the kind of ad we will use in the app, such as banner, interstitial, and rewarded. The following screenshot illustrates the types of banners and ad units:

The banner ad occupies the one fixed width in the app, whereas **Interstitial** is a full page, **Rewarded** is a category that can show video, and so on.

Android Studio and initializing the SDK

We need to initialize the SDK before we do any other actions. Now choose the action and make good use of the resources.

The following code snippet illustrates the SDK initialization:

```
public class MainActivity extends AppCompatActivity {
    ...
    protected void onCreate(Bundle savedInstanceState) {
        super.onCreate(savedInstanceState);
        setContentView(R.layout.activity_main);
        // Sample AdMob app ID: ca-app-pub-3940256099942544~3347511713
        MobileAds.initialize(this, "YOUR_ADMOB_APP_ID");
    }
    ...
}
```

In the layout XML design files, we can start using `AdView` as a component:

```
<com.google.android.gms.ads.AdView
        xmlns:ads="http://schemas.android.com/apk/res-auto"
        android:id="@+id/adView"
        android:layout_width="wrap_content"
        android:layout_height="wrap_content"
        android:layout_centerHorizontal="true"
        android:layout_alignParentBottom="true"
        ads:adSize="BANNER"
        ads:adUnitId="ca-app-pub-3940256099942544/6300978111">
    </com.google.android.gms.ads.AdView>
```

Also, `adUnitId` is supposed to pass as follows:

```
val adView = AdView(this)
adView.adSize = AdSize.BANNER
adView.adUnitId = "ca-app-pub-7635463545376453/76354763"
```

The official document at `https://developers.google.com/android/reference/com/google/android/gms/ads/package-summary` introduces all the new updates on the ad-related documentation.

Summary

AdWords and AdMob are powerful tools in the area of marketing and monetizing. In this chapter, we have gained a quick insight on what AdWords is and how to link an AdWords account to Firebase. We have explored AdMob for generating revenue using the concepts explained. We have discovered that playing video ads inside the application has some limitations such as network bandwidth, and so on. In the next chapter, we will focus on Cloud Firestore.

13
Flexible NoSQL and Cloud Firestore

"No matter how modern it looks, it just does the same old storage thing but efficiently."

— Unknown

Firestore sounds fancy enough! Well, what is Firestore doing in the Firebase toolchain? In October, 2017, Firebase released an **Release Candidate** (**RC**) beta tool called Firestore. Just a few months ago, this tool stepped into the developer world and has already created a huge buzz because of the kind of features it offers. It is well known as a document database. Firestore is a NoSQL document database for app development. Data in Firestore syncs app data on a global scale.

Cloud Firestore is an adaptable, versatile database for application development from Firebase and Google Cloud Platform. Like Firebase Realtime Database, it keeps your information in sync over different applications through real-time listener callbacks and offers offline help for versatile app development, so that you can build responsive applications that work regardless of network latency or internet availability. Cloud Firestore additionally offers consistent coordination with other Firebase and Google Cloud Platform products, including Cloud Functions.

Let's explore Firestore in detail. In this chapter, we will cover the following topics:

- Overview of Firestore:
    - Firestore versus Realtime
    - Usage, limits, and pricing
- Adding and managing data:
    - Data model
    - Structuring data
    - Data types
    - Adding data
    - Managing Firestore with a console
- Querying data
- Securing data
- Firestore offline data support

Cloud Firestore

Firestore has already created a great buzz in the developer community, and adjectives such as adaptable, versatile, and scalable are already a brilliant way of describing Firestore. Though it is still in a beta state, Firestore has proven a lot and developers have started to use this tool in production builds.

So, what makes Firestore stand out compared to Realtime Database? Well, Firestore is a document database, whereas Realtime Database is NoSQL. Firestore offers **better querying and more structured data**. Realtime Database is a JSON hashmap tree. Firestore is more structured and all user data consists of documents (which are basically key-value pairs) and collections (list of documents). Documents can point to a subcollection that holds other documents. **Designed to scale**, Firestore offers better scaling than Realtime Database. Firestore will perform faster, even with large datasets. **Easier manual fetching of data** similar to real-time database, Firestore offers to fetch our data. **Multiregion support** means more reliability as our data is shared across multiple data centers at once and that will not compromise the consistency. **Good pricing model**, Firestore charges based on the number of operations you perform.

Firestore has quotas and limits like a Realtime Database. The following table illustrates the beta tool limits:

Limit	Details
Maximum writes per second per database (at beta)	2,500 (up to 2.5 MiB per second)
Maximum concurrent connections for mobile/web clients per database (at beta)	100,000

Firestore free tier has its quota listed as follows:

Free tier	Quota
Stored data	1 GiB
Document reads	50,000 per day
Document writes	20,000 per day
Document deletes	20,000 per day
Network egress	10 GiB per month

In addition to all these limits, if you want to use Firestore for your production application keep in mind the limits that apply to your usage of Firestore.

Limitations on collections, documents, and fields:

- **Collections**:
    - Limitations of collection ID's:
        - Must be a valid UTF—eight characters
        - Must be no longer than 1,500 bytes
        - Cannot contain a forward slash (/)
        - Cannot solely consist of a single period (.) or double periods(..)
        - Cannot match the regular expression __.*__
    - Maximum depth for subcollections:
        - 100

- **Documents:**
    - Limitations on document IDs:
        - Must be a valid UTF—eight characters
        - Must be no longer than 1,500 bytes
        - Cannot contain a forward slash (/)
        - Cannot solely consist of a single period (.) or double periods(..)
        - Cannot match the regular expression __.*__
    - The maximum size for a document name:
        - 6KiB
    - The maximum size for a document:
        - 1 MiB

- **Fields:**
    - Limitation on the field names:
        - Must be a valid UTF—eight characters
    - The maximum size of a field name:
        - 1500 bytes
    - Limitations on field paths:
        - Must separate field names with a single period (.)
        - Must enclose each field name in backticks, but excluding the following exceptions:
            - The field name contains only the characters and underscore
            - The field name does not start with 0-9
    - Field value:
        - 1Mib-89 bytes
    - The depth of the field in a map:
        - 20

Similarly, Firestore has limitations on writes and transactions. A few important limitations are enlisted here:

Limit	Details
Maximum API request size	10 MiB
Maximum write rate to a document	One per second
Maximum write rate to a collection in which documents contain sequential values in an indexed field	500 per second
Maximum number of documents that can be passed to a **Commit** action or written in transaction	500
Time limit for a transaction	270 seconds, with a 60-second idle expiration time

Firestore has limitations on security rules as well. For more details on Firestore limitations on usage, please visit this URL: `https://firebase.google.com/docs/firestore/usage` .

Adding and managing data

Since Firestore is a NoSQL document-oriented database, it will not have rows and tables like an SQL database. You can store the data in the form of documents and collections. Every document contains a set of key-value pairs. Also, Firestore is optimized to store a large collection of the small document.

All documents should be stored in collections, and Firestore identifies the document by its location in the database. In Firestore, a document is a unit of storage. A document is a record that contains fields.

A data model allows developers to create a reference for documents. An example is shown as follows:

```
DocumentReference alovelaceDocumentRef =
db.collection("readers").document("firebaseMastering");
```

We can also create a reference to collections as follows:

```
CollectionReference usersCollectionRef = db.collection("readers");
```

You can create a subcollection called `chapter` as follows:

```
DocumentReference messageRef = db
        .collection("book").document("firebase")
        .collection("book").document("chapter")
```

Choosing a data structure for your Firestore project

For many use cases, having nested data in documents works well than with other structures. Similarly, before we go forward to implement the data structure plan, there are three main possibilities for the data structure, which are nested data in documents, sub-collections, and root level collections.

Firestore supports all the primitive data types and also some of the modern data types as well. Firestore supports array, boolean, bytes, date and time, floating point numbers, geographical points, integer, map, NULL, reference, and text string.

When the query involves fields with mixed types, Firestore uses deterministic ordering. The ordering is enlisted as follows:

1. Null values
2. Boolean values
3. Integer and floating point, sorted, numerical order
4. Date values
5. Text string values
6. Byte values
7. Firestore references
8. Geographical point values
9. Array values
10. Map values

Adding data to Firestore is straightforward. First, we need to add the document within the collection. The following code illustrates the process to create a document:

```
Map<String, Object> city = new HashMap<>();
city.put("name", "Los Angeles");
city.put("state", "CA");
city.put("country", "USA");

db.collection("cities").document("LA")
        .set(city)
        .addOnSuccessListener(new OnSuccessListener<Void>() {
            @Override
            public void onSuccess(Void aVoid) {
                Log.d(TAG, "DocumentSnapshot successfully written!");
            }
        })
```

```
        .addOnFailureListener(new OnFailureListener() {
            @Override
            public void onFailure(@NonNull Exception e) {
                Log.w(TAG, "Error writing document", e);
            }
        });
```

`LA` is the document of cities collection. Firestore lets you write the data with most of the data types enlisted previously. Consider the following example:

```
Map<String, Object> docData = new HashMap<>();
docData.put("stringExample", "Hello world!");
docData.put("booleanExample", true);
docData.put("numberExample", 3.14159265);
docData.put("dateExample", new Date());
docData.put("listExample", Arrays.asList(1, 2, 3));
docData.put("nullExample", null);

Map<String, Object> nestedData = new HashMap<>();
nestedData.put("a", 5);
nestedData.put("b", true);

docData.put("objectExample", nestedData);

db.collection("data").document("one")
        .set(docData)
        .addOnSuccessListener(new OnSuccessListener<Void>() {
            @Override
            public void onSuccess(Void aVoid) {
                Log.d(TAG, "DocumentSnapshot successfully written!");
            }
        })
        .addOnFailureListener(new OnFailureListener() {
            @Override
            public void onFailure(@NonNull Exception e) {
                Log.w(TAG, "Error writing document", e);
            }
        });
```

Firestore also allows users to add custom data types (apart from primitive data types). Consider the following example:

```
public class City {

    private String name;
    private String state;
```

```
    private String country;
    private boolean capital;
    private long population;

    public City() {}

    public City(String name, String state, String country, boolean capital,
long population) {
        // ...
    }

    public String getName() {
        return name;
    }

    public String getState() {
        return state;
    }

    public String getCountry() {
        return country;
    }

    public boolean isCapital() {
        return capital;
    }

    public long getPopulation() {
        return population;
    }

}
```

The preceding custom object can be added as follows:

```
City city = new City("Los Angeles", "CA", "USA", false, 5000000L);
db.collection("cities").document("LA").set(city);
```

If you want to add the cities to the same custom object, you can achieve it as follows:

```
Map<String, Object> data = new HashMap<>();
data.put("name", "Tokyo");
data.put("country", "Japan");

db.collection("cities")
        .add(data)
        .addOnSuccessListener(new OnSuccessListener<DocumentReference>() {
            @Override
```

```
        public void onSuccess(DocumentReference documentReference) {
            Log.d(TAG, "DocumentSnapshot written with ID: " +
documentReference.getId());
        }
    })
    .addOnFailureListener(new OnFailureListener() {
        @Override
        public void onFailure(@NonNull Exception e) {
            Log.w(TAG, "Error adding document", e);
        }
    });
```

Updating documents need to have a document reference without overwriting the entire document, so use the `updated()` method as follows:

```
DocumentReference washingtonRef = db.collection("cities").document("DC");

// Set the "isCapital" field of the city 'DC'
washingtonRef
    .update("capital", true)
    .addOnSuccessListener(new OnSuccessListener<Void>() {
        @Override
        public void onSuccess(Void aVoid) {
            Log.d(TAG, "DocumentSnapshot successfully updated!");
        }
    })
    .addOnFailureListener(new OnFailureListener() {
        @Override
        public void onFailure(@NonNull Exception e) {
            Log.w(TAG, "Error updating document", e);
        }
    });
```

Update a specific field as follows:

```
db.collection("users").document("Ashok")
    .update(
        "age", 26,
        "favorites.color", "Red"
    );
```

Developers can manage Firestore with the console, and perform most of the CRUD operations such as add, edit, delete, and so on. In the console, you can add the data by clicking on **ADD COLLECTION**, as shown in the following screenshot:

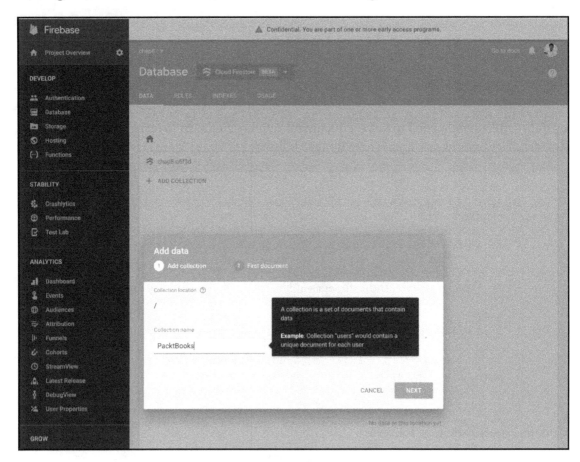

Once you enter the name for your collection, click on **NEXT**. There you can enter a specific document ID or you click on **Auto-ID** and start adding the fields for the data in documents. Click **Save** so that data appears in the data viewer. If you want to add more documents to the collection, click **ADD DOCUMENT**.

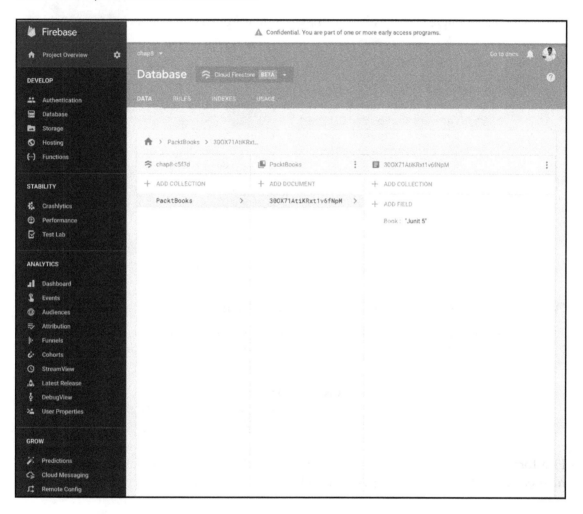

Querying data

In Firestore, there are two methods to retrieve data. Call a method to retrieve data and set the listener to receive the data change events.

The following example shows how to retrieve content from a document:

```
DocumentReference docRef = db.collection("cities").document("SF");
docRef.get().addOnCompleteListener(new
OnCompleteListener<DocumentSnapshot>() {
    @Override
    public void onComplete(@NonNull Task<DocumentSnapshot> task) {
        if (task.isSuccessful()) {
            DocumentSnapshot document = task.getResult();
            if (document.exists()) {
                Log.d(TAG, "DocumentSnapshot data: " + document.getData());
            } else {
                Log.d(TAG, "No such document");
            }
        } else {
            Log.d(TAG, "get failed with ", task.getException());
        }
    }
});
```

Developers can retrieve the data of a custom object as follows:

```
DocumentReference docRef = db.collection("cities").document("BJ");
docRef.get().addOnSuccessListener(new OnSuccessListener<DocumentSnapshot>()
{
    @Override
    public void onSuccess(DocumentSnapshot documentSnapshot) {
        City city = documentSnapshot.toObject(City.class);
    }
});
```

Firestore also allows retrieving multiple documents at a time with the help of the `where()` method. The following code snippet shows how to use the method:

```
db.collection("cities")
        .whereEqualTo("capital", true)
        .get()
        .addOnCompleteListener(new OnCompleteListener<QuerySnapshot>() {
            @Override
            public void onComplete(@NonNull Task<QuerySnapshot> task) {
                if (task.isSuccessful()) {
                    for (QueryDocumentSnapshot document : task.getResult())
```

```
        {
                        Log.d(TAG, document.getId() + " => " +
document.getData());
                    }
                } else {
                    Log.d(TAG, "Error getting documents: ",
task.getException());
                }
            }
        });
```

You can retrieve all the documents in a collection as follows:

```
db.collection("cities")
        .get()
        .addOnCompleteListener(new OnCompleteListener<QuerySnapshot>() {
            @Override
            public void onComplete(@NonNull Task<QuerySnapshot> task) {
                if (task.isSuccessful()) {
                    for (QueryDocumentSnapshot document : task.getResult())
{
                        Log.d(TAG, document.getId() + " => " +
document.getData());
                    }
                } else {
                    Log.d(TAG, "Error getting documents: ",
task.getException());
                }
            }
        });
```

In case of local changes using this method, we can check for pending writings to Firestore and perform the writings:

```
final DocumentReference docRef = db.collection("cities").document("SF");
docRef.addSnapshotListener(new EventListener<DocumentSnapshot>() {
    @Override
    public void onEvent(@Nullable DocumentSnapshot snapshot,
                        @Nullable FirebaseFirestoreException e) {
        if (e != null) {
            Log.w(TAG, "Listen failed.", e);
            return;
        }

        String source = snapshot != null &&
snapshot.getMetadata().hasPendingWrites()
                ? "Local" : "Server";
```

```
            if (snapshot != null && snapshot.exists()) {
                Log.d(TAG, source + " data: " + snapshot.getData());
            } else {
                Log.d(TAG, source + " data: null");
            }
        }
    });
```

Detaching listeners is as easy as follows:

```
Query query = db.collection("cities");
ListenerRegistration registration = query.addSnapshotListener(
        new EventListener<QuerySnapshot>() {
            // ...
        });

// ...

// Stop listening to changes
registration.remove();
```

If you notice any sort of array out of bound exception, you can use the Firebase console to identify the data structure problem.

Securing data

We explored match rules in `Chapter 5`, *Arsenal for Your Files, Firebase Cloud Storage*. Similarly, Firestore uses the same rules syntax and principles with a few updates.

Firestore rules always start with the following rule syntax:

```
service cloud.firestore {
    match /databases/{database}/documents {
        // ...
    }
}
```

The basic read/write rules will consist of a `match` statement of a specific document and allow expression for detailing when reading that specified data is allowed:

```
service cloud.firestore {
    match /databases/{database}/documents {

        // Match any document in the 'cities' collection
        match /cities/{city} {
            allow read: if <condition>;
```

```
            allow write: if <condition>;
        }
    }
}
```

Granular operations can be implemented with the help of `get` and `list` keywords, as shown in the following example:

```
service cloud.firestore {
    match /databases/{database}/documents {
        // A read rule can be divided into get and list rules
        match /cities/{city} {
            // Applies to single document read requests
            allow get: if <condition>;

            // Applies to queries and collection read requests
            allow list: if <condition>;
        }

        // A write rule can be divided into create, update, and delete
rules
        match /cities/{city} {
            // Applies to writes to nonexistent documents
            allow create: if <condition>;

            // Applies to writes to existing documents
            allow update: if <condition>;

            // Applies to delete operations
            allow delete: if <condition>;
        }
    }
}
```

Offline data support

Firestore supports offline data persistence, and when a network reconnects, it will push or synchronize local changes with the cloud changes. To enable offline support, use the following code snippet:

```
FirebaseFirestoreSettings settings = new
FirebaseFirestoreSettings.Builder()
        .setPersistenceEnabled(true)
        .build();
db.setFirestoreSettings(settings);
```

The preceding code will enable your application to function offline. Once you have enabled the offline persistence, your listeners will receive the events whenever the local cache data changes. Consider the following code example that listens to the offline event changes:

```
db.collection("cities").whereEqualTo("state", "CA")
        .addSnapshotListener(new EventListener<QuerySnapshot>() {
            @Override
            public void onEvent(@Nullable QuerySnapshot querySnapshot,
                                @Nullable FirebaseFirestoreException e) {
                if (e != null) {
                    Log.w(TAG, "Listen error", e);
                    return;
                }

                for (DocumentChange change :
querySnapshot.getDocumentChanges()) {
                    if (change.getType() == Type.ADDED) {
                        Log.d(TAG, "New city:" +
change.getDocument().getData());
                    }

                    String source =
querySnapshot.getMetadata().isFromCache() ?
                            "local cache" : "server";
                    Log.d(TAG, "Data fetched from " + source);
                }

            }
        });
```

Now when the device is offline, the application tries to retrieve the data from the cache. If not, it will return an error. Firestore can extend most of its functionalities with the Firebase functions.

Summary

Firestore is the next big thing in the Firebase toolchain. In this chapter, we have explored adding, managing, and querying the data, as well as some of the limitations. We have also explored the security rules for Firestore, enabling offline persistence, and so on. We looked at adding data to Firestore, updating the data, and managing the data through the Firebase console, and so on. In the next chapter, we will focus on the concept of predictions.

14
Analytics Data, Clairvoyant, Firebase Predictions

The best way to predict the future is to create it"

— *Peter Drucker*

Google Analytics for Firebase is a powerful part of the platform, and it also offers free insights on application usage and user engagement. Firebase Analytics helps developers to understand how their users are interacting with the application. From the data it captures, we can derive which part of the application is delightful to the users and which needs to be improved.

In addition to the analytics, what if we can go further and learn ahead of time which users can become active, which users can make in-app purchases, or create a dynamic user group of the application? Having this ability, we can use other Firebase tools such as notifications and remote config to give a customized user experience. Perhaps the whole process is not easy on its own. Google Firebase supports it with powerful machine learning algorithms to identify and predict a user's behavior ahead of time.

Firebase Predictions lets you anticipate which users are likely to churn and which are likely to make a monetary transaction. Firebase Predictions applies ML models to an application's analytics data and it automatically predicts user behavior. Also, the predictions are available for remote config, the notification composer, and A/B testing to assist developers to make the required changes in business logic according to the predictions.

In this chapter, we will explore the following topics:

- Firebase Predictions overview
- Optimizing monetization
- Optimizing promotions
- Preventing churn
- Risk tolerance

Firebase Predictions

Firebase Predictions uses analytics data to anticipate or predict user actions. Using Firebase Predictions with remote config, developers can increase conversions by providing custom experience based on the user type and analytics information.

Use Firebase Predictions with a notification composer to deliver the right message to the right user groups. Using remote config we can build multiple variants of the application and we can evaluate the effectiveness of the prediction strategies. We can make an application engaging by understanding the user's next move. Firebase Predictions dynamically segments your users based on their collected data. In the Firebase console, we can see that there are pre-populated cards including `churn`, `non_churn`, `spend`, and `non_spend` types and also a card to create a custom prediction. The default cards are explained in further detail here:

- CHURN: The CHURN group contains users who have been active from the last seven days, yet are anticipated to be inactive within the following seven days. So this is the imperative prediction that developers need to keep user attention.
- NON-CHURN: This group contains users who have been active during the last seven days and are predicted to stay active within the next seven days.
- SPEND: This group contains users who are predicted to make in-app purchases or e-commerce purchases in the next seven days.
- NON-SPEND: This group contains users who are predicted to not spend in the app in the next seven days.
- CUSTOM Prediction: This group is to create a prediction by using analytics events to mark events as conversions. It can take up to 24 hours for new conversion events to show up.

Firebase Predictions includes some influential key features such as Google's Advanced Machine Learning to your data. This boosts the conversion rate in a dynamic and more customized manner, increasing the retention with smarter notifications and creating custom predictions.

Firebase Predictions is available for both iOS and Android platforms and it includes the analytics SDK. By default, Firebase Predictions provides two key pieces of information:

- Churn: Predicts which users will be inactive in the next seven days (app has not been opened for a long time, neither have the notifications).
- Spend: Anticipates the user buying information such as in-app purchases. Firebase Predictions also allows us to create a custom conversion analytics events.

Firebase Predictions gives you a chance to modify the risk tolerance of a prediction so you can strike the correct balance between focusing on fewer users with more precision, or more users with less precision, and it demonstrates to you what level of your user base will be focused at each risk tolerance level. The machine learning model for your application enhances as the sum and pertinence of information gathered utilizing analytics increases, and as your number of users increases. What's more, the precision of the model for a particular user will be enhanced after that user has used the application for no less than a couple of days.

The following metrics are provided for each event:

- **Event count:** Number of times the event was triggered.
- **Users:** Number of users who triggered the event.
- **Count per user:** Average number of times per user that the event was triggered.
- **Value:** All value parameters provided with the event. Utilize this context-delicate metric to track any information that is significant to your application (for example, income, time, and distance).

Now let's explore how to take analytics and predictions forward.

Setting up Firebase Predictions

To use Firebase Predictions with the application, we have to follow these steps:

1. Add analytics and custom events to your application.
2. We need to enable analytics data sharing in the application.
3. Create and evaluate predictions.
4. Supervise the effects of risk tolerance levels.
5. Use Firebase Predictions with remote config and notifications composer.

By default, Firebase Predictions assumes that the application uses `churn`, `spend`, and `configured`. We can also create custom events.

Add analytics to your project. For more information on adding the analytics, you can follow `Chapter 9`, *Application Usage Measuring and Notification, Firebase Analytics and Cloud Messaging* and add additional events that you want to use to predict your apps, such as `spend_virtual_currency` or share.

On the Firebase console navigation bar, click on the **Project Settings** and go to the **Data privacy** tab to make sure that you have enabled Google Analytics for Firebase data sharing.

The following screenshot shows the **Data privacy** tab in the Google console:

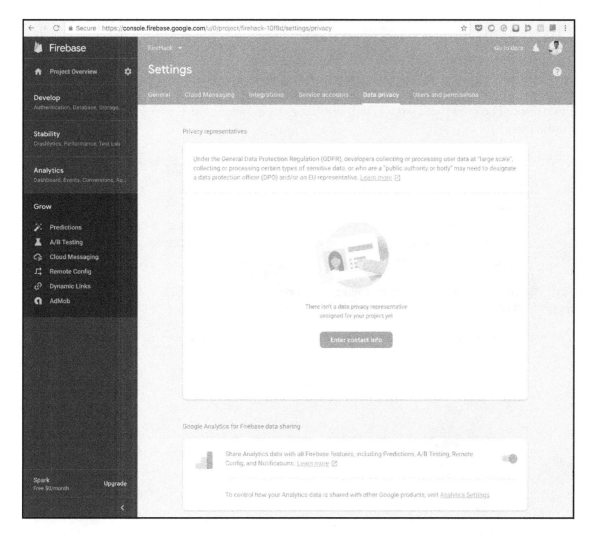

Now you are free to use the predictions options from the **Grow** facility, as shown in the preceding screenshot. Before proceeding, try to understand the different risk tolerance and start using tools such as remote config and notification composer.

Optimizing monetization

Predictions make it straightforward to give customized user experience depending on the user actions. For instance, we can remove or disable in-app advertisements if the user is likely to buy the premium service. However, before implementing such strategies it is important to be sure that changes will not have any adverse difference in retention of the application user.

Now let's explore using monetization with Firebase A/B Testing:

- Enable data sharing in the Firebase console
- Explicitly log the spend events
- We need to have sufficient data to make meaningful predictions (typically 10000 monthly active users and 500 positive and negative examples)
- Share a good amount of data to process

Start predicting user spending. In the Firebase console, go to **Predictions** and agree to the terms and conditions to see the following screen.

The following screenshot depicts the **Predictions** dashboard in the Firebase console:

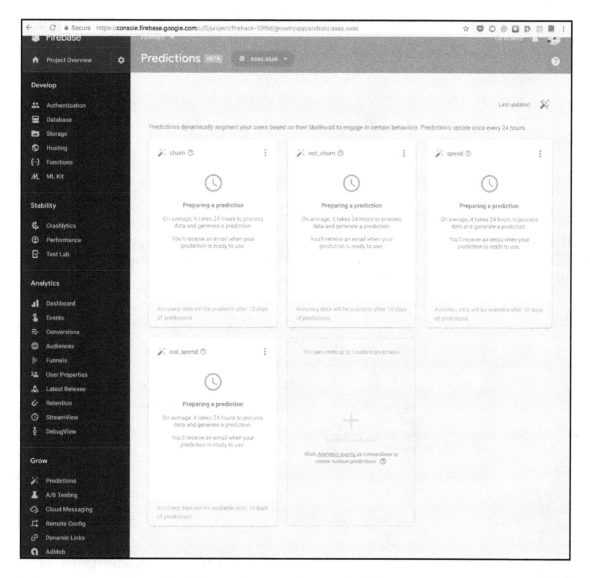

Now create a project and add the analytics and remote config to your application. Create a monetization strategy as follows:

```
mFirebaseRemoteConfig = FirebaseRemoteConfig.getInstance();

Map remoteConfigDefaults = new HashMap<String, Object>();
remoteConfigDefaults.put("ads_policy", "ads_never");
mFirebaseRemoteConfig.setDefaults(remoteConfigDefaults);
```

```
// ...

mFirebaseRemoteConfig.fetch(cacheExpiration)
    .addOnCompleteListener(this, new OnCompleteListener<Void>() {
        @Override
        public void onComplete(@NonNull Task<Void> task) {
            if (task.isSuccessful()) {
                mFirebaseRemoteConfig.activateFetched();
            }
            executeAdsPolicy();

            // ...
        }
    });
```

If the application retrieves the `ads_policy` string then the user would get the advertisements. If it receives the `ads_never` string then we will not show the advertisements, rather we will make the application richer:

```
private void executeAdsPolicy() {
    String adsPolicy = mFirebaseRemoteConfig.getString("ads_policy");
    boolean will_not_spend =
mFirebaseRemoteConfig.getBoolean("will_not_spend");
    AdView mAdView = (AdView) findViewById(R.id.adView);

    if (adPolicy.equals("ads_always") ||
        (adPolicy.equals("ads_nonspenders") && will_not_spend)) {
        AdRequest adRequest = new AdRequest.Builder().build();
        mAdView.loadAd(adRequest);
        mAdView.setVisibility(View.VISIBLE);
    } else {
        mAdView.setVisibility(View.GONE);
    }

    FirebaseAnalytics.getInstance(this).logEvent("ads_policy_set", true);
}
```

The preceding code illustrates the way to enable remote config to handle advertisements. Let's explore how to optimize promotions.

Optimizing promotions

Optimizing the in-app promotions to each individual user based on their interests and other facts is straightforward now. Prediction developers can optimize the promotions in so many different ways. For instance, if you have an e-commerce application, you can recommend one expensive product to one set of users and a less expensive product to another set of users. This can also be A/B tested by conducting product level experiments and seeing how this prediction-based method affects the revenue.

Now let's explore using promotions with Firebase A/B Testing:

- Enable the data sharing in the Firebase console
- Explicitly, any generic spend events may be paid podcast
- We need to have sufficient data to make meaningful predictions (typically, 10000 monthly active users and 500 positive and negative examples)
- Share a good amount of data to process

Start predicting user spending habits based on the analytics data and you can create custom spend events to create custom predictions. Later, you can add the remote config with `predicted_will_spend`. We can now make this a boolean and set the value to true if the user will buy, if not we will set it to false:

- Always promote the basic bundle features for every user (control group)
- Always promote the premium bundle
- Promote suitable bundles depending on the spending prediction for the group

Now we can create A/B tests from the Firebase console, and we also need to write the remote config code in the application. For more details on remote config, please read `Chapter 10`, *Changing Your App - Firebase Remote Config and Dynamic Links*.
You can define three variants in the A/B testing dashboard with `promoted_bundle` as a parameter, now the three variants are `basic`, `premium`, and `predict` to the prediction-based variant.

Choose a purchase revenue as the metrics for prediction and select additional metrics that support the predictions. Let's now look at a small code example:

```
mFirebaseRemoteConfig = FirebaseRemoteConfig.getInstance();

Map remoteConfigDefaults = new HashMap<String, Object>();
remoteConfigDefaults.put("promoted_bundle", "basic");
mFirebaseRemoteConfig.setDefaults(remoteConfigDefaults);

// ...
```

```
mFirebaseRemoteConfig.fetch(cacheExpiration)
    .addOnCompleteListener(this, new OnCompleteListener<Void>() {
        @Override
        public void onComplete(@NonNull Task<Void> task) {
            if (task.isSuccessful()) {
                mFirebaseRemoteConfig.activateFetched();
            }
            // Remote Config
            mPromotedBundle = getPromotedBundle();

            // ...
        }
});
```

Now the preceding code can retrieve the values from the parameter and we can set the promotions as follows:

```
private String getPromotedBundle() {
    FirebaseAnalytics.getInstance(this).logEvent("promotion_set", true);

    String promotedBundle =
mFirebaseRemoteConfig.getString("promoted_bundle");
    boolean will_spend =
mFirebaseRemoteConfig.getBoolean("predicted_will_spend");

    if (promotedBundle.equals("predicted") && will_spend) {
        return "premium";
    } else {
        return promotedBundle;
    }
}
```

Customizing promotions can be helpful for e-commerce and other applications and it will help developers to have an active user base and also the marketing team can promote the needful purchases to the users.

Now using predictions, how can we engage users and make a big difference in user retention? Let's explore that in the following section.

Preventing churn

In Firebase, churn is a term used for users who are dropping off from your application. To such users, we need to start giving them attention by promoting strategic engagement activities. Firebase Predictions can help in identifying the users who are likely to be inactive users. And predictions help to retain such users. For instance, if your application is a mobile game and if there is churn, you can offer gift levels or small upgrades to make the user use the application again.

Now let's explore using promotions with Firebase A/B Testing:

- Enable analytics data sharing in the Firebase console
- Explicitly log any analytics events and try logging most of the events that make sense
- We need to have sufficient data to make meaningful predictions (typically, 10000 monthly active users and 500 positive and negative examples)
- Share a good amount of data to process

Now using prediction we can start predicting the user churn. In Firebase Remote Config, add new parameters such as `will_churn`. If churn is predicted we can make this remote config value as `true`, and if not, `false`.

We can now go ahead and create retention strategy experiments, such as:

- Never grant gifts/upgrade game levels (control group)
- Grant gifts based on their game achievements
- Grant gifts when players are predicted to churn

In the experiment, we have to create a `game_policy` parameter, of which we can have three different versions. Namely, `gift_never` to the control group, `gift_achievement`, and the last variant as `gift_likelychurn` to the prediction-based variant. This parameter can be used to determine when to give gifts and to which user.

The following code describes the preceding process:

```
mFirebaseRemoteConfig = FirebaseRemoteConfig.getInstance();

Map remoteConfigDefaults = new HashMap<String, Object>();
remoteConfigDefaults.put("gift_policy", "gift_never");
mFirebaseRemoteConfig.setDefaults(remoteConfigDefaults);

// ...
```

```
mFirebaseRemoteConfig.fetch(cacheExpiration)
    .addOnCompleteListener(this, new OnCompleteListener<Void>() {
        @Override
        public void onComplete(@NonNull Task<Void> task) {
            if (task.isSuccessful()) {
                mFirebaseRemoteConfig.activateFetched();
            }
            executeGiftPolicy();

            // ...
        }
    });
```

Now you can execute the gift policy based on the parameters you retrieved. At this time we can log the policy and set the policy as follows:

```
private void executeGiftPolicy() {
    String giftPolicy = mFirebaseRemoteConfig.getString("gift_policy");
    boolean will_churn = mFirebaseRemoteConfig.getBoolean("will_churn");

    if (giftPolicy.equals("gift_achievement") {
      grantGiftOnLevel2();
    } else if (giftPolicy.equals("gift_likelychurn") && will_churn) {
      grantGiftNow();
    }

    FirebaseAnalytics.getInstance(this).logEvent("gift_policy_set", null);
}
```

It takes a couple of days to see the results and understand if offering a gift will help in user retention.

Predefined predictions

By default, predictions define four sets of groups that are dependent on analytics data and are dynamically populated with machine learning algorithms.

Churn predictions contain users who are active in the last seven days, but are predicted to become inactive within the next seven days. Churn is different from uninstalling the application. Users may churn long before they uninstall the application. Most users will not uninstall the application until they replace the phone or factory reset the phone. However, predictions use uninstall as one of the values for predictions.

The `not_churn` group contains the users who have been active during the last seven days and are predicted to continue to be active over the next seven days. For instance, say your application is a language learning platform, `not_churn` addresses the point that the user will come back to the app, but doesn't guarantee the revenue.

Sometimes wizards predictions also go wrong. Similarly, when the `churn` and `not_churn` groups are not mutually exclusive, predictions might make some errors.

Spend predictions will have two groups, `spend` and `not_spend`. The `spend` group contains users who are predicted to make transactions, such as in-app purchases, e-commerce buy out, and so on. Predictions advanced machine learning would be learning these purchases.

The `not_spend` group contains the users who are predicted to not spend in the next seven days. As with the `churn` rule, membership in the `not_spend` group is different from not being a member of the `spend` group.

 Generally, we do not target users based on them not being a member of the particular group.

Predictions and risk tolerance

When predicting using predictions on user behavior, there is always scope for the uncertainty that requires some trade-off, you must decide whether to include fewer users in a predicted group for the maximum accuracy or to include more users for minimum accuracy.

We can decide some of the uncertainty that might occur and we can tell predictions how much uncertainty we can tolerate by choosing risk tolerance level. Based on the prediction and number of available analytics events, you will see the following risk tolerance levels:

- **High-Risk Tolerance:** This tolerance level targets more users than other risk tolerances with a minimum level of accuracy. When there is no other risk tolerances, high-risk tolerance will be present.
- **Medium-Risk Tolerance:** This risk tolerance level targets a moderate number of users with a moderate level of accuracy.
- **Low-Risk Tolerance:** This tolerance level targets minimum users with a maximum level of accuracy.

You can set these tolerance levels using a slider in the Firebase console, and when it is set to one of the preceding tolerances for a prediction, the tile for that prediction in the Firebase console shows the following metrics:

- Percentage ratio of your app's user base who can be targeted with those predictions at that risk tolerance level
- The total number of app users who can be targeted with that prediction at that risk tolerance

Losing your users is all about losing the audience for your show. Please understand the risk level before you make any decision based on prediction data. Just a heads up, Firebase Predictions is still in beta, but it is good enough for medium-scale predictions. The Firebase team is continuously working on making the tool more accurate and better.

Summary

After learning about Firebase Predictions in this chapter and once you have a good amount of expertise with the tool, do you think you will be considered a wizard? Perhaps you need to explore the tool more by looking at other possible examples and use cases. In this chapter, we have explored the possibilities of predictions and also understood the certain limitations that predictions have. We have explored how to optimize monetization and promotion, prevent churn, and we have also explored what risk tolerance is. In the next chapter, we will look at ML Kit, which was introduced in Google IO 2018.

Training Your Code and ML Kit

15

"What we want is a machine that can learn from experience."

— Alan Turing

Machine learning (ML) can be defined as an ability to learn without programming, and ML and **Artificial Intelligence (AI)** are the most happening buzzwords in recent times. The terms AI and ML are from the same branches of a tree, but both are quite different. AI is the more extensive idea of machines having the capacity to do tasks in a way that we would consider "smart", whereas Machine Learning is an application of AI based on the possibility that we should simply have the capacity to give machines access to data and let them learn for themselves.

In Google IO 2018, Google officially announced some new, cutting edge technology to build great mobile and web applications. This includes a beta version of ML Kit. ML Kit is an exclusive mobile software SDK that helps in building ML-based applications. Currently, Firebase ML Kit supports iOS and Android.

Even though ML Kit is powerful, it is straightforward to use in applications. If you are an expert or beginner in the area of Machine Learning, ML Kit offers a wide range of support for everyone. Software developers can start learning ML Kit without profound knowledge of neural networks, model optimization, and so on. These are the topics that drive Machine Learning to a greater height.

ML Kit offers lightweight APIs that help you to use TensorFlow Lite models with your mobile applications.

In this chapter, we will explore the following topics:

- Overview of ML Kit
- Vision:
    - Recognizing text
    - Detecting faces
    - Scanning barcodes
- Custom models:
    - Using a custom model

Firebase ML Kit

Ever since Google announced ML Kit, it has widely experimented with SDK, and the coding style for ML is as simple as any other Firebase toolchain service, which will ensure that experts and beginners are on the same page in understanding the tool better. ML Kit has some key capabilities, such as we can use the current beta release for the production applications for use cases such as recognizing text, detecting faces, identifying landmarks, and so on.

ML Kit's selection APIs execute within mobile devices or in the remote cloud. The on-device APIs work quickly and draw the results even when the mobile phone is disconnected from the network. On the other hand, cloud-based APIs utilize the power of **Google Cloud Platform** (**GCP**) to produce very accurate and a higher level of results. ML Kit APIs cannot cover all the unique problems and use cases. To fill the gap, ML Kit offers a way to consume TensorFlow Lite models. Developers have to upload the models to the Firebase console and the rest is handled by Firebase since ML Kit acts as an API layer to any custom model.

ML Kit is the smartest way that one can experiment with or use Google services such as Google Cloud Vision API, Android Neural Networks API, and so on in one single SDK. ML Kit features offline capabilities using on-device models; also, using cloud, it features a powerful processing.

Let's understand which service can be on-device and which is in the cloud:

Feature	On-Device	Cloud
Text recognition	Yes	Yes
Face detection	Yes	No
Barcode scanning	Yes	No
Image labeling	Yes	Yes
Landmark recognition	No	Yes
Custom model inference	Yes	No

At the time of writing, Firebase officially mentioned that they are working on backwards-incompatible ways and they are not subject to any agreements such as deprecation policy.

Using ML cloud features is subject to use of GCP and can be billed accordingly. Currently, ML Cloud APIs are available for preview.

To start exploring ML Kit and integrating it into Android projects, we need to follow these steps:

- Integrate the SDK
- Prepare input data
- Apply the ML models
- Ready to use APIs include text recognition, face detection, barcode scanning, and so forth

A typical ML Kit library for adding in the app-level `build.gradle` file is shown as follows:

```
implementation 'com.google.firebase:firebase-ml-vision:16.0.0'
```

Google offers a great number of examples through Google Codelabs for Firebase.

```
http://g.co/codelabs/mlkit-android
```

Now let's understand what ML Kit Vision has to offer us.

Vision

ML Kit offers two distinct services. One is for processing images and retrieving the results or any information on the image. The second service is using custom models such as TensorFlow to process the data for the results.

In ML Kit Vision, we have essential, ready-to-use models, which are listed as follows:

- Recognizing text
- Detecting faces
- Scanning barcodes
- Labeling images
- Recognizing landmarks

Let's explore what it is like to recognize text using ML-Kit.

Recognizing text

ML Kit offers powerful text recognition APIs. It can recognize any Latin-based language on an on-device basis, perhaps more when connected to a cloud. Text recognition can automate numerous data works. Using cloud-based APIs, we can extract text from different documents. Identifying the train schedule by PNR number on the ticket, we can write a model to set a reminder immediately or two hours before train departure, and in many more use cases.

Since recognizing text offers on-device and cloud-based features, it has a usage quota. To find out more about this usage quota, please refer to Firebase documentation and pricing schemes.

On-device support is also powerful enough to identify the shapes, text, and so on, whereas with cloud-based support, we can have more details, such as identifying the places, locales, and more.

 Most of the cloud processed data and content abides by Apache 2.0 License. For more details, you can visit Firebase ML Kit support and understand the policies.

Setting up ML Kit for recognizing text

ML Kit follows the same standards of other Firebase tools in the toolchain, which means to adding Firebase SDK to your application and then adding the tool dependency as required.

Check out `Chapter 1`, *Keep It Real - Firebase Realtime Database* to find out how to add Firebase SDK to your Android Studio project. After completing that successfully, you can add the following ML Kit dependency:

```
dependencies {
  // ...

  implementation 'com.google.firebase:firebase-ml-vision:16.0.0'
}
```

Firebase recommends adding the following metadata tag if you are using an on-device API. It helps to download the ML model to the device from Play Store services:

```
<application ...>
  ...
  <meta-data
      android:name="com.google.firebase.ml.vision.DEPENDENCIES"
      android:value="text" />
  <!-- To use multiple models: android:value="face,text,model2,model3" -->
</application>
```

If install time model downloads are not enabled, the models will be downloaded at the first run of the on-device detector.

 Though ML Kit is brilliant and jaw-dropping in so many use cases, it still has limitations such as all requests without downloading the models will not produce any results. Also for cloud-based models, you need blaze level plans for the Vision API.

In the following section, we will look at on-device and cloud-based text recognition.

On-device text recognition

On-device text recognition models need to run `FirebaseVisionTextDetector` to detect the text in the image, and the process involves a method called `detectImage`. Before processing text, we need to capture the picture and convert that into a bitmap file and we shall pass it to `FirebaseVisionImage`. Look at the following steps to understand the Vision API for texts:

1. Create a `FirebaseVisionImage` object from bitmap:

```
FirebaseVisionImage image = FirebaseVisionImage.fromBitmap(bitmap);
```

2. We should determine the phone and camera orientation matches.

3. Create a `FirebaseVisionImageMetadata` object that contains the pictures height, width, color, encoding format, and rotation:

```
FirebaseVisionImageMetadata metadata = new
FirebaseVisionImageMetadata.Builder()
        .setWidth(1280)
        .setHeight(720)
        .setFormat(FirebaseVisionImageMetadata.IMAGE_FORMAT_NV21)
        .setRotation(rotation)
        .build();
```

4. We should also pass context and URI:

```
FirebaseVisionImage image;
try {
    image = FirebaseVisionImage.fromFilePath(context, uri);
} catch (IOException e) {
    e.printStackTrace();
}
```

5. Get the instance of `FirebaseVisionTextDetector`:

```
FirebaseVisionTextDetector detector = FirebaseVision.getInstance()
        .getVisionTextDetector();
```

6. Now pass the image to the `detectInImage` method:

```
var result = detector.detectInImage(image)
        .addOnSuccessListener(OnSuccessListener<FirebaseVisionText>
{
            // Task completed successfully
            // ...
        })
```

```
        .addOnFailureListener(
OnFailureListener {
                // Task failed with an exception
                // ...
        })
```

7. Extract text from blocks of recognized text:

```
for (FirebaseVisionText.Block block:
firebaseVisionText.getBlocks()) {
    Rect boundingBox = block.getBoundingBox();
    Point[] cornerPoints = block.getCornerPoints();
    String text = block.getText();

    for (FirebaseVisionText.Line line: block.getLines()) {
        // ...
        for (FirebaseVisionText.Element element:
line.getElements()) {
            // ...
        }
    }
}
```

The preceding code snippets and steps illustrate the process of using on-device based text recognition. Now let's understand what would be the process to do cloud-based text recognition.

Cloud-Based text recognition

To use the cloud-based text recognition model, we need to configure the text detector as follows:

> ML Kit offers preview APIs for developers for cloud-based models. For production cloud-based models, please fully understand the billing details before opting in.

1. Configure the text detector:

```
FirebaseVisionCloudDetectorOptions options =
    new FirebaseVisionCloudDetectorOptions.Builder()
.setModelType(FirebaseVisionCloudDetectorOptions.LATEST_MODEL)
        .setMaxResults(15)
        .build();
```

2. Run the text detector. In order to run it, we have to follow all the rules we followed for on-device based models.

3. Create a `FirebaseVisionImage` object from a Bitmap instance:

```
FirebaseVisionImage image = FirebaseVisionImage.fromBitmap(bitmap);
```

4. We should determine that the phone and camera orientation matches.

5. Create a `FirebaseVisionImageMetadata` object that contains the pictures height, width, color, encoding format, and rotation:

```
FirebaseVisionImageMetadata metadata = new
FirebaseVisionImageMetadata.Builder()
        .setWidth(1280)
        .setHeight(720)
        .setFormat(FirebaseVisionImageMetadata.IMAGE_FORMAT_NV21)
        .setRotation(rotation)
        .build();
```

6. We should also pass context and URI:

```
FirebaseVisionImage image;
try {
    image = FirebaseVisionImage.fromFilePath(context, uri);
} catch (IOException e) {
    e.printStackTrace();
}
```

7. Now, get the instance of `FirebaseVisionCloudTextDetector` or `FirebaseVisionCloudDocumentTextDetector`:

```
FirebaseVisionCloudTextDetector detector =
FirebaseVision.getInstance()
        .getVisionCloudTextDetector();
// Or, to change the default settings:
FirebaseVisionCloudTextDetector detector =
FirebaseVision.getInstance()
        .getVisionCloudTextDetector(options);
```

8. We are ready to pass the image to the `detectInImage` method as follows:

```
var result = detector.detectInImage(image)
.addOnSuccessListener(OnSuccessListener<FirebaseVisionCloudText> {
            // Task completed successfully
            // ...
        })
        .addOnFailureListener(OnFailureListener {
```

```
                          // Task failed with an exception
                          // ...
                  })
```

9. Extract text from the blocks as follows:

```
String recognizedText = firebaseVisionCloudText.getText();

for (FirebaseVisionCloudText.Page page:
firebaseVisionCloudText.getPages()) {
   List<FirebaseVisionCloudText.DetectedLanguage> languages =
           page.getTextProperty().getDetectedLanguages();
   int height = page.getHeight();
   int width = page.getWidth();
   float confidence = page.getConfidence();

   for (FirebaseVisionCloudText.Block block: page.getBlocks()) {
       Rect boundingBox = block.getBoundingBox();
       List<FirebaseVisionCloudText.DetectedLanguage>
blockLanguages =
                  block.getTextProperty().getDetectedLanguages();
       float blockConfidence = block.getConfidence();
   }
}
```

The preceding code illustrates how to use cloud-based text recognition. Let's understand how to use ML Kit to detect faces and process data.

Face detection

Face detection! Definitely sounds like wizards' work. ML Kit's face detection API helps to identify key facial features, using these developers can generate avatars and process selfies, portraits, and so on. ML Kit can perform face detection in real time. The key capabilities of face detection are recognizing and locating facial features, and recognizing facial expressions such as smiling, anger, crying, and more. ML Kit face detection can track faces across video frames.

Setting up ML Kit for face detection

Face detection also depends on Firebase SDK, so the first important step is to make sure that your project is connected with Firebase SDK. Now you can choose to add the vision dependency mentioned in the text recognition chapter of this chapter.

You can use the following metadata tag to your application scope, and it will also fetch the ML models from the Play Store:

```
<meta-data

 android:name="com.google.firebase.ml.vision.DEPENDENCIES
 "
         android:value="face" />
```

In case for whatever reason we need to change the default face detection settings, please do it in the `FirebaseVisionFaceDetectorOptions` object. The following table illustrates the different features available:

Settings	
Detection mode	FAST_MODE (default) | ACCURATE_MODE Favor speed or accuracy when detecting faces.
Detect landmarks	NO_LANDMARKS (default) | ALL_LANDMARKS Whether or not to attempt to identify facial "landmarks": eyes, ears, nose, cheeks, mouth.
Classify faces	NO_CLASSIFICATIONS (default) | ALL_CLASSIFICATIONS Whether or not to classify faces into categories such as "smiling" and "eyes open".
Minimum face size	float (default: 0.1f) The minimum size, relative to the image, of faces to detect.
Enable face tracking	false (default) | true Whether or not to assign faces an ID, which can be used to track faces across images.

For instance, consider the following code snippet that describes the changing default face detection settings:

```
FirebaseVisionFaceDetectorOptions options =
        new FirebaseVisionFaceDetectorOptions.Builder()
.setModeType(FirebaseVisionFaceDetectorOptions.ACCURATE_MODE)
.setLandmarkType(FirebaseVisionFaceDetectorOptions.ALL_LANDMARKS)
.setClassificationType(FirebaseVisionFaceDetectorOptions.ALL_CLASSIFICATION
S)
                .setMinFaceSize(0.15f)
                .setTrackingEnabled(true)
                .build();
```

Now the face detection process is also almost similar to what we have learned in text recognition, the small change is we will be passing the bitmap image to `FirebaseVisionFaceDetector`'s `detectInImage` method.

After following the process for recognizing text, we can extract the information about the detected faces. If the Vision API succeeds, then a list called `FirebaseVisionFace` will return the data. Consider the following example:

```
for (FirebaseVisionFace face : faces) {
    Rect bounds = face.getBoundingBox();
    float rotY = face.getHeadEulerAngleY();  // Head is rotated to the
right rotY degrees
    float rotZ = face.getHeadEulerAngleZ();  // Head is tilted sideways
rotZ degrees

    // If landmark detection was enabled (mouth, ears, eyes, cheeks, and
    // nose available):
    FirebaseVisionFaceLandmark leftEar =
face.getLandmark(FirebaseVisionFaceLandmark.LEFT_EAR);
    if (leftEar != null) {
        FirebaseVisionPoint leftEarPos = leftEar.getPosition();
    }

    // If classification was enabled:
    if (face.getSmilingProbability() !=
FirebaseVisionFace.UNCOMPUTED_PROBABILITY) {
        float smileProb = face.getSmilingProbability();
    }
    if (face.getRightEyeOpenProbability() !=
FirebaseVisionFace.UNCOMPUTED_PROBABILITY) {
        float rightEyeOpenProb = face.getRightEyeOpenProbability();
    }

    // If face tracking was enabled:
    if (face.getTrackingId() != FirebaseVisionFace.INVALID_ID) {
        int id = face.getTrackingId();
    }
}
```

The preceding code snippet describes how to work with the Vision API for extracting the facial features information. Now let's understand how ML Kit extends its help in extracting barcode information.

Barcode scanning

The barcode standard formats can be processed through ML Kit. Barcodes are a convenient way to pass information such as product pricing, expiry details, and so on. ML Kit automatically recognizes the barcode and QR code patterns and parses the data. ML Kit barcode scanning includes key capabilities such as reading most standard formats, automatic format detection, extracting structured data, working with any orientation, and much more.

Setting up ML Kit for barcode scanning

Barcode scanning also depends on Firebase SDK, so the first step is to make sure that your project is connected with Firebase SDK. Now you can choose to add the vision dependency mentioned in the text recognition section of this chapter.

You can use the following metadata tag to your application scope and it will also fetch the ML models from the Play Store:

```
<meta-data

 android:name="com.google.firebase.ml.vision.DEPENDENCIES
"
    android:value="barcode" />
```

Configuring the barcode detector to change any default settings needs to be changed in the FIrebaseVisionBarcodeDetectorOptions instance, as shown in the following snippet:

```
FirebaseVisionBarcodeDetectorOptions options =
        new FirebaseVisionBarcodeDetectorOptions.Builder()
        .setBarcodeFormats(
                FirebaseVisionBarcode.FORMAT_QR_CODE,
                FirebaseVisionBarcode.FORMAT_AZTEC)
        .build();
```

The rest of the steps follow the sequence. Instead of text detection and face detection, we use FirebaseVisionBarcodeDetector:

```
FirebaseVisionBarcodeDetector detector = FirebaseVision.getInstance()
        .getVisionBarcodeDetector();
```

We can extract the barcode information from the `FirebaseVisionBarcode` class as follows:

```
for (FirebaseVisionBarcode barcode: barcodes) {
    Rect bounds = barcode.getBoundingBox();
    Point[] corners = barcode.getCornerPoints();

    String rawValue = barcode.getRawValue();

    int valueType = barcode.getValueType();
    // See API reference for complete list of supported types
    switch (valueType) {
        case FirebaseVisionBarcode.TYPE_WIFI:
            String ssid = barcode.getWifi().getSsid();
            String password = barcode.getWifi().getPassword();
            int type = barcode.getWifi().getEncryptionType();
            break;
        case FirebaseVisionBarcode.TYPE_URL:
            String title = barcode.getUrl().getTitle();
            String url = barcode.getUrl().getUrl();
            break;
    }
}
```

The preceding code snippet illustrates barcode scanning and getting the information from the barcode. Now let's explore what custom models have to offer.

Custom models

ML developers who are skilled in the area of writing Machine Learning code can use TensorFlow Lite and can write models with ML Kit. The models can be hosted in a Firebase cloud. The few key capabilities of custom models are Firebase cloud hosting, on-device ML inference, automatic model fallbacks, automatic model updates, and so on.

To build custom model ML Kit projects, the following steps need to be carried out:

- Train your ML model
- Convert the model to TensorFlow Lite for working with ML Kit
- Host the model in the Firebase console
- Use the models for inference

Before we focus on the custom model, we need to make sure that the project is connected to Firebase SDK and also add the following dependency:

```
dependencies {
  // ...

    implementation 'com.google.firebase:firebase-ml-model-interpreter:16.0.0'
}
```

Now we are almost ready to explore the custom models. To host the models in a Firebase cloud, follow these instructions:

- Visit the Firebase console, go to the ML Kit section, and click on the **Custom** tab
- Now you will notice a button to **Add custom model**
- You can name the model anything of your choice, but the extension needs to be `.tflite`
- Now in the manifest file, add the internet permission and read/write to external storage

All the models in the Firebase cloud can be added locally in the app. If and only if the model is lightweight, create an asset folder and add the model files. After adding the asset folder, add the following code:

```
android {

// ...

    aaptOptions {
        noCompress "tflite"
    }
}
```

Using a `FirebaseCloudModelSource` object, specify the name for the model, add a model to cloud resource, and now register with the `registerCloudModelSource` method as follows:

```
FirebaseModelDownloadConditions.Builder conditionsBuilder =
new FirebaseModelDownloadConditions.Builder().requireWifi();
if (Build.VERSION.SDK_INT >= Build.VERSION_CODES.N) {
// Enable advanced conditions on Android Nougat and newer.
    conditionsBuilder = conditionsBuilder
            .requireCharging()
            .requireDeviceIdle();
}
FirebaseModelDownloadConditions conditions = conditionsBuilder.build();
```

```
FirebaseCloudModelSource cloudSource = new
FirebaseCloudModelSource.Builder("packt_cloud_model")
.enableModelUpdates(true)
.setInitialDownloadConditions(conditions)
.setUpdatesDownloadConditions(conditions)
.build();
FirebaseModelManager.getInstance().registerCloudModelSource(cloudSource);
```

We can perform inference on input data by creating a `FirebaseModelInputs` object:

```
byte[][][][] input = new byte[1][640][480][3];
input = getYourInputData();
FirebaseModelInputs inputs = new FirebaseModelInputs.Builder()
.add(input)  // add() as many input arrays as your model requires
.build();
Task<FirebaseModelOutputs> result =
firebaseInterpreter.run(inputs, inputOutputOptions)
.addOnSuccessListener(
new OnSuccessListener<FirebaseModelOutputs>() {
    @Override
    public void onSuccess(FirebaseModelOutputs result) {
        // ...
    }
})
.addOnFailureListener(
new OnFailureListener() {
    @Override
    public void onFailure(@NonNull Exception e) {
        // Task failed with an exception
        // ...
    }
});
```

So far we have seen everything in words. Let's now explore ML Kit in action by writing a simple text recognition project.

ML Kit and text recognition

Before we plunge into writing the application, let's understand the functionality. When the picture is captured through camera intents, we will convert the picture to bitmap and send it to ML Kit. I have used two buttons, `ImageView` and `TextView`.

The following layout is the intended design for this project:

```xml
<?xml version="1.0" encoding="utf-8"?>
<LinearLayout xmlns:android="http://schemas.android.com/apk/res/android"
    xmlns:tools="http://schemas.android.com/tools"
    android:layout_width="match_parent"
    android:layout_height="match_parent"
    android:orientation="vertical"
    tools:context=".MainActivity">
    <ImageView
        android:id="@+id/imageView"
        android:layout_width="match_parent"
        android:layout_height="250dp" />
```

Within the same layout lets create a scrollview that helps us to capture the image and detect the texts in it.

```xml
<ScrollView
    android:fillViewport="true"
    android:layout_width="match_parent"
    android:layout_height="match_parent">
    <LinearLayout
        android:layout_width="match_parent"
        android:layout_height="wrap_content"
        android:orientation="vertical">
        <LinearLayout
            android:layout_width="match_parent"
            android:layout_height="wrap_content"
            android:orientation="horizontal">
            <Button
                android:id="@+id/snapBtn"
                android:layout_width="match_parent"
                android:layout_height="wrap_content"
                android:layout_weight="1"
                android:text="Capture" />
            <Button
                android:id="@+id/detectBtn"
                android:layout_width="match_parent"
                android:layout_height="wrap_content"
                android:layout_weight="1"
                android:text="Detect" />
        </LinearLayout>
        <TextView
            android:id="@+id/textView"
            android:layout_width="match_parent"
            android:layout_height="match_parent"
            android:textColor="@android:color/holo_orange_dark"
```

```
                         android:textSize="20sp" />
              </LinearLayout>
         </ScrollView>

    </LinearLayout>
```

Connect the project to the Firebase console to add Firebase SDK. Add the dependency as follows:

```
dependencies {
    implementation fileTree(dir: 'libs', include: ['*.jar'])
    implementation"org.jetbrains.kotlin:kotlin-stdlib-jre7:$kotlin_version"
    implementation 'com.google.firebase:firebase-ml-vision:16.0.0'
}

apply plugin: 'com.google.gms.google-services'
```

Next, straight away connect the UI to the `activity` class and then add the `FirebaseVisionText` classes as follows:

```
class MainActivity : AppCompatActivity() {

    internal lateinit var bitmap: Bitmap
    private val CODE = 15

    override fun onCreate(savedInstanceState: Bundle?) {
        super.onCreate(savedInstanceState)
        setContentView(R.layout.activity_main)
        FirebaseApp.initializeApp(this);
        snapBtn.setOnClickListener {
            val intent = Intent(MediaStore.ACTION_IMAGE_CAPTURE)
            startActivityForResult(intent, CODE)
        }
        detectBtn.setOnClickListener {
            val image = FirebaseVisionImage.fromBitmap(bitmap)
            val detector = FirebaseVision.getInstance().visionTextDetector
            detector.detectInImage(image).addOnSuccessListener {
firebaseVisionText ->
                val textdata = firebaseVisionText.blocks
                if (textdata.size > 0) {
                    var displaydata = ""
                    for (myblock in firebaseVisionText.blocks) {
                        displaydata = displaydata + myblock.text + "\n"
                    }
                    textView.text = displaydata
                } else {
                    Toast.makeText(this@MainActivity, "Failed to detect any
```

```
text.", Toast.LENGTH_SHORT).show()
            }
        }.addOnFailureListener { Toast.makeText(this@MainActivity, "No
text detected in the given image.", Toast.LENGTH_SHORT).show() }
    }
}
```

Now, In onActivity result method we will get the data that we can set to our imageview as shown below.

```
    override fun onActivityResult(requestCode: Int, resultCode: Int, data:
Intent) {
        super.onActivityResult(requestCode, resultCode, data)
        if (requestCode == CODE && resultCode == Activity.RESULT_OK) {
            val bundle = data.extras
            bitmap = bundle?.get("data") as Bitmap // the default key is
'data'
            imageView.setImageBitmap(bitmap)
        }
    }

    companion object {
        private val CODE = 15
    }
}
```

Now we are all good to compile the code and see the output.

The following screenshot depicts the scenario of when a user presses on the capture, which will open a native camera intent:

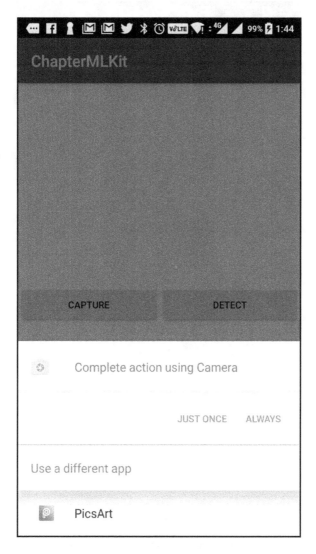

The following screenshot depicts the processed image:

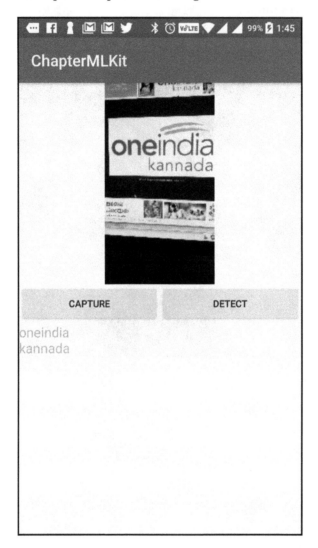

Once we start exploring ML Kit, we realize that it is very straightforward and convenient compared to other platforms.

Summary

Well done! We have reached the final chapter and have learned about the latest tool introduced in Firebase. In this chapter, we have explored text recognition, face detection, and also barcode scanning. We have understood on-device and cloud-based models. We have also looked at creating TensorFlow Lite custom models.

Time led us here to explore ML Kit. We started by writing a real-time database and then we focused on understanding the file storage mechanism, push notifications, analytics and Test Lab, and so on.

By now, you should know which tool to use for the problem you are trying to solve using Firebase. This book has focused on all 18 tools. Each and every tool plays a major role in making your app better. It also addresses the famous categories in Firebase, which are development tools, stability tools, analytics tools, and growth tools.

If you have any queries the tools in Firebase, feel free to reach out to me at *ashokslsk@gmail.com* You can also find me on GitHub and other social media platforms under the username *Ashokslsk*. Thank you for reading this book. With a little more practice, you will be able to be the expert you always wanted to be.

Other Books You May Enjoy

If you enjoyed this book, you may be interested in these other books by Packt:

Mastering Android Development with Kotlin
Miloš Vasić

ISBN: 9781788473699

- Understand the basics of Android development with Kotlin
- Get to know the key concepts in Android development
- See how to create modern mobile applications for the Android platform
- Adjust your application's look and feel
- Know how to persist and share application database
- Work with Services and other concurrency mechanisms
- Write effective tests
- Migrate an existing Java-based project to Kotlin

Hands-on Full Stack Development with Angular 5 and Firebase
Uttam Agarwal

ISBN: 9781788298735

- Understand the core concepts of Angular framework
- Create web pages with Angular as front end and Firebase as back end
- Develop a real-time social networking application
- Make your application live with Firebase hosting
- Engage your user using Firebase cloud messaging
- Grow your application with Google analytics
- Learn about Progressive Web App

Leave a review - let other readers know what you think

Please share your thoughts on this book with others by leaving a review on the site that you bought it from. If you purchased the book from Amazon, please leave us an honest review on this book's Amazon page. This is vital so that other potential readers can see and use your unbiased opinion to make purchasing decisions, we can understand what our customers think about our products, and our authors can see your feedback on the title that they have worked with Packt to create. It will only take a few minutes of your time, but is valuable to other potential customers, our authors, and Packt. Thank you!

Index

A

AdMob
  about 312, 314
  Android Studio 315
  reference 316
  SDK, initializing 315
AdWords Editor
  download link 309
AdWords
  about 308
  account, creating 309
  linking, to Firebase 310
  reference 309
  used, for app conversion 312
Analytics Triggers 127
Android application
  creating, Realtime Database used 30
  logic 35, 38, 42
  user interface design 30, 33
Android projects
  Firebase, configuring 9
Android Studio
  using, with Test Lab 217
App Indexing
  about 293, 294
  personal content indexing, enabling 298, 301
  public content indexing, enabling 295, 297
  reference 294
  user actions, logging 301
Application Not Responding (ANR) 95
Artificial Intelligence (AI) 347
automatic traces
  App Background 229
  App Foreground 229
  App Startup 229
  Network Requests 229

B

BaaS (Backend as a Service) 7
barcode scanning
  ML Kit, setting up 358
Bitrise
  reference 202
Buddy build
  reference 202

C

CI systems
  using, with Test Lab 214
Cloud Firestore Triggers 122, 123, 124, 125
Cloud Firestore
  about 318
  data structure, selecting for project 322, 325, 327
  data, adding 321
  offline data support 331, 332
  reference 321
  used, for querying data 328
Cloud Functions
  connecting 193, 195, 197
  development environment, setting up 113
  using, tools 112
Cloud Messaging, using in Android
  about 248
  device registration token, accessing 249
Cloud Messaging
  about 246, 248, 251
  first notification, sending 251
  notification, sending 254, 255
  using, in Android 248
Cloud Pub/Sub Triggers 131
Cloud Storage 140
Cloud Storage Triggers 129

Continous Integration (CI) 214
Crash Reporting
  about 96
  Crashlytics, upgrading from 103
  custom logs, creating 100
  disabling 102
  ProGuard labels, deobfuscating 100
  setup 97
  support for multiple APK 101
crash reports
  creating 98
Crashlytics Trigger 127
Crashlytics
  about 96, 103
  and functions 109
  Crash Reporting, migrating to 105
  debug mode, enabling 107
  implementation, validating 106
  reports, customizing 107
  setup 103
  upgrading, from Crash Reporting 103
custom attributes, monitoring
  about 232
  Logcat output, enabling 233, 235
custom domain
  connecting to 191, 193
custom models 359

D

data
  querying 328
  securing 330
database rules
  customizing 26
  data security 27
  data validation rules 25
  indexing rules 25
  types 25
default variables
  auth 28
  data 29
  newData 29
  now 29
  root 29
  RuleDataSnapshot, methods 29

development environment, Cloud Functions
  custom logs 119
  functions, reviewing 119
  project structure 116
  project, deploying 118
  reference 113
  required modules 117
  setting up 113
development environment
  Firebase, configuring in Android projects 9
  prerequisites 9
Dynamic Links, use cases
  content, sharing between users 277
  mobile web users, converting to native app users
    276
  reward referrals, using Firebase 278, 281
Dynamic Links
  about 274
  anatomy 282
  creating 283
  receiving 284
  use cases 275

F

face detection
  ML Kit, setting up for 355
Facebook login service, FirebaseUI
  about 74
  App secret 71
  Facebook App ID 71
  project configuration 75, 77
  reference 72
file metadata
  about 158
  common errors, handling 161
  files, deleting 161
  retrieving 158
  security and rules 162
  updating 158, 160
files
  data, downloading through URL 155
  downloading 143, 152
  downloading, into local file 154
  downloading, into memory 153
  downloading, issues 156

existing files, uploading 144
form data, uploading in memory 146
images, downloading with FirebaseUI 155
monitoring and managing 149, 152
reference, creating 153
upload, managing 147
upload, monitoring 148
uploading, as stream 145
Firebase Analytics, using for Android
  about 241
  events, debugging 244
  functions 245
  user properties, setting 242
  using, in WebView 242, 243
Firebase Analytics
  about 240
  using, for Android 241
Firebase Authentication Triggers 127
Firebase Authentication
  about 44
  failures 92
  Firebase SDK 47
  FirebaseUI Auth 46
  setting up 45
FireBase Console
  reference 165, 262
  using, for performance monitoring 235, 236
  using, with Test Lab 206, 210, 211
Firebase functions
  Cloud Functions, for firing push notification 133,
    137, 138
  writing 131
Firebase Hosting 184
Firebase Invites
  receiving, from Android applications 289
FireBase Invites
  receiving, from Android applications 292
Firebase Invites
  reference 292
  sending, from Android applications 292
Firebase Predictions
  about 334
  and risk tolerance 345
  cards 334
  churn, preventing 343

events, metrics 335
monetization, optimizing 338, 340
predefined predictions 344
promotions, optimizing 341
setting up 336
Firebase Realtime Database
  rules 22
  writing to 10
Firebase SDK social networking site authentication
  Anonymous Authentication method 90
  Facebook login method 85
  failures 92
  Google sign-in method 84
  multiple Auth providers, linking 91
  phone number sign-in method 89
  Twitter sign-in method 87
Firebase Storage
  using 170, 177, 181
Firebase
  configuring, in Android projects 9
  development environment , setting up 9
  reference 9
FirebaseUI Email Authentication
  about 48
  configuring, for Email Authentication 48, 50
  Email/Password Authentication, enabling in
    Console 52
  initializing 53
  project, finalizing 54, 56
FirebaseUI social networking site Authentication
  about 65
  Facebook login 71
  Google Sign-in 66
  phone number sign-in method 82
  Twitter sign-in method 77
functions
  triggering 122

G

game loop testing, Test Lab
  about 221
  project, creating 223
  Test Loop Manager, using 222
gcloud CLI
  reference 212

using, with Test Lab 212
Google Cloud Platform (GCP) 348
Google Sign-in, FirebaseUI
  about 66
  code, for Google provider 68, 70
  SHA-1 fingerprint 66, 68

H

hosting behavior customization
  about 197
  headers 199
  hosting priorities 199
  redirects 198
  rewrites, using 198
HTTP Triggers 129

M

Machine learning (ML) 347
ML Kit Vision
  about 350
  barcode scanning 358
  face detection 355
  text, recognizing 350
ML Kit
  about 348
  reference 349
  setting up, for face detection 355
  setting up, for text recognition 351
  setting, up for barcode scanning 358
  text recognition 361, 365
ML Text
  text recognition 366

N

Node.js
  reference 185

P

performance monitoring, for Android
  automatic traces 229
  steps 227, 229
performance monitoring
  about 226
  counters 230

custom attributes, monitoring 232
custom trace 230
for Android 227
for Android performance 231
phone number sign-in method, FirebaseUI
  about 82
  project configuration 82, 83
Plain Old Java Object (POJO) class 35
prelaunch reports 224

R

Realtime Database Triggers 126
Realtime Database
  about 8
  and lists 19
  data, deleting 21
  data, offline capabilities 22
  data, structuring with objects 13
  data, updating 17
  database reference 10
  DataSnapshot object, parsing 17
  HashMaps, writing to Realtime database 18
  objects, reading from 15
  reading from 12
  reading to 10
  used, for creating Android application 30
  value changes, reading 16
  writing into 11
Release Candidate (RC) 317
Remote Config, setting up for Android
  about 259
  conditions 265
  Google Analytics 267
  in-app parameters 260
  parameters, accessing 261
  parameters, activating 265
  parameters, fetching 263
  rules 265
  server-side parameters 261
  singleton object 259
  values 265
Remote Config
  A/B testing, using with 268, 269, 273
  about 258
  setting up, for Android 259

Representational State Transfer (REST) 11
reserved URLs 200
risk tolerance, levels
  high-risk 345
  low-risk 345
  medium-risk 345
rules, Firebase Realtime Database
  about 22
  custom variables 28
  database rules and types 25
  default security rules 22, 25
  default variables 28

S

SDK Email Authentication
  about 57
  existing users, signing in 58
  new users, signing up 57
  users, managing 59
  users, managing through console 63
security
  Request and Resource Evaluation 168
  rules 162
  security rules, general syntax 163
  user files, securing 166
storage reference
  creating 141
  limitations 142
  properties 142
storage
  and functions 169

T

Test Lab, for Android
  about 203, 204
  device type, selecting 206
  Robo test, playing out 205
  test results, reviewing 206
  testing method, selecting 205
Test Lab, using with CI systems
  about 214
  global security settings, configuring 216
  Jenkins project, creating 216
Test Lab, using with gcl CLI

gcloud commands, scripting 213
  test configurations, selecting 212
Test Lab
  about 202
  available device list 220
  Firebase Console, using 206, 210
  for Android 203, 204
  game loop testing 221
  prelaunch reports 224
  results 219
  using, with Android Studio 217
  using, with CI systems 214
  using, with FireBase 211
  using, with gcloud CLI 212
text recognition
  about 350
  Cloud-Based text recognition 353
  ML Kit 361, 366
  ML Kit, setting up for 351
  on-device text recognition 352
triggers
  about 122
  Analytics Trigger 127
  Cloud Firestore Triggers 122
  Cloud Pub/Sub Triggers 131
  Cloud Storage Triggers 129
  Crashlytics Triggers 127
  Firebase Authentication Triggers 127
  HTTP Triggers 129
  Realtime Database Triggers 126
Twitter Sign-in method, FirebaseUI
  about 77
  project configuration 80
  reference 78
  Twitter Api key 78

U

user actions, App Indexing
  implementations, testing 302
  latest APIs 303, 305
  logging 301
  reference 303
  search performance 303, 305
user management
  about 59

forgot password notification 61
profile 60
provider-specific user profile details 60
Smart Lock 65
through console 63
user, deleting 62

verification email, sending 61

W

website
  deploying 185, 187, 190

www.ingramcontent.com/pod-product-compliance
Lightning Source LLC
Chambersburg PA
CBHW080609060326
40690CB00021B/4632